SLICE OF LIFE

Slice of Life

The British Way of Eating Since 1945

Christina Hardyment

BBC BOOKS

ACKNOWLEDGEMENTS

This book was written to accompany the BBC television series *Slice of Life*, which was conceived by Jane Root of Wall to Wall Television. The many people interviewed for the series provided invaluable 'vox pop', extending my own understanding enormously, and research undertaken for the series has informed my own considerably. Everyone in their team has helped me, but I am especially indebted to Catherine Lucas, Kate Norbury, Lucy Richer, Fiona O'Doherty, Victoria Stable and of course Jane Root herself. The BBC Books production team (Heather Holden-Brown, Doug Young, Tessa Clark, Frances Abraham and Linda Blakemore) could not have been more helpful, supportive and inspired.

I would also like to thank the food historian John Burnett for looking kindly on the project (its limitations are of course no fault of his), Beatrice McLeod for her invaluable specialized knowledge of James Bond's eating preferences, Eleo Gordon of Viking Penguin for giving me special leave from the book I should have been writing, and Gill Coleridge for her constant support and encouragement.

This book is published to accompany the television series
Slice of Life which was first broadcast in 1995.
The series was produced by Wall to Wall Television for the BBC.

Executive Producer: Jane Root   Producer: Catherine Lucas

Published by BBC Books, an imprint of BBC Worldwide Publishing.
BBC Worldwide Limited, Woodlands, 80 Wood Lane, London W12 0TT

ISBN 0 563 37087 4

Set in Ehrhardt by BBC Books
Printed and bound in Great Britain by Butler & Tanner Limited, Frome, Somerset
Colour separations by Radstock Reproductions Limited, Midsomer Norton
Jacket printed by Lawrence Allen Ltd, Weston-super-Mare

CONTENTS

FOREWORD: FOOD FOR THOUGHT

The object of this survey of how our eating habits have changed since the war is to show how much the way we eat reveals changes in the way we live, and to encourage debate as to eating patterns to come. I make no dramatic claims for food's role in creating society, or indeed for society's role in creating food, but there are I hope plenty of ingredients to stimulate discussion about what exactly is happening in a country where the food industry is one of the few growth areas in the economy, and eating out seems set fair to becoming more common than eating in.

The first chapter of the book describes the lean gastronomic pickings of the decade after the war when, for all our theoretical victory and the glorious egalitarian measures of Beveridge's welfare state, British larders remained bare. Only saints could have refrained from grumbling: we didn't. Housewives revolted over the 1947 rationing of bread in an extraordinary episode which revealed just how much power they could wield if they chose to get organized. Chapter two charts the extreme reaction when the good times of the 1950s finally arrived. A nation of women who had grown accustomed to coping with everything from riveting battleships to tilling the fields raced back to their own kitchens to create a claustrophobic world of vol-au-vents and Vim which soon had them reaching for the valium. Chapter three shows how outside influences brought in a breath of fresh air (to say nothing of the reek of garlic). The teen scene rocked the night away in coffee bars while the twenty-some-things made romantic assignations in trattorias with no thought of marriage in mind. And Elizabeth David's gospel of good simple European food did as much to prepare middle-class minds for the idea of a united Europe as any diktat from Brussels.

Chapters four and five move from chronology to survey. Chapter four charts the role food played in the arrival and survival of the new British, and our gradual adoption of a multiethnic approach to eating. Chapter five focuses on healthy eating: the causes of the new fashion for vegetarianism, the history of the concern for animals' wellbeing which has dogged the rise of intensive animal farming methods ever since its post-war beginnings, and our growing fear of food and concern with dieting. Finally chapter six examines the way we eat now. Is family life really dwindling away in favour of daily TV doses of imaginary antipodean neighbourhoods, or have we never had it so good?

Since the time span of the book is that of my own life, I have found it a nostalgic personal odyssey to recall my tiny weekly ration of butter as a four-year-old, that first illicit visit to a coffee bar (*L'Auberge*, on Richmond Hill), and fashioning nutmeat turkeys with celery stick drumsticks to celebrate Christmas in the grim year in which my parents became converted to the compost-heap approach to nutrition. Then there was the thrill of discovering Italian and Indian food as an undergraduate, the painstaking folding of napkins into bishops' mitres for dinner parties as a young bride, tearing my hair out over the children's fads and fancies as a harassed mother of four, and finally enjoying the astonishing speed with which a really very respectably tasty meal can be rustled up these days. All in all, I remain an optimist in the kitchen – which does not mean that we don't have to be vigilant against the abuses of factory farming, the mania for dieting, and our exploitation by the ever more powerful supermarket Lords of the Aisles.

CHAPTER ONE

Bread and Bureaucrats

*Every morning, clouds of women came down from the little Georgian houses and smug
cottages of Bridbury, they poured in from the surrounding villages, they stripped the counters bare.
After eleven, for those in the know, the little town had nothing much to offer. Sorry, the shaken heads
would signal to those foolish virgins who came late with their baskets to seek the
rare orange, the potted plaice, the yellow and unyielding bun.*

MOLLY PANTER DOWNES, *One Fine Day* 1947

*I am the chap who has to eat the grub. When I was going to work before the war,
the wife would give me sandwiches and she would say, 'here you are, you know what
you've got.' You do not know what you get in some of these restaurants.*

HERBERT HODGE, in *The Listener* 1946

*There is much good social discipline to be learnt at the common table,
and school feeding will be as great an educational benefit as it will be a material one.*

LORD WOOLTON to the Warwickshire Women's Institute 1945

*Snoek and porpoise defeated him, although, protein-starved as they were, the family ate his dishes; after
several attempts he felt he had mastered whale meat though the family did not wholly agree.*

JOHN POSTGATE, *A Stomach for Dissent: A Biography of Raymond Postgate* 1994

*What I say is, this Government has taken all the fun out of women's work ... Something has
gone from a nation that thinks of 'custard' as a concoction of coloured cornflour.*

Housewives Today 1950

Bread and
Bureaucrats

O n 30 April 1945 the Russians surrounded Berlin, Adolf Hitler shot his mistress and committed suicide, and a roaring drunk Lord Haw-Haw grabbed the microphone for the last time. 'You may not hear from me for a few months,' he said. 'Heil Hitler and farewell.'

But faring well was not to be the lot of the British people straight away, literally or metaphorically. For all the partying that broke out when news of the Germans' official surrender on 8 May was heard on the radio, seven lean years of austerity stood between VE day and the boom years of the middle and late 1950s. Recovery was a good deal less glorious than victory. There was a world shortage of food, famine in India and severe hunger - even rumours of cannibalism - in Europe. We might have won the war (with a little help from our friends across the Atlantic), but we still had to win the peace.

Informing the Kitchen Front: a Ministry of Food poster issued to stress the importance of food conservation during the war

The Second World War was a catalyst for an uneasy new relationship between the public and the state, forged over dinner. In the drive for sensible eating to ensure that the men and women of Britain had enough energy to work and fight, food had stopped being a matter of personal, regional and class preference and had become 'a munition of war': an issue of national concern, a domestic 'science' to be learnt and practised in every home in the land.

The biggest shock of the First World War had been the discovery that only three in nine conscripts were classed as fully fit after their medical examination. Of the remaining six, two were below average, three were completely unfit and one was a chronic invalid, undernourished and unsuitable for service. As storm clouds darkened over Europe in the 1930s, the lesson was not forgotten. Food moved into the front line. In 1931, Professor John Drummond, the nation's pre-eminent food guru, headed an advisory committee on nutrition. New marketing schemes were established to encourage farmers to produce more food for the home market. Printers were approached for estimates for ration books as early as 1935. In 1934, the Milk in Schools scheme was initiated and, by 1939, health departments were giving mothers and infants free milk, cod-liver oil and vitamins.

When war was declared, a huge and highly organized bureaucracy swung into action. The aim of the Ministry of Food under the able management of Lord Woolton was not simply to share fairly what was available but actually to improve the health of the men and women on whom the war effort depended - and to ensure that children, the nation's stake in the future, would grow up healthy into the bargain. There was a three-pronged offensive: making sure that as many people as possible had at least one substantial, balanced and nutritious meal a day by establishing canteens, civic restaurants and school kitchens; directing consumption of food by using price control and rationing; and educating housewives about the right sort of food to use to feed their families cheaply and well.

To sugar the pill of hard work and spartan meals, the wartime coalition Government under Winston Churchill painted a bright new vision of the future in a report by the economist William Beveridge. A total of 635 000 copies of the report and its official summary were sold within two weeks of its publication in December 1942. 'I've been up all night reading the first chapter of a book called *Gone With the Want* by that stout fellow Beveridge,' announced the famous comic Tommy Handley in his wartime role of 'His Fatuity the Minister of Social Hilarity'. A Gallup poll one week later established that 19 out of 20 people had heard of the report and 9 out of 10 believed that its proposals should be adopted.

Beveridge recommended that the scanty patchwork of existing social insurances should be gathered into an overall scheme that would cover the citizen in a cosy State-made security blanket from cradle to grave. He proposed family allowances for all children, a National Health Service and a future in which mass unemployment could be avoided. The only cloud was over prospects of pensions for the elderly, a commitment so expensive that this part of the scheme could not be fully implemented for 20 years.

Although the New Jerusalem was not quite conditional on accepting the spartan conditions of the Home Front in the 1940s, it was certainly an incentive to the war effort. But as yet, all the jam was to be tomorrow. Meat was more difficult to buy in 1945 than in 1944 (it did not finally come off the ration until 1954). The amount of bacon and lard allowed shrank by a third. Rumours of fat cat capitalists gorging themselves behind the polished mahogany doors of Pall Mall clubs accelerated the landslide shift to socialism. 'I am worried about this damn election,' Churchill said to his doctor in June that year. 'I have no message for them now.'

He was right. In July, in defiance of all electoral predictions, Clement Attlee's Labour Government came into power on a tide of hope. A new era in Britain's history was about to begin. Ernest Bevin, an ex-miner, was foreign secretary, Aneurin Bevan was Minister of Health and the cadaverous and vegetarian Stafford Cripps was President of the Board of Trade. They lost no time in putting into execution the Beveridge plan and fulfilling their election promises to nationalize Britain's basic industries and so benefit the workers.

But it was clear that wartime controls would have to continue if economic disaster was to be averted. The war had cost the country around a quarter of her national wealth, and lost her two-thirds of her export trade. As Fortress Britain lowered her drawbridges, an export drive was essential. Advertisements for soap, food and the much longed-for new domestic appliances were more promissory notes than hidden persuaders. A 1949 advertisement in *Good Housekeeping*:

Ice tomorrow: an advertisement for Prestcold refrigerators in *Good Housekeeping*, 1949. The majority of the exciting new appliances were being sent abroad as part of Britain's vitally important export drive

Our milk chocolate is wonderful! Unfortunately, Cadbury's are only allowed the milk to make an extremely small quantity, so if you are lucky enough to get some, do save it for the children.

The burning question after the war was whether the British people would remain the obedient servants of a nanny State or revert to independence. For many the decision was the difference between communism and capitalism, totalitarianism or freedom. How far should the State legislate for the family? Would we feed for ever in its canteen-style restaurants or return to our own kitchens?

MEALS EN MASSE

> *Psychologically, tea breeds contentment. It is so bound up with fellowship and the home and pleasant memories that its results are almost magic . . . worth its weight in gold at 1d a cup.*
>
> C. G. GARDINER, *Canteens at Work* 1941

> *The Duchess shook her head. 'We mustn't let go,' she said stolidly, as she had so many times before. 'I'd sooner starve than have to eat my breakfast in the kitchen. When I can't have my breakfast in the breakfast-room any longer, I shall give up the struggle completely, and go and look for a British Restaurant right away.*
>
> MARGHANITA LASKI, *Love on the Supertax* 1944

Eating out had increased enormously because of the war. In May 1941, we were eating 79 million midday meals a week in factory canteens, school dining-halls and subsidized restaurants; by December 1944, 170 million. Communal eating was a deliberate stratagem by government to improve the nutrition and the productivity of its citizens at a stroke. Woolton called it 'one of the greatest social revolutions that has taken place in the industry of our country'. He may not have foreseen that it would influence family life in quite uncalculated ways. 'British Restaurants', factory canteens and school kitchens transformed the habit of coming home for lunch, and shifted a quarter of the average individual's leisure time away from the home base.

A 1941 article in *Housecraft* gives a vivid picture of the arrangements that were typical of the small wartime canteens set up to cope with war workers and casualties of the Blitz alike.

It is the one catering establishment in this town where the hungry can be sure of food and hot drinks on Sundays and week-days alike, from 7.30 in the morning to 10 o'clock at night. It is the first place to which people coming to the town from bombed areas, workmen on Government work, lorrymen, soldiers and airmen travelling, or on leave, are directed.

This canteen was started in early September 1940 to provide meals for a small group of schoolchildren from a danger zone, and six months later it was providing 1000 meals a day. The room was sprayed with disinfectant between meals, but there were homely touches – jade green tables with green oilcloth to match, and fresh flowers on every table. This home-from-home feel was reinforced by the provision of a piano, a radio-gramophone ('always in use'), a writing table and a library 'for the use of the troops'. The staff were part voluntary, part paid, and cakes and pastry were baked on the premises. Waste was eliminated by careful planning: scrapings from the plates were sold to helpers who kept poultry, and vegetable refuse went to a pig-keeper.

Breakfast was the first meal, served to firewatchers, busmen and buswomen, workmen and evacuees. At midday, 60 grammar school boys arrived to eat lunch – typically braised beef, vegetables and dumplings, followed by Victory Pudding, an eggless sponge plumped out with grated carrot, potato and breadcrumbs. Then came the civil servants living in billets, evacuees and war workers. All hot food was served 'really hot', kept that way with makeshift equipment that ranged from tin-hat plate warmers to a locally made bain-marie. Cake, watercress sandwiches and sardines on toast featured at tea-time. At supper there were vegetable pies, savoury Yorkshire puddings, steamed puddings (ginger sponge was a favourite) and milk puddings. The *Housecraft* article continues: 'Very little meat is used in the evenings, but occasionally we are able to get liver and serve a Poor Man's Goose, or make Baron's Pie or rissoles from remains of a joint.'

As Minister of Food, Frederick Marquis, Lord Woolton, masterminded operations. As early as 1940, using contacts from his pre-war days as head of the Lewis department store chain, he had envisaged a network of restaurants across the country. 'I planned kitchens in an array of buildings that ranged from ladies' boudoirs to churches,' recalls draughtsman Harry Lambert, seconded from designing department stores. In 1942, local authorities were given grants to assist in

Benign, and always quick with an encouraging word, the wartime Minister of Food Lord Woolton samples the soup in a mobile field kitchen

setting up British Restaurants (the name was Churchill's improvement on the original Community Feeding Centres) which offered three-course meals for a shilling. In Cambridge, the University's exclusive Pitt Club was requisitioned as one, while in Nottinghamshire, several were opened in converted battery-hen houses. Local art students designed murals to brighten up walls; volunteers provided flowers and gay tablecloths as well as their own services.

By 1945, British Restaurants were cooking 50 million meals a week. Although they provided cheap comforts, they were never intended for pleasure. While many appreciated a cheap hot meal, others loathed their institutional character, as Edmund Blishen pointed out in *A Cack-Handed War* (1972):

> Maybe the little café round the corner served nothing much better in the way of food, but you felt that Mrs Bolton's variations on the theme of Spam and chips were by some indefinable advantage of individuality and privacy an improvement on the anonymous offerings of the British Restaurant. Eating there was awfully like being fed by the Government – positively by the Minister of Food himself.

The fact that the main meal of the day was provided outside the home was of considerable assistance to the overworked and underpaid housewife-worker. But women had a good deal of personal pride invested in their skill as cooks, and men were uneasy at the loss of home comforts. 'The way a woman can cook when she is cooking just for one or two people … can't compare with all this mass-produced belly-fodder,' complained a correspondent in a 1946 issue of *The Listener*.

Few mass-eating facilities were provided by industry in the late 1930s, although the fact that factory canteens made good sense not just in war but in peace was well known. Research reported by C. G. Gardiner had discovered that 'many of the problems of industry, not only output, but absenteeism and health, accidents, labour turnover and contentment, were found to be related to not breaking the long spell at work with a midshift refresher.' In 1940, the Ministry of Labour required any factory employing more than 250 people to provide a suitable canteen in which hot meals could be bought.

The huge wartime increase in women factory workers made the need for canteens more urgent. According to Gardiner, they tended to be set to work at exceptionally tedious, repetitive jobs and so needed 'more frequent relief than men'. Moreover, they often arrived at work without having eaten any breakfast. 'In about two hours time, a decided flagging is noticed, cases of fainting occur, and the accident rate may go up as much as two and a half times, while the output rate goes down.'

Enthusiasm for canteens was not universal. Conservatism in eating habits led many working men to reject both what the Government thought was good for them and any attempt to brighten the wartime table with imaginative innovations. The Wartime Social Survey records the despair of a former hotel chef who managed a factory canteen in Birmingham.

He said that the workers at the factory only wanted fish and chips, cream cakes, bread and butter, and brown gravy over everything. They had protested when he made white sauce with boiled beef and carrots. They would not eat salads, did not like savouries – 'Birmingham people do not understand food'.

Nowhere did old habits die harder than in the mining areas. Miners were used to returning home for a substantial evening meal. Their union asked for them to be given larger rations at home to meet the needs of their physically exhausting labour, but the Government imposed a strict wartime policy of 'feeding on the job', and decided to offer the supplement at midday instead. Unfortunately, it did not consider working conditions when it planned the meals. David Robertson, a Member of Parliament, supervised various experiments for transporting hot meals underground and serving a meal of meat, vegetables and pudding in the middle of a shift. But even though the meals were heavily subsidized, the take-up rate was tiny (4 per cent at Haigh Colliery in south Yorkshire, for example). It was too hot and dusty to eat underground. Pithead canteens were much more successful, but what miners wanted at midday were sandwiches, meat pies or Cornish pasties.

A miner is served in the new canteen at Manvers Main pit near Doncaster in 1947. This was part of the experiment to make the working lives of the miners happier and less arduous. But the workforce preferred their traditional stodgy diet to the chef's sauces and green salads

In 1945, the National Union of Mineworkers again asked for larger rations at home for miners, and was refused. But in 1946, the Government cracked. 'The miner is a conservative individual,' it declared, and increased the amount of meat that miners could obtain on their ration books.

WE SHALL EAT AGAIN

'Canapé Cheval' appeared on the House of Commons dinner menu in 1943, and even this candour was surpassed after VE day, when 'Chicken (literally) Ancienne' was offered.

ANGUS CALDER, *The People's War* 1982

I used to make a kind of mayonnaise with flour and water put into the mixing machines with vinegar, mustard and a bit of powdered egg. It made me shudder to serve it.

MARIO GALLATI manager of the Ivy restaurant in CHRISTOPHER DRIVER,
The British at Table 1983

Those with the money to indulge their inclination could escape the prosaic good-for-you public eating of the canteen and the British Restaurant. Hotels and restaurants provided expensive food off the ration for those who could afford it, and there were murmurings about the way they snapped up unrationed luxuries such as lobsters, chicken and rabbits. In 1942, restaurant meals were officially restricted to one main course and a five shilling maximum charge. Luxuries were still to be had but if you plumped for oysters at four shillings a dozen at Simpson's in the Strand, you would have to go (officially at least) straight to pudding. But, claims historian Angus Calder, 'many of the classier establishments were exempted, particularly if fulfilling the important war work of feeding Westminster's statesmen.'

Expensive eating-out continued all through the war, but was severely curtailed. Smart London night-life centred on a very small number of restaurants which might have to be booked as much as a fortnight ahead. On one occasion, the fashionable Café de Paris suffered a direct hit. Bizarre and unpleasant incidents were reported in the ensuing mêlée: a woman had a broken leg washed in champagne, and looters pulled rings from the fingers of the dead and wounded.

Insistence on maintaining pre-war pretensions may have led the rich and privileged to do themselves down. The emperor's new clothes were as nothing to the contrivances of the snob chefs, and it was considered bad form to comment on 'ersatz' substitutions. Marghanita Laski's amusing wartime satire, *Love on the Supertax*, contrasts the fictional Mimosa in Curzon Street with a Lyons Corner House. In the first, her upper-class heroine Clarissa, unused to anything better,

… enjoyed her *Shellfish Cocktail*, which was shredded cod covered with a pink sauce made from cochineal and the water a lobster had once been cooked in; she appreciatively ate the rabbit with the ends of sprue that was called *Poulet Supreme,* and savoured to the full the *Crème au Chocolat* that was whipped up custard powder flavoured with cocoa. They drank Vin Rosé that was watered Palestine port and finished with reheated coffee … As they lit their cigarettes, Sir Hubert remarked, 'Lousy meal, isn't it?'

Clarissa stared at him. She had never questioned the convention that found such meals the height of luxury eating.

When she is taken out for a much more plebeian meal by the real love of her life, socialist Sid Barker, she found far better food at the Corner House. The long queue winding down the stairs was in sharp contrast to that 'at the Savoy, or Boulestin's … no pushing, no shoving, no wheeling in of favoured patron', and there was decent cooking to boot.

There were none of the cryptic elaborations she expected to find (*Boeuf Viennois* – hot Spam; *Boeuf Haché à l'Américaine* – cold Spam). Every dish looked as if it might represent real solid food and none of them was crossed out … Sid ordered omelettes, chops and *Sachertorte,* and two lagers … Clarissa, when she ate, had no words. She had completely forgotten what it felt like to feel entirely satisfied and when the last dish and the last drop of magnificently iced lager had gone, she turned to Sid and said spontaneously, 'Wasn't that too utterly marvellous?'

The torch of British gastronomy was kept alight by one man more than any other. André Simon had started the Wine and Food Society in 1933, and he managed to keep its quarterly magazine coming out as regularly as a dinner gong even during the war years. A collection of its articles published in 1944 gives a vivid picture both of the delights of pre-war eating and the determination with which gourmets pursued their pleasures despite wartime adversity in localities as diverse as Chad, Warsaw and Wessex. In his introduction, Louis Golding pays tribute to Simon's achievement in 'deepening and enriching' a whole generation's 'sense of good wine and good food'. He is also touchingly premature in anticipating the return of plenty.

The meal was confined within the strict Wooltonian framework. On the other hand, it is likely that M. Simon had made certain suggestions to the chef who had carried them out with passion and piety. 'We shall eat and drink again', I said; and (I confess it without shame) my heart danced for joy. One would be permitted to eat both fish and meat at the same meal in a public place. Decently, and in order, there would be as much butter as one cares for, eggs, cream, sugar and spice. Wine would flow again, as much wine as the enemy had spared us, along the parched and reviving conduits … and turning suddenly on my host, I added, 'And it's got an awful lot to do with you'.

PILLARS OF THE STATE

> *Nations are born out of nurseries. Children are like houses; if they are jerry-built, they never recover.*
>
> CHARLES HILL, Radio Doctor (1942)
>
> *The whole ground floor of the Empire Hall is entirely devoted to children's interests. Several Ministries have co-operated to show what is done for young people in the modern State, from the time they are born up to school-leaving age.*
>
> RUTH DREW at the Ideal Home Exhibition, *Good Taste* (1948)

Besides taking on a unparalleled degree of responsibility for providing the main family meal of the day, the wartime Government was concerned to ensure the health and well-being of children. The need for paternalism was the more acute because the men were away and so many women were, in effect, single parents. 'In the next thirty years housewives as mothers have vital work to do in ensuring the adequate continuance of the British race and of British ideals in the world,' announced Beveridge in 1942. State directives on feeding and bringing up children paved the way for the avalanche of advice on bringing up babies which has been such a feature of the last 50 years.

Evacuation at the beginning of the war was a violent intervention between parent and child. Although many mothers accompanied their tots to more or less satisfactory rural sanctuaries, in the summer of 1939 hundreds of thousands of children found themselves suddenly alone in strange environments in which everything from food to accents was strange. Many returned home almost as soon as they arrived. But meeting them opened the eyes of upper- and middle-class families to the degree of deprivation and poverty that existed in the cities. It created widespread enthusiasm for the measures later taken by the State to improve welfare, diet and education for all children. As a consequence, post-war children were, according to Susan Cooper in *The Age of Austerity:*

> A large and healthy generation, guarded by regulation orange juice, halibut oil and milk … Unable to remember a time without shortages, they were not haunted by the ghosts of freedom and bulging shops and real cream.

School meals, supplies of milk and the insistence on regularly taking vitamin supplements were official interventions that had undoubted benefits for children, but which were felt by some to question the competence of mothers. For all his often-stated respect for the family, Lord Woolton could not conceal his authoritarian instincts in a speech on the subject which he gave to the Warwickshire Women's Institute in 1945.

Don't let us throw out the baby of sound nutrition with the cold bath-water of restriction and control ... the young need protection and it is proper that for them the State should take deliberate steps to give them opportunity ... Feeding is not enough, it must be good feeding. The food must be chosen in the light of knowledge of what a growing child needs for the building of a sound body. And when the food has been well chosen, it must be well cooked. This is a task that calls for the highest degree of scientific catering; it mustn't be left to chance.

The Housewives League (of which more below) pointed out the insult implicit in the refusal of the authorities to provide milk for children during school holidays. 'It was as though you could get things via institutions, but not ... via your mother and father,' recalls Mary Blakey, a Lancashire housewife and League member. In later years it has been realized that a generation of children may have had their teeth rotted by sugar added to vitamin-rich drinks and that a considerable number of them may

Schoolboys watch as their lunch arrives at a London school in 1947

have been allergic to cow's milk. But at the time the benefits seemed easily to outweigh the disadvantages. Clearly, mothers no longer knew best.

Universal school meals were a wartime innovation which continued to be a central part of school life until they were effectively abandoned by Margaret Thatcher's Government in 1980 (see page 202). Before the war, only 5 per cent of children who were classed as malnourished qualified for school meals. Most of the rest went home to eat or brought a packed lunch. By June 1949, nearly 3 million children were eating at school every day, 53 per cent of the total school population. School dinners were seen as a matter of national importance, too much for the Board of Education to undertake, and so the erecting of canteens, generally prefabs, fell to the responsibility of the Exchequer.

More than lunch was available. Tea was served to those doing after-school activities and for children staying on for fire-watch practice. Schools even provided breakfast, and meals at weekends and holidays. It was recognized that this was not just for the health of the child but to alleviate the load on women's shoulders at a time when the Government was very keen to attract mothers back to work.

Meals were also seen as an important opportunity for social training. At grammar schools, boys and girls were segregated for eating. Primary school children were supposed to wash their hands and comb their hair before settling down to eat up their greens and semolina. By 1945, 1 in 3 schoolchildren had their main meal of the day at school, compared with 1 in 36 before the war, and the stage was set for the younger generation to spend more of its waking day away from its parents than it ever had before.

School meals for all echoed the extension of the school day to all. The 1944 Butler Education Act made free secondary school education available for all children (in 1938 only 14 per cent of the proportion eligible by age gained admission to secondary school) and raised the school-leaving age from 14 to 15 (effected in 1947). It was the beginning of a qualitative shift in perspective, a clearer split between the generations than Britain had ever known. The unlooked-for effect of extending educational opportunities to boys and girls of all backgrounds was to distance children from home.

At the time, Lord Woolton insisted that we should 'never forget that children are the children of parents, not of the State, and the home is the centre of their lives and the source of their strength and the foundation of their characters.' But the Government he served under did more than any other in British history to remove them from it. Fifty years later, we take the school's responsibility for the socialization of children so for granted that it is a commonplace to blame the decline of table manners on the ending of formal school dinners.

Breaktime in a primary school in 1949. The daily ration of milk did wonders to improve the physique of the nation's children. School children enjoyed its benefits free until 1980, when Margaret Thatcher cancelled the order

THE MAN IN WHITEHALL ████████████████

> *Not long ago I overheard a conversation between two women shopping at a counter,*
> *'After all, housewives are war workers the same as everybody else, aren't they?' They are.*
> *And that is why I present this book to them. I hope they find it a serviceable weapon.*
>
> LORD WOOLTON, *Food Facts for the Kitchen Front* c.1942
>
> *In peacetime, exhortations to work hard for the sake of the nation lacked the moral*
> *authority they had possessed during the war. The rhetoric of economic crisis was at odds with the*
> *popular experience of abundant employment and better working conditions. Worse, there was a*
> *hectoring element, an implicit criticism of the working classes as lazy, and a veiled threat of*
> *penalties to come unless they pulled their socks up.*
>
> PAUL ADDISON, *Now the War is Over* 1985

Besides providing meals for her men and her children outside the home, the powers-that-be were concerned with re-educating the housewife herself. The wartime coalition Government had negotiated the challenge of invading the Englishwoman's kitchen without being summarily rapped over the knuckles with a wooden spoon with admirable tact. This was largely thanks to the organizational flair of Lord Woolton, a large and amiable man with a face not unlike the potato he prized so highly for its nutritional quality, and a personal charisma that could bring whole halls of housewives spontaneously to their feet.

'The Government can and will build houses, but only women can build homes,' he told the 'domestic war workers' he respected as 'community leaders'. His introduction to a popular collection of lectures on dietetics called *The Nation's Larder and the Housewife's Part Therein* ('A Book of National Importance') was addressed to 'The housewife, and all those in a community of any kind - village or town, institute or society - who are acting or can act in any way as leaders with regard to this now vital matter of food.' It emphasized that no one yet knew all there was to know about dietetics, and that it was a mistake to get bogged down in calorie counts. But,

> We can probably be certain that if we took an East End child and put him on
> a midday meal of cheese, vitaminized margarine, wholemeal bread, milk and
> an orange, he would, at the end of three months look fitter and be
> clearer skinned - and possibly more vivacious and naughtier - than one who
> had regularly had his cut from the joint and two vegs followed by pudding.'

The evident truth of this had been proved by the innovative Peckham Experiment undertaken in south London before the war, although this had offered whole families, rather than just children, the opportunity of eating an 'Oslo' breakfast of this sort, and of exercising well. It was also underlined by the improved health of evacuee children, and by the change that came over men and women who joined the forces. Mary Lee Settle, who enlisted as an airwoman in 1942, remembers how her fellow conscripts were transformed by army life.

> All these very young products of the dole, then the war, of white bread, 'marge' and strong tea, of a hard city life, already had the shrunken upper body, the heavy-set thighs, white and doughy, of mature women. After a few weeks of basic training, the girls around me had begun to fill out and glow. Air, exercise, regular meals and the very act of sleeping above ground for the first time in years were making the blood run better in their veins.

Woolton gave a sense of patriotic purpose to domestic life. To this day, many of the generation who listened to him in their twenties and thirties are inescapably wedded to habits of thrift. And to gardening. This was the age of the useful garden, of digging for victory regardless of sex or class. In *Come Into the Garden Cook* (1942), Constance Spry wrote:

> I write this book for … people who are ready and able to spend thought and energy on growing food in the garden with which to supplement adequate rations. I am thinking also of the women who, perhaps for the first time in their lives, will go into the kitchen and cook, bringing to bear on cooking the intelligence and judgement which hitherto they may have reserved for other occupations

By the end of the war, over half of all manual workers kept either allotments or vegetable gardens, to say nothing of tomato-filled window-boxes and mushroom-scented cellars. Rows of runner beans, carrots and cabbages decked the moat of the Tower of London. Pig clubs started up all over the country to supplement declining meat production as farmers turned away from pasture to the high-intensity farming of wheat and potatoes. A daily dawn chorus of cluckings and crowings was heard from the 11½ million hens kept in Britain's back gardens, allotments, schools and even cages attached to the windows of flats. Peter Rabbit was suddenly a welcome guest - 'meat from waste' according to a Ministry of Food factsheet. 'In a single tame rabbit four and a half months old, there is the nutritive value of 4½ pounds of best beef, shoulder of mutton or of pork.'

The new medium of radio was essential in spreading the new good food gospel. During the war 'listening in' became a national priority. Eighteen million people tuned in to the five-minute programme *The Kitchen Front*, broadcast daily at 8.15 a.m., a time calculated to make it as much a national institution as the weather forecast. Marguerite Patten, who became one of the most popular television cooks of the 1950s, was part of a team which also included 'radio doctor' Charles Hill, Mabel Constans-Duros and Grandma Buggins. They gave daily advice on what food was seasonally available and how to cook it to best advantage. There were debates on the best way of ridding cormorant of its salty taste and much criticism of the murderous

British way with vegetables. Hill, according to the social commentator Ann Valery, was especially concerned to keep Britain regular.

> Doctor Hill's lugubrious tone and flights of rhetoric brought the nation's obsession with its bowels to its peak, and it was no surprise when he became head of the BBC some years after. After all, a man who can comprehend the tortured contortions of the British Inside will hardly be stumped by the Byzantine ramifications of Broadcasting House.

In his introduction to the 'book of the series', *Food Facts for the Kitchen Front*, Lord Woolton declared that, 'its lessons in cookery and food values hold good for times of peace and plenty.' The Ministry of Food's 1945 *ABC of Cookery* also emphasized that the methods of cooking it recommended were 'useful in times of plenty as well as in times of rationing ... If important foods from the wartime rations are made the foundation of our peacetime meals, and if salads, vegetables and energy foods are added, the diet will be excellent.'

Wishful thinking. Nothing could have gone more over the top than the techni-colour age of gourmet entertaining with processed foods that was to come. The gloriously varied range of salad vegetables suggested in 1945 ('raw cabbage heart, savoy, spinach, sprouts, young leaves of kale and young turnip tops, cauliflower, broccoli, watercress including the stalks, parsley, young dandelion leaves, mint, nasturtium leaves, young celery leaves, green tops of leeks or spring onions, chives, mustard and cress, all green herbs, lettuce and endive') was thinned down in the 1962 edition to a suggestion that tomato, carrot and beetroot, or cold potato, would add 'variety of colour and texture to lettuce'.

Woolton was a hard act to follow, and it was undoubtedly more difficult to inspire an exhausted post-war population than it had been to arouse the Blitz spirit when the country had its back to the wall. Although the habit of obedience instilled by five years of national emergency meant that the British people put its collective shoulder to the wheel of Labour's export drive with remarkably little protest, as the years dragged on and there seemed no let-up even after the war, more and more grumbles were heard. Emigration rates to Australia, Canada, New Zealand and South Africa soared. GI brides were offered special quarters on transatlantic liners.

The housewife, once the loyal ally of the Government, was now dangerously disaffected. 'Ration figure', the consequence of women eating too much carbo-hydrates because they were giving high-protein foods to their children and menfolk, was common. Queues still took up at least an hour of the day. Frequent power cuts led to heating, the radio and the iron being cut off, soap was non-existent, prices were rising. Just when things were worst, the sweet ration was halved and the instant comfort of sugar lost. Resentment against civil servants and shopkeepers smouldered. 'We won the war,' says the housewife dramatized in a *Picture Post* feature, 'Mrs Average' in 1947. 'Why is it so much worse? ... Mrs Average wants more leisure, more colour, more food and clothing, less weary work. But most of all she wants hope. That is why she is sadder now than during the war.'

But it is also clear that the post-war Labour Government's attitude to housewives was uninspiring and patronizing. 'Housewives as a whole cannot be trusted to buy all the right things where nutrition and health are concerned', Douglas Jay, Economic Secretary to the Treasury, wrote as early as 1937 in *The Socialist Case*, his pre-war outline for a Labour-led future. 'This is really no more than an extension of a principle according to which the housewife herself would not trust a child of four to select the week's purchases. For in the case of nutrition or health, the gentleman in Whitehall really does know better what is good for people than the people themselves.'

HOUSEWIVES' REVOLT

> *We are suffering from mental exhaustion, irritation and frustration. The smiling mother of yesterday is the bad-tempered mother of today, and the understanding partner is now the nagging wife ... We are under-fed, under-washed and over-controlled.*
>
> CONSTANCE HILL, Liverpool Townswomen's Guild 1946

> *We are sick and tired of your rudenesss, and of fawning and simpering to get honest value for money from you. What has happened to English courtesy?*
>
> MARGUERITE STEEN, 'Open letter to some shopkeepers' 1945

Jay's image of the housewife as a child of four was not calculated to appeal. In fact, women had never been better organized. Membership of both political women's organizations and non-partisan groups such as the Women's Institutes and Townswomen's Guilds soared in the 1940s, and as 'Food Leaders' many of their members played a vital part in the dissemination of Ministry of Food information and directives. All acted together to lobby Whitehall during the peak years of disillusion with the Government, the 1946/7 winter of discontent.

One group was more radical than the rest. Irene Lovelock, founder of the British Housewives League, was a lively south London vicar's wife with three small children. She had voted Labour in the general election, but, angered by the sight of elderly and pregnant women in queues, she began a purely local protest called the Anti-Queue Association in Croydon in June 1945. It was primarily an attack on shopkeepers, 'domineering, petty tyrants, who treat women like children'. Alfreda Lansdau, a Neasden rabbi's wife, did the same, and the two then united to form the British Housewives League. A total of 17 000 signatures was collected on a petition to Parliament. The *London Evening News* ran a series of front-page stories on the League and the *Sunday Graphic* invited Lovelock to write a weekly column. 'But the housewives' revolt was not simply an invention of the right-wing press,' says historian James Hinton, whose research on this little-publicized subject I have found invaluable:

Editors were as much responding to the rage of a section of their female readership (expressed in the very large numbers of letters which flooded their offices when housewives' protests were reported) as engaging in any calculated attempt to manufacture protest for partisan purposes. Indeed the first wave of protest had taken off at a time when nobody knew who would be running the next Government.

When Marguerite Steen published that 'open letter to shopkeepers' in the *London Evening News,* the paper announced six days later that she had provoked 'our heaviest postbag for months'.

Worse was in store. In February 1946, Ben Smith, then Minister for Food, announced cuts in bacon, poultry and egg rations and, in an attempt to gain a bargaining counter in the renegotiation of the American lend-lease shipments that had been ended with brutal suddenness in August 1945, withdrew dollar-costly dried eggs, perhaps the most important staple of the wartime larder, from the shops. He was attacked from every side, not least for his lily-livered defensiveness. 'They seem to be so afraid,' complained Nelly Last, a Mass Observation diarist. 'Winston Churchill never hesitated to tell us the worst, and you felt brave and strong with him.'

Women's organizations howled in protest and speakers stressed their non-partisan and classless nature. 'We don't care two hoots – most of us – what party is in,' said Constance Hill, a moving spirit in the Liverpool Townswomen's Guild, at a rally in the city. A telegram from 600 members of the Govan Tenants Associations threatened to 'force our husbands to strike if our rations are reduced'. On the day the issue was to be debated, several hundred members of the British Housewives League

turned up at the House of Commons. Banner headlines in the newspapers recorded Smith's withdrawal in disarray and the restoration of dried eggs to the shops. Thousands of housewives sent subscriptions to the Lovelocks' Croydon vicarage to celebrate what was arguably the first-ever political victory for organized domesticity, and an official League newsletter, *Housewives Today*, began to be circulated. In this sprightly journal a wide range of abuses were condemned, including that of luxury eating in restaurants.

Some months later, first the threat and then the reality of rationed bread produced another outcry. During the war, this most essential of staple foods had never been rationed, but fears of worldwide harvest failure led a cautious Government to limit supplies of both loaves and flour in 1946. This time women's groups from Buckinghamshire and Liverpool, Bristol and Glasgow, Cheltenham and London sent in petitions, and the revolt took on a genuinely national character. By July, Lovelock could claim to have 600 000 signatures on the petition the League presented to the Ministry of Food. Even Enid Blyton was moved to a Lorena Bobbitt-like ferocity:

I wish I were an MP's wife.
I'd lead him such an awful life . . .
Has no MP an angry wife
Who threatens with a carving knife
And vows that if he rations bread
She'll see that boys and girls are fed,
And he must give up half his share
Because HE made the cupboard bare?

Below:Women's groups from all parts of the country marched on Westminster in 1946. Led by Irene Lovelock (centre) they brought a petition signed by 600 000 housewives
Bottom right:The ascetic and vegetarian Chancellor of the Exchequer Sir Stafford Cripps had none of Lord Woolton's charm

"Now don't forget – anyone hanging around with a wistful look in their eye – let 'erm have it – bang, bang!"

The Labour Government came close to climbing down again, but Attlee decided to face out the protests, confident (rightly) that they would die away once people realized that the reality of bread rationing would not mean shortages. Certainly, news of the rationing of bread increased sympathy for Britain in the United States at a time when the vital American 'lend-lease' contributions to Britain's food supplies had been suspended. It undoubtedly contributed to Congress's approval on 15 July of the loan negotiated by Maynard Keynes which formed the seed corn for Britain's eventual industrial recovery.

But all this was still in the invisible future. Matters were worsened by the freezingly cold winter of 1947. Parsnips had to be dug out of the ground with pneumatic drills, thousands of sheep died in Scotland and 20 000 acres of winter corn was destroyed. In the spring of 1948, floods gutted potato clamps and destroyed 80 000 tons of tubers. In all, 32 per cent of Britain's hill sheep died, as did 30 000 cattle. The smell of burning corpses floated across Wales. Concessions to the unions for shorter working weeks for men, at a time when women were being urged to go back to work in the factories at the customary fraction of male pay, led to further outcry. 'The Government is trying to get a 40-hour week for men at the expense of an 80-hour week for mothers,' complained *Housewives Today* in February.

At this point, extremists took over the public face of the League, now rumoured to be a million strong. A year earlier the unpleasantly anti-Semitic Eleonara Tennant had attempted to hijack its demonstration in Trafalgar Square with a protest against German refugees; now the distinctly upper-class Oxford Philosophy, Politics and Economics graduate Dorothy Crisp soared to prominence and, in Hinton's words, 'inverted the core identity of Mother as carer and coper to Mother as wielder of the rod of correction'. Lovelock disliked Crisp's rabble-rousing and her politics, but she also admired her: 'There is something Elizabethan about Dorothy,' she wrote in her autobiography. However, Crisp's attempt to achieve real political power by negotiating for an alliance with the Conservatives (she admitted an ambition to be Britain's first woman prime minister) has led to the League being dismissed by some as a tool of the Tory party. This is to distort its true purpose. Hinton again:

> It was in defence of the home, not merely of their interests as consumers, that the League called on women to organize. A leading objective was 'to show that over-control by the State is not in the interests of a free and happy home life and the development of personality in accord with the Christian traditions'.

It was, said Irene Lovelock, 'a spiritual movement', which aimed 'to put into public life the same spirit shown by women in home life, unselfishness and readiness to serve.' Women, 'bound up with the home and children, and the simple lasting experiences of life', were better placed than men to 'know what's worth preserving in Britain and what wants changing.' The sanctity of home has been destroyed,' she added, now that 'hordes of officials have the right to enter your home at any time.'

She also presciently questioned the annexation of children's lives by schools, and objected to homework on the grounds that it prevented them being taught 'the things that mattered, the way to run a home and cook and make clothes, to be true citizens.' Today, concerned as we are over 'family values', we read this with more respect than it received at the time.

The League's political position is best understood by drawing a parallel with the Green Party today. In conception, it was no more Tory than the Greens are socialist. What the League did stand for was middle-class values. And in this lies the clue to a deeper cause of discontent than food shortages and queues: the humiliation experienced by women who had once been able not only to run attractive homes but to enjoy interesting lives of their own. The Government could point to a rise in living standards at the end of the 1940s, but although working-class women were qualitatively better off even during the age of austerity, the same was far from true for the middle classes. In *Housewives Today* (January, 1950), Joyce Mew accurately defined the profound changes in the domestic set-up that Betty Friedan would in time call 'the problem which has no name'. The only difference is that Mew saw rationing and State interference with the traditional handing-down of domestic expertise as the source of the problem, while Friedan blamed women's exclusion from the male sphere of work. In the past, wrote Mew,

> Women have been on the whole contented with their lot chiefly because their daily routine has included a considerable amount of creative work. The care of children can be, apart from the inevitable small exasperations, a deeply satisfying experience. There is a sense in which a perfect apple pie is comparable with a landscape by Turner, or a poem by Keats; the difference is one of calibre, not in essence.
>
> As the opportunity for creative work in the home recedes, so we find women becoming dissatisfied and eventually vociferous. They are demanding that the 'fun' be put back into their work again. In the meantime, there are three things we can do about this. First, we can be intolerant of poor quality in materials over which we have control. Secondly, we can let the youngsters (boys as well as girls) 'have a go' in the kitchen, even at the risk of wasted rations. And thirdly, we can make a point of having, at least once or twice a week, some dish made from a traditional recipe, followed exactly, so that the family keeps on remembering what good food is.

In the 1940s, people saw more clearly than they would do in the 1950s and 1960s that the housewife was criminally overworked. A survey in 1951 revealed that the average housewife in Britain worked 75 hours a week, not including the work she did at weekends. Discontent was undoubtedly heightened when middle-class wives were put into the same boat as working-class women by the flight of domestic servants from the home. In her introduction to Molly Panter Downes' 1947 novel, *One Fine Day*, Nicola Beauman calls the 1940s 'the era when servants were a vanished species, but labour-saving devices hadn't arrived'. During the war, it was

Half-way through the morning—FLOP!

Every woman knows that sinking feeling—so apt to drag at you in the middle of the morning. *That's* the moment for a cup of Bovril. Bovril refreshes. Invigorates. Warms. Gives you fresh energy for the daily round.

BREAKFAST SPECIAL

Fry cooked potatoes and any left-over vegetables until well browned underneath. Dot the top with Bovril, and fold over like an omelette.

FREE

The Mr. & Mrs. Cook Book, 46 pages of recipes and kitchen hints. Send now for your copy to : Bovril Ltd., Old Street, London, E.C.1

BOVRIL *prevents that sinking feeling*

A 1950s comment on the drudgery of house-work – an advertisement for 'invigorating' Bovril

accepted that extraordinary domestic efforts had to be made; after it ended, people began to put their minds more seriously to the problems of home management. At the 1946 Labour party conference, Ian Mikardo suggested that central kitchens with a hot meal delivery service should be provided for the benefit of housewives. He also talked of taking the drudgery out of housework by introducing kitchen floors designed to reduce dirt and dust, like those in modern factories, properly staffed nurseries and central playrooms, district heating centres and even communal sewing centres. Beveridge wrote in 1948 that

> The housewife's job with a large family is frankly impossible, and will remain so unless some of what has now to be done separately in every home - washing all clothes, cooking every meal, being in charge of every child for every moment when it is not done at school, can be done communally outside the home.

But in the long run, housework was not nationalized along with the rest of Britain's industries. The wartime nurseries closed, as did the bulk of the British Restaurants. The solution to the housewife's overloaded agenda was to be consumer goods: women had to go out to work for the products that would save them time and effort in the home.

TOGETHER AGAIN

For some people it was bliss when their husband came back. But in some cases, they weren't the same person. Some women had to get used to a different person coming back into their life, which is very disconcerting.

MARGUERITE PATTEN

No one can pretend that the approaching mass transfer is going to be easy, even if it is helped for a short space by the heady champagne of victory. It is one of those major operations which ought not to be performed with any other anaesthetic than the will and consent of the people affected.

MASS OBSERVATION SURVEY, *The Journey Home* 1945

The model fictional wives of the war, Jan Struther's *Mrs Miniver* and E. M. Delafield's *Provincial Lady in Wartime,* greeted their returning spouses with open arms. But the truth was that prolonged separation and the tension of never quite knowing whether a spouse or fiancé was even alive put enormous strains on couple relationships. The jolly group life of camp, barracks and factory canteen had encouraged freedom and irresponsibility; both women and men found it difficult to adapt to the petty privations of the domestic scene. Nostalgic depictions of the post-war years as a golden age of the family emphasize the baby boom of the mid-1940s rather than the 50 000 couples who were queuing up to get divorced when the war ended. Even Jan Struther, whose heroic Mrs Miniver was reputed to have been of considerable influence in persuading the United States to enter the war, divorced her husband and married an American after the war.

Phoebe and Laurence Bendit's *Living Together Again* (1946) was a sensitive little paperback on this much-discussed problem.

> The seeds of trouble were waiting to spring into life, if, when the boys did come home, they found that their wives and sweethearts did not expect to settle into their little houses, or flats, and become once more domestic servants, or pet animals, who are not expected to have a life of their own.

The strains of the situation had more influence than is generally recognized on the instability that has been a characteristic of marriage in Britain ever since. In a qualitatively new departure from pre-war books on marriage, the Bendits asserted that 'marriage is a fifty-fifty proposition, where both sides have rights and both sides have duties'. Their book firmly recommended parting if couples no longer found it possible to see eye to eye. For the majority of people, the economics of austerity made it financially ruinous to separate, and there was still a profound social stigma to divorcing if children were involved.

But even where marriages did not formally end, many children of that generation remember the lives of their mothers and fathers as cold war conflicts at best, with occasional outbreaks of guerrilla warfare or even wholesale battles. Sitting round a table 'as a family' was much rarer than we assume it was. Children ate straight after school and were shushed away so as not to disturb Dad when he came in for his own meal. Women tended to grab a bite when they were hungry, probably in the kitchen, standing up.

The middle classes found it exceptionally difficult to adapt. Molly Panter Downes' *One Fine Day* is a requiem for a life style. The whistling butchers' boys, the nannies with starched apron fronts, the 'caps and aprons in the kitchen shrieking with laughter over their bread-and-cheese elevenses', have all disappeared. Stephen and Laura ('wretched victims of their class, they still had dinner. Without the slaves, they still cherished the useless lamp') experience the house as a tyrant, that binds Laura 'to the kitchen, Stephen, when he was home, to the lawn mower and the woodpile, the dirty boots and the devilish bindweed.'

Bread and Bureaucrats

During dinner, Stephen would expand, glow, visibly enjoy himself. Then a cloud of irritation descended on his brow, he took off his coat and hung it up without a word. The least he could do for her, he said, was that. He fetched the coal, stoked the boiler, cleaned shoes. Sometimes the wicker chair in the kitchen gave a loud creaking report as they worked together straightening out the mess. Occasionally Laura wondered …whether the chair was creaking beneath the ghost of some former cook – Mrs Abbey, perhaps, who had been killed in the London Blitz. An ectoplasmic Mrs Abbey rolled against the faded cushions, clapping her hand across her splitting mouth at the sight of Stephen, with a dishcloth round his middle, frowning at a smear of grease on a glass, He was so good, so kind. But he was a neat man, hating mess and hugger-mugger. He could not take it all in his stride as she could.

In default of an ideal man, dreams of ideal children and an ideal home moved to the forefront of feminine thinking. 'Have women forgotten how to fall in love?' challenged Barbara Vise in 1949 in *Good Taste* magazine.

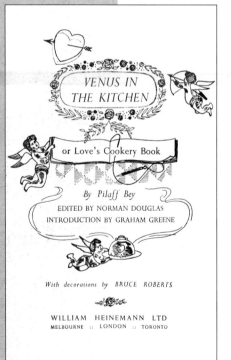

The title page illustration for Norman Douglas's Venus in the Kitchen

Today women seem so much occupied with material complexities, with the ambition for material comfort and easy-thinking, with the full-time business of making a living, paying their taxes and finding the next meal, that they have little time to live in this illusion which is a greater reality than all the rest. Their focus is changed. Today it is set more by everyday arithmetic than by the imagination which lets one look into the far and enchanted countries of the spirit … It seems to be a modern policy to keep skimming over the surface and playing at things by taking them all at their outer value. After all, it is much easier – it doesn't matter so much – just to be thinking whether you will be having a new refrigerator in your nice, spotless kitchen in your new home, with your bridegroom as background, than be caught in a spell by him.

'Forgotten' was not the right word. What this article, like thousands of others along similarly sentimental lines in the next few years, was doing was rejecting the wartime free-for-all when [haughty sniff] 'propinquity seemed to have stronger bonds than loyalty', and announcing a new script for the future. Instead of seeing themselves as independent workers in their own right, who deserved to have the domestic chores taken off their shoulders, women were to present themselves as sex objects, *femmes fatales*. It was entirely appropriate that one of the first of the flood of post-austerity cookery books published in the 1950s was Norman Douglas's collection of aphrodisiac recipes, *Venus in the Kitchen*.

GRUMBLINGS

When the war finished, Britain expected, not perhaps the lap of luxury, but at least a few bananas, a few more cigarettes, a range of cloths to choose suits from, a car maybe or a trip abroad, the odd bottle of whisky to celebrate the expanding horizons which were already closing in. No arguments from the front bench ever quite persuaded the people that they could not be given these things; somewhere sadists were at work, or puritans. Almost unwillingly, and half-guiltily, the public looked to the spivs to correct the balance. Even if no whisky materialised, the snook had to be cocked.

DAVID HUGHES, in *The Age of Austerity* 1963

During the war it was considered unpatriotic to support the 'spivs'; by 1951 it was a popular pastime . . . Faith in State control as the instrument of obligatory equality broke against the rock of human nature.

JAMES McMILLAN, *The Way it Changed* 1987

By 1947, rations were lower than they ever had been during the war. The average adult's weekly allowance was just 13 ounces of meat, 1½ of cheese, 6 of butter and margarine, 1 of cooking fat, 8 of sugar, 2 pints of milk and 1 egg. The long, hot summer might have cheered people up if it hadn't caused drought in Wales and nearly exhausted Manchester's water supply. The Government, desperate for popularity, made one last try to titillate the nation's jaded palates. It began to import whale meat.

At first this had some degree of success. It was, at least, different. Marguerite Patten gave a recipe for whale stew on her first appearance on the newly established *Woman's Hour.* She remembers that 'the smell was awful – a cross between liver and rather strong meat, with a very fishy and oily smell as well.' But by September, Lyons Corner Houses reported that they were serving 600 whale steaks a day. The Caterers' Association declared that 'the public will take all that we can give them'. Vast refrigerated ships brought in both fresh meat and canned. But the novelty wore off, especially once the meat ration was upped. In 1950, 4000 tons of unwanted whale meat were towed to and fro across the North Sea. Even when arguments with Argentina reduced the meat ration to a shilling a week, there were no takers.

But by then a new delicacy was supposed – by the Ministry of Food at least – to be all the rage. Ten million tins of a mysterious fish called 'snoek' arrived from South Africa to replace sardines, a restricted import after the devaluation of the pound had created exchange problems with Portugal. Susan Cooper *(The Age of Austerity)* remembers that

The name, of course, was a gift. Before it even arrived in the shops, it was seized upon with cries of delight by cartoonists and comedians ... Research revealed that the snoek was a large, ferocious, tropical fish, like a barracuda, that it was dangerous to bathers, had rows of fearsome teeth, and when displeased hissed like a snake and barked like a dog.

Undeterred, the Government spent nearly £900 000 on advertising the new product. Dr Edith Summerskill presided over a snoek-tasting party at the Ministry of Food in May 1948, and a rash of unlikely recipes were produced.

Snoek piquante:
4 spring onions, chopped;
liquid from snoek;
4 tablespoons vinegar;
½ can of snoek, mashed;
2 tablespoons of syrup;
salt to taste;
½ teaspoon of pepper.

Cook the onions in the fish liquor and vinegar for five minutes. Add the snoek, syrup and seasoning and mix well; serve cold with salad.

Newspapers produced polls suggesting that snoek was widely regarded as unpalatable, but the Ministry persevered, not least because contracts had committed them to importing eight million more tins. A new batch from Australia was described as barracuda, but sold no better. Judgements ranged from 'tasteless and unpalatable' and 'abominable' to 'one of the dullest fish I have ever eaten' (this from the Minister for Food himself).

Prices were cut from 1s 4 ½d to a shilling a can. Finally, snoek came off points altogether. 'Decently obscure mists closed around the piles of tins,' Susan Cooper recalls. But 18 months later, 'a mysterious quantity of tinned fish for cats came on the market . . . it cost tenpence a tin, and its origins were left muffled in tact.'

Attlee's austere yet dedicated Labour Government was being made to look increasingly ridiculous, not least by the efforts of Lord Beaverbrook, who once said memorably to the Royal Commission on the Press that he 'ran the paper [the *Daily Express*] purely for propaganda, and for no other purpose.' Films also had an effect. Newsreels continued to back Britain with hearty slogans, but Hollywood made us greedy for glamour and the famous Ealing comedies sent up the Government unmercifully. The historian Peter Hennessy has speculated on the extent to which the story of the brave little inner London state run so successfully as a ration-free zone by Stanley Holloway in *Passport to Pimlico* 'fanned resentment of rationing in 1949 and contributed to the dramatic shrinking of Labour's majority the following year'. Certainly, the scriptwriter, T. E. B. 'Tibby' Clarke was made an OBE by Churchill in 1952.

Whisky Galore's unforgettable story of the hijacking of a shipwrecked cargo of Scotch intended for export to the United States spoke directly to the public's resentment that the whole of the world, including its former enemies, seemed to be enjoying luxuries while Britain, the supposed victor, was mired in gloom. 'Almost all the whisky made in the land of the leal is hurtling across the Atlantic as fast as it can, and now we hear that £4 000 000 worth of kippers are to follow', ran a furious newspaper report in November 1950. 'We shall get the dyed kippers, while the Lowestoft cured go on a voyage.'

Left: The film of the play *Whisky Galore* highlighted the widely-felt sense of grievance at the export of the best British products. Right: Black market profiteering in London's Oxford Street. A spiv selling nylons is caught by a policeman

The phrase 'under the counter' was a wartime coinage. There had been grumblings of discontent during the war about the flourishing black market that was known to exist in chocolate, nylons and perfume, but the compulsory national solidarity allowed few to surface. When the *Daily Mirror*'s columnist Cassandra launched a 'Gutskrieg' against lavish eaters in restaurants in 1941, the newspaper was reproved and Cassandra was called up to join the Army shortly afterwards. Frank Owen of the *Evening Standard*, another articulate critic of spivvery and under-the-counter practices, was also suddenly de-reserved in his late thirties.

The longer the post-war depression continued, however, the more the black market gained acceptability. Visitors to the Continent came back to write angry letters to the newspapers declaring that on holiday in Austria, 'an ex-enemy country, still under military occupation', they had found that, 'in all zones of occupation, anyone can go into any sweet shop he likes and buy as many bars of Cadbury's milk chocolate as he likes, at a price approximating to what we pay in England.'

'Sacrifice is no longer necessary or fashionable,' said *The Spectator* in 1945, 'lawlessness is in the air . . . History tosses up wide boys as the face erupts boils, to force poisons out of the body politic.' Glamorous 'Black Max' Intrator was pictured in the papers with his arms round a mysteriously veiled woman, sipping champagne. The crime rate soared. *The Recorder* of London referred to a 'distemper of dishonesty which has swept over the country in the last few years until people have lost sight of the difference between right and wrong.' During 1947, £13 million worth of property disappeared compared to only £2.5 million in 1938.

In 1948 *The Times* deplored the failure of the police to search positively for 20 000 deserters with no rights to ration books who 'formed a pool of lawbreakers'. It warned that, 'They have been taught techniques of violence in wartime and were bitter enough to exercise them now.' In 1950, a legal paper stated that the ordinary citizen no longer felt safe in his own home. 'Old people tremble when they hear a knock on the door.'

A Mass Observation report on delinquency is enough to disabuse anyone who thinks that juvenile crime is a modern invention. The peak age of offending in 1950 was 14. The report also quotes a 13-year-old boy saying to his 8-year-old partner: 'Keep your bloody mouth shut, I'll do the talking.' Every large school had on its register a couple of active criminals who had no fear of the police. 'One small boy sneered on arrest, "You can't touch me, mate, I'm under eight."'

BANANARAMA

When Mrs Prout turns up, winking, sighing 'There's bananas in the village,'
do I not drop everything, leap for the bicycle, arrive panting at the shop, agonized with fear
in case Victoria shall be the only child at Miss Grant's not happily peeling one of
those over-rated things?

MOLLY PANTER DOWNES, *One Fine Day*

When bananas first turned up after the war, they were greeted with incredulity. The Home Secretary had to show children how to eat them - like ice-cream cones rather than corn on the cob. As rationing dribbled to a close between 1949 and 1954, the Government could boast proudly of its social achievements but the return to normality proved painfully slow. On the plus side, the nation as a whole had never been as well fed, lean and fit, albeit resigned to a diet as uniformly greige in appearance as Utility clothing and as lacking in flavour as those infamous tins of snoek. A Rowntree survey of poverty in 1936 had found that one-third was due to unemployment and one-third to inadequate wages. By 1950, none was due to unemployment, only 1 per cent was the result of inadequate wages and only 2.77 per cent of the working class were living in poverty as it had been defined in 1938. Welfare state expenditure was the main reason for this great improvement.

Children from the Bristol
area getting their first taste
of bananas. The first
shipload from Jamaica
since the end of the war
arrived at Avonmouth

But the economy itself was still as stagnant and unimaginative as the contents of the average housewife's soon-to-be-redundant larder. In his final summing up of the immediate post-war period, Peter Hennessy quotes the social theorist Ralf Dahrendorf as saying,

> What the post-war Labour Government really did at the crucial period was to complete the interwar policies of redistribution rather than prepare the ground for a new period of growth. 1945-51 is a postscript to the interwar period. All they did was wonderful but clearly wrong – right in social terms, wrong in economic terms. There was something great about the post-war Government. But it was the right Government at the wrong time.

In the long run, the snapping of an ancient tradition of domestic independence would have quite unlooked-for social consequences in terms of women's position in society, children's relationships with their parents and, of course, on the way we eat. In the short term, Hennessy concludes,

> Britain had never - and still hasn't - experienced a progressive phase to match 1945-51. It is largely, though not wholly, the achievement of these years – and the wartime experiences, the crucial platform on which those advances were built – that 1951 Britain, certainly compared to the UK of 1931, or any previous decade, was a kinder, gentler and a far, far better place in which to be born, to grow up, to live, love, work and even to die.

CHAPTER TWO

Aspic and Aspirations

I could almost see the family sitting round the table in our kitchen dining-room. Two, three, four children, perhaps more, beating spoons and with gravy on their mouths. Donald presiding and myself bringing the pudding from the cooking end. This was how home should be.

VERILY ANDERSON, *Spam Tomorrow* 1956

In the centre of the table stood the three pineapples, flanked on all sides by plates of fish and chips, more coloured blocks of ice-cream, pots of raspberry and strawberry jam, bottles of tomato ketchup and Guinness, bottles of Worcester sauce and cups of tea, chocolate biscuits and piles of iced buns.

H. E. BATES, *The Darling Buds of May* 1958

Liberated at an early age from cradle-watching, spending not only the household's money but her own (one-third of wives, twice the 1939 proportion, having jobs), fashion's eager slave, the woman of the Fifties possessed at once the time, the resources and the inclination to bring to perfection the new arts of continuous consumption.

HARRY HOPKINS, *The New Look* 1963

It seemed like a bright new world, the 1950s. There wasn't the sophistication of the years to come, the 1960s. It was a time of hope. There wasn't the all-one-ness of the 1940s, but after all the drama and emergencies, it was like coming into dry land, to peace.

MARGUERITE PATTEN

Shortly after the Tory victory in October 1951, the prime minister Winston Churchill confided to his private secretary John Colville that his policy was going to be 'houses, red meat, and not getting scuppered'. Austerity was out of fashion: a vote-loser that no government could afford to pursue. The days of wine and roses were under way, though it would be three more years before meat came off the ration in 1954. But the nation was more than ready to relish the contrast between the 100 clothing ration points allotted to Princess Elizabeth for her wedding dress in 1947 and the splendour of the Coronation procession along a Mall trimmed with flowers by Constance Spry in June 1953.

'The biggest excitement was in 1952, the first year that I could stand up and say, "I'm going to show you how to make a perfect Christmas cake and Christmas pudding" ', remembers Marguerite Patten, the most popular television cook of the age. 'The Ministry had allowed people to buy more on their ration, and released more dried fruit, and so for the first time I wasn't making pseudo things.' In nothing was the country's self-indulgence more celebrated than sweetness: when sugar came off the ration in 1949 consumption rocketed. By 1960 total consumption of raw sugar in the United Kingdom was estimated at 57 kg (126 lb) per capita a year, an amount second only to that consumed in Greenland.

In 1953, Butler's 'New Look' budget cut income tax and purchase tax and the scene was set for a consumer boom in the high street. The years between 1945 and 1970 saw a greater improvement in standards of living than any previous quarter century – 30 per cent up between 1955 and 1961 alone. State welfare provision, pressure from ever more powerful unions (*I'm Alright, Jack* hit cinemas in 1959) and the increasing availability of part-time work for women all contributed to the new prosperity. Between 1955 and 1965 the number of families owning cars, televisions, vacuum cleaners and washing machines doubled.

Nowhere was the boom reflected more quickly than in the kitchen. Food consumption rose dramatically, especially of processed foods which were now for sale in previously unheard-of variety and quantity. There could be no greater contrast to the grey-coloured and coarse-textured National Loaf of the age of austerity than the foamy white, feather-light slivers of Mother's Pride, the famous wrapped sandwich loaf which was first put on the market in the early 1950s. It and the frilly floral apron were the icons of the age. The book most in tune with the times was H. E. Bates's loving celebration of rural domesticity, *The Darling Buds of May*, published in 1958. At least one, usually several, exceptionally lavish meals are demolished in every chapter.

In the long run, gearing industry for home-sold consumer goods and turning away from exporting and the modernization of heavy industry would create spectacular weaknesses in our industrial infrastructure, not least in the decline of a car industry that never measured itself properly against international competition. But none of this was obvious at the time. When the Conservative prime minister Harold Macmillan adapted the American trades-unionist George Meany's campaigning phrase 'Most people have never had it so good', it won him the 1959 election.

Our concern was with immediate gratification rather than solid worth. Elaborate icings on bought cake-mixes, preferably as American as the dollars of the Marshall Plan, succeeded the skimpy powdering of sugar over honestly home-made carrot cakes. *Nouveau riche* vulgarity was the order of the day. The distinctly *déclassé* self-made millionaires, Lord and Lady Docker, gorging on pink champagne and caviare as they rode along in their gold-plated Rolls-Royce, were the darlings of the tabloids. This was an age in which everybody had aspirations. And professional persuaders had no hesitation in using magazines and television to make sure that we knew how to fulfil them. Independent Television hit our screens in 1956.

A WOMAN'S PLACE? YES, IT IS!

> *I have had more satisfaction out of making a good steamed pudding than in any speech I have ever made from the front bench of the House of Commons.*
>
> FLORENCE HORSBRUGH, former Minister of Education

> *Surely there is nothing more uplifting to the soul or more joyful to the spirit than well-flavored, well-prepared food ...The preparation of good food is merely another expression of art, one of the joys of civilized living.*
>
> DIORE LUCAS, *Cordon Bleu Cook Book* 1951

Of all the exhibits at the 1951 Festival of Britain, it was the Home of the Future that pulled the greatest crowds. With its clean, uncluttered lines, electrical appliances and 'contemporary' colours it promised cleaning chores cut to a minimum and a concentration on the most important symbolic marital act outside the bedroom: the preparation of dinner for the returning breadwinner. Matrimony was as much in fashion as Formica. What brides wanted were dream homes – and thanks to the highly efficient combination of Harold Macmillan and Ernest Marples at the Housing Ministry, over 300 000 flats and houses were being built every year. Fourteen new towns were under construction. By 1958 10 million people, a fifth of the population, were living in new post-war homes.

At the heart of every dream home was the kitchen, formerly the scene of so much miserable penny-pinching and contriving. 'This is the room which more than any other you love to keep shining and bright,' trilled a 1950s editorial in *Woman's Own*. 'A woman's place? Yes, it is! For it is the heart and centre of the meaning of home. The place where, day after day, you make with your hands the gifts of love.' The new fashion for domesticity was not seen as a retreat from the freedoms won by those now slightly eccentric-seeming old maids, the suffragettes. It was billed as a positive choice. Work for women had been easy to come by in the 1940s, and remained so right through to the 1960s. The assumption of the young women who were marrying earlier, and in greater numbers, than ever before or since was that it would be easy to pick up jobs again when and where they wished.

That the majority of the jobs available to them were not especially well paid, and lacked prospects of promotion and pensions, did not matter much to women who confidently believed that a home for their husband and children was the most important thing in life. For the moment, everything in the larder looked cosy. Femininity had succeeded feminism. 'Ours is certainly not the era of the "career girl"', commented Viola Klein drily in *Working Wives* (1959). 'The growth in married women going out to work is the result of the smaller size of families and the general reduction of housework – owing to the modernization of household techniques – combined with a striving to improve their own standard of living. It is not due to an urge for "emancipation".'

To understand the general enthusiasm for home making at all levels of society, we have to bear in mind how deprived women had been both of normal home life and of any opportunity to express their own individual domestic creativity during and after the war years. Once the Welfare State had taken over such traditional kinship duties as educating children, caring for the sick and providing for the elderly, the actual feeding of the family assumed new importance. It was the most important remaining arena in which a woman could publicly show her prowess as a wife and mother. 'One of the main responsibilities of a wife,' wrote Joan Robins in 1953 in *Common Sense Cooking and Eating*, is 'the proper care of the health of her family by feeding them to their wholesome satisfaction and general enjoyment.' Although she conceded that 'in these days of working women, many newly married wives choose to continue to work,' the evening meal together 'will be the main family event of the day and will be cherished and planned as such.'

But the education of girls alongside boys set in train by the 1944 Education Act would prove a time bomb at the heart of the model new families in their model new homes. Nora Riddington had an interest in electricity which would have made her an

Mother's home cooking made the evening meal the focus of 1950s family life

electrical engineer today. Instead, she became a housecraft demonstrator in the 1950s. She points out that, 'Obviously, during the war a lot of women went out to work and, at various strata, women have always gone out to work. But with more girls going to college, more to university, they had bigger horizons, they could expand their life. They didn't just have to work in a shop or work locally; they could go away and work and seek more interesting jobs. After they'd been to college they didn't just want to be shut in looking after children. They wanted children, but they wanted a wider horizon.' In the 1950s, however, such ambitions still came a poor second to domestic joys.

Home life was also highly valued by men. For all the promotion of factory canteens, in 1955, six out of every ten still went home for a midday meal. Even lunch-box food was usually prepared by the wife the evening before. The majority of men remained wedded to the expectation of finding a wife and a 'proper meal' waiting for them when they returned in the evening. This is a tradition which was still very evident among the Welsh mining families interviewed by the sociologist Anne Murcott in 1982. 'It's a pleasure to cook for him,' said one of the miners' wives. 'There's nothing he likes more than coming in the door and smelling a nice meal cooking. I think it's awful when someone doesn't make the effort ... I think, well if I was a man I'd get really fed up if my wife never bothered.' Convenience foods had their place as snacks, but they were firmly outlawed when it came to a cooked dinner.

THE APPLIANCE AGE

The desirability of domestic appliances reached farcical heights when a House of Lords debate of 20 December 1953 discussed the blasphemous implications of a display in the Warrington showroom of the Electricity Board featuring the Three Wise Men bearing gifts of a washing machine, an electric cooker and a refrigerator.

HARRY HOPKINS, *The New Look* 1963

When timers came in I was one of the many people who painted a picture of putting food in the oven in the morning, going to work, and finding the meal all ready by magic when you came home. We did think in years to come that perhaps leaving food in a shut-up oven for hours and hours wasn't the most hygienic thing. But it was a lovely vision: woman being free and the cooker taking over almost like a robot.

MARGUERITE PATTEN

The drudgery of housework was enormously alleviated by the domestic appliances produced by the booming white goods industry that developed after the war, first for export, then for the housewife. In 1938, 65 per cent of houses had been wired for electricity. This rose to 86 per cent in 1948. Although 81 per cent of Londoners

The newly available electric
appliances promised to
transform the overworked
housewife into the Queen
of the kitchen

cooked on a gas stove or a gas ring in 1942, in rural Gloucestershire the figure was only 3 per cent. Ownership of electric cookers rose from 6 per cent of houses in 1936 to 18.6 per cent in 1948, 30 per cent in 1961 and 46 per cent in 1980. Prosperity meant that women could use their wages to lighten their load at home instead of merely supplementing inadequate family diets and saving for clothes. Spending on electrical goods was six times higher than on other consumer items. At first there was still the familiar concern with thrift and durability that had stood generations of housewives in good stead. The Thor machine, a reliable old trooper if there ever was one, washed clothes and dishes (not at the same time, of course). But soon there was a rash of new gadgets, from the restyled Kenwood mixer to the economical pressure cooker. In the last 50 years the kitchen has changed more than any other room in the house.

Electricity makes life **EASIER**

Issued by the British Electrical Development Association

"The Kenwood you bought me prepared this wonderful meal"

With A KENWOOD in the kitchen, cooking becomes a new thrill: meals a gay adventure — and what a proud possession for every modern housewife! At the flick of a switch, the Kenwood becomes the Chef! It will do 101 jobs in the kitchen and save you time and trouble in cooking preparation — and makes so many appetizing meals possible which would otherwise rarely reach the table!

Write now for the illustrated Kenwood folder containing full details of this wonderful machine, plus 10 exciting recipes; also the name of your nearest stockist to Kenwood Electrics Ltd. (Dept. D.1) 1-4 New Audley Street, London, W.1.

Most Versatile Kitchen Help

Kenwood
"YOUR SERVANT MADAM!"

at the touch
of a switch it . . .
mixes · minces · whips
creams · grinds
mashes · beats · peels
blends · purees · juices

* * * * * * * *

To help women cope with these changes, and to protect them against the blandishments of the advertisers, the Electrical Association for Women had been set up in 1924. In the 1950s it had over 10 000 members who held local meetings and cookery competitions. It trained thousands of girls from domestic science and technical colleges to become the proud possessors of the EAW Diploma in Electrical Housecraft. EAW graduates were assured of jobs as kitchen demonstrators in electricity showrooms around the country. They ran courses on how to use electricity properly, and issued leaflets – including one on kitchen design called 'Towards Perfection'. Nora Riddington, who had taken the EAW exams at college, worked for the electricity board in the 1950s.

There were no other consumer groups at the time, other than the Townswomen's Guild and the Women's Institute; certainly no one who specialized in electricity. We were like magicians to some people! ... The audience was very varied. You could have the lady of the manor and the farm worker's wife, and then you'd have a few people who worked as cleaners, and women who worked in towns.

In January 1953, the EAW carried out a survey to guide manufacturers on what women wanted from their new appliances – interviewees included 'mainly housewives, with some business and professional women, and some men who had personal knowledge of household duties.' The survey reported 'a large measure of satisfaction', particularly over the durability of existing appliances – among them a 30-year-old iron, 25-year-old wash boiler, 24-year-old cooker and 20-year-old washing machine. One hundred and twenty-eight electric fires had been in use for over 20 years, and 100 refrigerators for over ten. A 40-year-old bowl fire had required only one new element and replating, a 37-year-old kettle one new element and new flex and a 30-year-old vacuum cleaner only an occasional new belt.

This particular message was ignored in favour of planned obsolescence. Before long, fashions in appliances were changing as fast as fashions in hats. Competing designers emphasized up-to-date 'features' that could be easily superseded and colours that could go out of style instead of the omnipresent white or sensibly mottled grey of an earlier age.

But the all-electric future was by no means obvious in the early 1950s. When Nora Riddington went to technical college in 1955, she was taught to iron with gas irons and flat irons as well as electric ones. 'They insisted that we might one day live in a house without electricity.' But as the magazines filled with advertisements for electric appliances, keeping up with the Joneses was only possible by 'going electric'.

'Buying a cooker was such a personal thing to a woman,' remembers Nora. 'It was a big event. I think the worst thing I had as a demonstrator was when a wife was in hospital having a child and her husband had decided to give her a treat by coming in to buy a cooker. So when she came out of hospital there was a new cooker waiting for her. But the chances were that she had her heart set on a Belling, and he bought her a Creda.'

'It was love at first sight!' runs the text of a 1950s cooker advertised in the magazine *Woman's Own* , 'I fell for the New World Gas Range the moment I set eyes on it! It really is a beauty.' And, added the small print, it could be hers 'so easily' on 'the best possible Hire Purchase terms'. The future began to be put in hock to the domestic present. Doreen Hunt was 'over the moon' when she got her own 'ultra modern' New World cooker. Forty years later, she can still remember every detail of it.

> The grill folded down flat, then you pulled it up when you wanted to grill. It had two doors and one opened into a hot oven you could put plates in on racks to warm them up before you dished up the meals ... It was white and the handles were sort of longish, and you just pressed down. There were no knobs to fall off like they used to on the old ovens. It was really nice: my pride and joy.

While cookers were obviously desirable, refrigerators called for a little more persuasion. Frigidaire records that Britain was regarded as something of a challenge: 'The hard sell was probably essential in a Britain which regarded ice as only an inconvenience of wintertime and cold drinks as an American mistake.' The first British Frigidaire was sold in 1924 and by 1927 the number of household and commercial models had risen to 20. Government action banning the use of certain preservatives in food gave the company a useful springboard for their 1928 advertising campaign:

> When Pure Food is NOT!
> Preservatives used to retard the natural processes of decay. Most women think it is perfectly easy to detect decay in time. The truth is far different. It is there 36 hours before you can detect it. Would you let your family eat such food, mouldy food, DECAYING food?

After the war, refrigerators steadily became more covetable, although only 2 per cent of houses had electric ones in 1948, and only 3.5 per cent in 1953. Instead of presenting them as luxury items, useful only for making ice for the newly popular cocktails, chilling trifles and freezing ice-creams, their manufacturers began to market them as necessities for busy, efficient housewives. Capacity was emphasized as frozen food became more popular and central heating made larders less effective. To save space, new houses were built without larders. The implicit assumption was that the new owner ought to have a refrigerator.

The final touch in the ideal kitchen was to create a unified and distinctly modern look by covering every imaginable surface with Formica. This new wonder material was invented in the United States by Daniel O'Connor and Herbert Faber in the 1930s. The tough, heatproof surface was made from resin-impregnated paper, thermal set under 8300 tons of pressure applied at 150°C (300°F). By the 1940s, their Ohio factory had occupied an area of 22 acres. Formica was available in every imaginable colour, perfectly suited to the 'contemporary' look and a newly hygiene-conscious age.

The first British factory opened in 1951 and before long the old labour-intensive wood and oil-cloth-covered kitchen worktops were trimly clad in eye-catching colours. Dust-catching door mouldings and banisters were boarded over, spindly coffee tables constructed, refrigerators clad. Jungle patterns in green, white and black, and squiggly lines in the shape of boomerangs were popular. Gold-sequined Formica was introduced in 1955 (it has never been deleted from the manufacturer's list). Advertisements featuring the Formica Girl – dressed in an outfit made from every colour available – suggested that husbands should find a shade the colour of their wife's eyes.

Formica was essential to the 'contemporary' look of the 1950s kitchen

Time and motion experts delighted in revealing new ways for housewives to save time and energy by rationalizing how the kitchen was arranged. Judith Hubback remembers 'watching a programme in which someone analysed the number of movements that a woman did in the kitchen. It was completely amazing what a lot of waste and effort there was, because she wasn't planning it carefully. I used to look with great envy at the adverts in the magazines for improved kitchens, and I was interested in being as scientific as possible, and working out what the relationship between the fridge and the sink and the cooker should be.'

This new professional approach to kitchen management, and the machines in the kitchen, meant that men could empathize with domesticity more easily than when it was an arcane mystery handed from mother to daughter. Husbands took a great interest in the new appliances, going with their wives to the gas or electricity showrooms. But there was no mistaking who was making the decisions. 'Now home has become the centre of his activity and most of his earnings are spent on or in the home, his wife becomes the chooser and spender and gains a new status and control – her tastes form his life,' observed sociologist Mark Abrams in 1959.

Marguerite Patten points out that many women earned their own money which they could, and did, spend on new appliances. 'You didn't have to wait for husbands to say, "Well, I'll let you know, dear, if you may have a dishwasher." You could say, "Look here, chum, I'm paying half, or I'm going to pay for it, so let's go and look at it".' Her husband insisted on taking dirty plates with a cooked breakfast – mustard and all – dried hard on them to the electrical shop to see if a dishwasher could live up to its claims to shift even dried food. 'He was rather disconcerted when it did!'

THE WAY TO HIS HEART

'It's not the way mother used to heat fish-fingers!'

I used to do features such as making a pie like mother used to make, because this was what they wanted to recapture. Maybe their husbands said, 'Oh, I never ate a pudding like my mother or granny cooked,' when in fact those dishes that were probably made by the family cook!

DOREEN FULLELOVE of *Woman*'s Wooden Spoon Club

Well, you'd be an idiot of a man, wouldn't you, if you didn't like a wife or a girlfriend who could jolly well serve you meals?

MARGUERITE PATTEN

A 1950s' bride's first duty was to cook just like her mother-in-law. Food was an important bridge between the old life style and the new for the millions of men and women – one-fifth of the population – who moved from their childhood localities to new towns and estates after the war. In the first few weeks after families moved in, local doctors received many night-time calls, due to 'feelings of insecurity'. A postwar survey of the Oxhey Estate near Watford showed anxiety neuroses running at twice the national figure. Sleep disturbances and undue tiredness were four times as high, headaches three times and duodenal ulcers two and a half times.

Cooking stews as tasty, cakes as light and pies as flaky as they were back home was a challenge which made many young wives who had grown up eating in NAAFI kitchens and British restaurants distinctly insecure. 'With both my parents working, I didn't have a clue how to cook,' remembers Doreen Hunt. 'I really wasn't into food, because in those days you could go into the old Express Cafés and Lyons Corner Shops and get meals there. When I first got married, I couldn't even boil an egg. It would either be too soft and runny or else too hard. It was a case of trial and error!'

The war had broken the old oral tradition of mothers teaching their daughters to cook, not only because of food shortages and the temporary family break-ups caused by warwork and evacuation, but because the constant barrage of Ministry of Food directives on the use of the allotted rations had educated the public in quite new habits of eating. After the war, new rules about diet, new forms of food, the virtual disappearance of servants and, last but not least, new levels of literacy, meant that young wives were more aware than ever before of how much they had to learn about domestic management. Day and evening classes in cookery were popular and well attended. Cookery books and domestic magazines became important sources of advice and inspiration for all levels of households rather than just for a middle-class élite. *Woman* magazine started its Wooden Spoon Club in the early 1950s for the benefit of the women it regarded as its typical readers: 'Young, married, two children, and not a lot of money to get going after the war'.

BBC TV's *Cookery Club* began in the mid-1950s. It was a cosy institution compèred by its 'president', Marguerite Patten. Each week a challenge was issued to the

Marguerite Patten, Britain's first 'Kitchen Agony Aunt', and president of BBC TV's *Cookery Club,* taught housewives to aim for ever more perfect results

viewers – a meal for three people for under five shillings, a children's party, a dinner party for twelve. Patten tried out the entries and announced a winner, who came to the studio and talked about her recipes. So many letters arrived in response to the programmes that the BBC elected Patten an official 'Kitchen Agony Aunt'. Her afternoon show became something of a national institution, advising on everything from household budgets and foolproof bread recipes to ideas for children's packed lunches.

'I was talking to two sorts of people,' she recalls. 'Young women who had left school, gone straight into the Forces and then got married had never had a chance to do any cooking at all, and they wanted to learn. And mums, who had been good plain cooks before and during the war, wanted to take a higher grade, to be really special cooks.'

THE PERFECT CAKE

We dare not ask for the grace of humility, but perhaps we don't need to when it is so often thrust upon us, thought Sophia, beating together eggs and sugar for a sponge cake, knowing that her cake would not rise so high as Sister Dew's. When she took it from the oven she was pleased with it, but later, placing it on the trestle table in the hall where refreshments were to be served, she saw that Sister Dew's was higher. 'So you've made one of your sponges,' said the latter in a patronising tone. 'It looks quite nice.'

BARBARA PYM, *An Unsuitable Attachment* 1965

The making of a feather-light sponge cake symbolized more than any other single culinary skill a sort of perfect womanliness. Perhaps it was merely a reaction against the shortage of eggs and butter during the war that did it; perhaps the 'depth psychologists' watching the baby boom get under way were right to interpret this eagerness literally to put buns in the oven as sublimated maternal longings.

'When I went to the various women's institutions and clubs, they often used to have a cookery competition and the thing that always turned up was the Victoria sandwich,' recalls Nora Riddington. 'And really, it was very important that even if you didn't win your Victoria sandwich looked as good as, or almost as good as, the next person's. I was usually asked to judge, which was really quite an onerous task, because hints might be dropped that Mrs So-and-so always won, and I'd be thinking, goodness me, which is Mrs So-and-so, and will it be awful if she doesn't win this week? And another part of you was saying, well, someone else ought to have a chance. And then I'd cut them in half – I wouldn't know whose was whose – and the chances were that this lady either won or was second. So honour was not lost!'

Which of us cheated and used a cake mix instead of elbow grease, history does not relate. Advisedly. 'A woman who spends her day at an office cannot devote the same amount of care to the preparation of meals as a full-time housewife,' warned Viola

Klein. 'Her cakes, bought at a shop or made from a ready-mix, will not compare with those her husband remembers with nostalgia from his mother's home.' The advertisers certainly knew that the secret should not be allowed to escape. 'When your friends call in for tea, what a pleasure it is to have a really splendid cake to hand around,' announced a Mary Baker advertisement in *Woman's Own*. 'And isn't this especially so when it's your very own home-made!' The 'home-made' nature of the cake was the egg which the cook was asked to add to the mixture herself 'for that personal touch of real home-made goodness'.

Less confident women could attempt to make Weston's 'perfectly risen dream of a cake … Light, white and luscious! It's something never seen here before! A delicious, delicate-textured white cake that practically makes itself … in just four minutes.' All they had to do was add water – this time those eggs had been 'expertly blended in' already.

The makers of the cake mixes and the new 'soft, fluffy' proprietary fats such as Cookeen and Stork took great care to sell their products as enabling women to achieve ever higher 'professional' or 'expert' standards, rather than merely saving time. Advertisements suggested transforming simple sponge mixtures into

Making a feather light sponge cake symbolized a sort of perfect womanliness. The cheat's way of achieving it was with one of the new mixes which promised that 'home-made' taste'

NEW Mary Baker CAKE MIXES GIVE YOU...

Home Sweet...

Home made Cakes

'mouthwatering extravagances'. A 'double-decker Apple Blossom Cake' offered by the Stork Cookery Service in 1958 was to have pale blue-tinted icing with a cocoa-coloured 'tree' piped over it. This was to be decked with angelica 'leaves', glacé cherry 'buds' and 'blossoms' made from triangles cut from thin slices from the top of marsh-mallows (sliced off with scissors dipped in hot water) and finished with mimosa 'balls'. All in an afternoon's work.

LOOKING IN

Mum, her eyes bright with excitement, appeared with a tray of tea and sandwiches. *'Quick, dear,' said Daddy, 'we're just going to switch on.' They all gazed rapturously at the screen.* *'Thank goodness I had time to make sandwiches,' Mum thought. 'I wouldn't have wanted to miss a moment of this.'*

'The day the TV set arrived', advertisement for Sunblest bread, 1953

TV Dinners? Terrible stuff! I think it must have been donkeys we were eating.

SANDY HUNT

It was a shrewd move to link the by no means initially popular new sliced bread with the equally novel, but enormously coveted television. The ultimate romance of the decade was one that included the whole family. Affluence made it easier to keep the home warm and comfortable, and the family well fed. Television made it into a place that could provide its own fireside entertainment. At a time when all the programmes were family ones, and transmission closed down for the 'toddler truce' between six and seven so that the children could be put to bed, it also strengthened the family circle. Sunday was easily the most popular evening for 'looking in'. In *A 100 Years of Eating,* the food historian James Johnston has even suggested that it prevented a return to the higher drinking levels that had characterized previous post-war eras – certainly it contributed to a decline in men disappearing to the pub in the evenings. In 1953, thousands took the plunge and bought a television set in order to view the Coronation in their own sitting-rooms. By 1955, when ITV started broad-casting, there were 3 million sets ready to receive it.

Initially, television was of distinctly secondary importance to 'the wireless' and news of its progammes occupied only four pages at the end of the *Radio Times* (not unlike the proportion of the magazine allotted to radio programmes today). The wartime habit of education on the air died hard – *The Archers* continues its wartime function of disseminating improving tips to the present day. 'There was a strong flavour of evening classes run by a well-endowed Workers' Institute about the BBC,' writes historian Peter Lewis. Television gardener Fred Streeter told us when to put in cabbage seedlings, TV chef Philip Harben outlined 'foolproof' dinners for young brides, Bill and Ben consulted Little Weed. Everyone puzzled over Christmas-party-

There's always
time for

NESCAFÉ

So quick to make — you don't miss a thing. And what rich,
fragrant coffee! Yes, for coffee you're proud to serve, rely on
Nescafé; put a spoonful in the cup, add near-boiling water. As
good as only Nestlé's know how to make it, Nescafé gives you
coffee with roaster-fresh fragrance and flavour
whenever you want it.

*Nescafé is a soluble coffee product composed of coffee solids, combined and
powdered with dextrins, maltose and dextrose added to protect the flavour*

ANOTHER OF NESTLÉ'S GOOD THINGS 64KA

A cup of the newly-
invented instant coffee
served while watching the
equally novel television set
was the forerunner of whole
meals eaten in front of
popular programmes

style guessing games such as *What's My Line*, and closedown was at the respectably early hour of 10.30 p.m., just nicely in time for a cup of Ovaltine and the Home Service's *Book at Bedtime*.

As habits of viewing took hold, the middle-aged began eating their evening meal with trays across their knees – viewing was distinctly higher among the over-40s. Though TV dinners were on offer surprisingly early, they had a poor reputation and it was more likely that the housewife had had a shot at one of the 'simple to serve and eat' menus suggested by cookery books in their new chapters on 'Television Entertaining'. Simple was a very relative term. It was just as well that interludes ('There will now be a short intermission') with restful rural images were numerous. A 'casual' TV tray described in *Woman's Own* in 1957 contained ham and tongue darioles, small sausage rolls and sherry trifle. Another recommended combination was creamed haddock savouries, vanilla ice-cream with ginger, and tongue canapés. On Saturday night, another item could be added: perhaps anchovy eggs, hot dogs, celery and watercress, and pineapple islands. Mass Observation 1957 showed that housewives with television sets spent on average half a day more a week preparing meals than those without.

Television had other unlooked-for effects. Ownership of a set correlated with fewer leisure activities outside the home. It encouraged passivity and reduced the speed with which women carried out such creative activities as knitting and sewing. When ITV was launched, its jolly jingles and frankly aspirational advertising created even more incentives to consumerism. TV cooks were especially prone to encouraging women to attempt highly professional levels of cuisine and dining elegance. None was more spectacular than Fanny Cradock, whose fur stoles, *décolleté* necklines and playful domination of her dinner-jacketed husband Johnny formed a comedy of Cordon Bleu manners that played to packed houses – and the cameras.

KEEPING UP APPEARANCES

The great desire was to shrug off wartime restrictions and return to happier days – the good old days. So great was the desire that the speed of execution provided a foundation of status rather than stability; a situation that has only recently been questioned.

GRAHAM KERR, *The Galloping Gourmet* 1966

People wanted to be correct in what they did, and in the way they laid the table.

NORA RIDDINGTON

We had supper … well, dinner, really, because there was soup, though I think it was tinned.

BARBARA PYM, *Some Tame Gazelle* 1950

Aspic and
Aspirations

A new breed of television
cooks brought professional
standards of culinary
glamour into the home
Left: Husband-and-wife
team Fanny and Johnny
Cradock

Below: Philip Harben tosses
a pancake for a crêpe suzette

Constance Spry's
championship of 'civilized
living' and 'the homelier
arts' inspired ambitious
visions of domestic
elegance

By 1960, a quarter of the adult population was white-collar and the mood of the times was extrovert and upwardly mobile. Prosperous ages need authoritative experts in etiquette for those aspiring to gentility. Books on such subjects date back to the Renaissance and beyond: their numbers are an accurate register of the rise and rise of the middle class. Isabella Beeton, the most famous nineteenth-century adviser on domestic affairs, claimed that the rank which people occupied in the grand scale could be gauged by how they took their meals. The introductory chapters of her 1908 *Household Management* offered 'kitchen outfits' for four distinct styles of home: 'any mansion', 'a good-class home', 'a middle-class house' and 'a very small house'.

Mrs Beeton's post-war successor was Constance Spry, whose family was in itself an essay in upward mobility. Her father had been a printer's devil in the East End with such fever to learn that he attended every evening class going. The Workers' Educational College ended up offering him a job. By 1891, he was its headmaster. He became an education inspector and was transferred to Ireland to advise on teaching the working classes. Constance herself ran a college for early school-leavers in London until her friends' enthusiasm for her fantastic floral arrangements encouraged her to open a shop in Albemarle Street. The rest is history, but Spry remained an inspired teacher all her life, running the school of domesticity which she set up at Winkfield Place after the war.

The *Constance Spry Cookery Book*, co-authored by Rosemary Hulme, was first published in 1956. It remained the most essential item on a well-heeled bride's list for the next three decades. This telling passage, which makes it clear how deliberately emancipated 'good-class' women of the pre-war years stepped back into the kitchen, is from its introduction.

> Since it would seem to be the simple duty of any woman with a home to run, or those with any sort of civic conscience, to understand about food and cooking, it is strange how low the subject ranks in the estimation of many academically-minded people. The influence of good food in the bringing up of children, its importance in the building up of a strong people, the contribution it makes to the harmonious running of a home, may be acknowledged theoretically, but there is still a tendency to consider the subject suitable primarily either for girls who cannot make the grade for a university or for those who intend to become teachers. As a training for home life, as a necessity for civilized living, as a serious consideration for the mentally clever girls, it is not always accorded approval. Possibly many scholarly women remember, as I do, the fight made for equality in education, and it may be natural for them to see only certain of the bright facets of learning. In gaining so much and gaining it with courage and tenacity, the homelier arts may have been eclipsed for a short space of time, but surely now intelligent people recognise them for what they are, the basis of balanced living.

Judith Hubback's memories echo this. 'My mother was a very creative person artistically, but not in food. I mean she could boil an egg, but not much more than that, I don't think. I don't believe she ever peeled a potato. One of my earliest memories as a small child was spending time in the kitchen with the cook.'

She remembers how useful people found the booming new women's magazines. 'They helped with the choosing and presentation of the meal, and that seemed important, because the aesthetic side clearly was valuable. 'We were fascinated by the exquisitely beautiful young women shown in *Vogue*, but a bit scornful of them. We tended to enjoy *Good Housekeeping* – it was very proper and respectable and full of very valuable advice.'

The 1950s were the age of the mass magazine. *Woman* went from 1 million copies in 1946 (price 3 pence, 20 pages) to 2.25 million in 1951 (40 pages and a larger format). In 1957, it had 100 pages, cost 4½ pence and its circulation had peaked at an all-time record for all magazines of nearly 3½ million. Advertising revenue had increased from £1.1 million in 1951 to £5.3 million in 1958. Women who didn't buy magazines read them with close attention on their weekly visit to the hairdresser. Recipes were clipped and entered into the personal recipe book that was an indispensable friend on the kitchen shelf.

'Attitudes of mind which were hopelessly out of her reach and experience before the war were within her ken now,' wrote Mary Grieve, then editor of *Woman*, of her average reader. 'An immense amount of her personality is engaged in her function as the selector of goods, and in this she endures many anxieties, many fears. Success in this function is as cheering and vitalising to her as it is to a man in his chosen career, failure as humiliating.'

The ultimate aspiration was Cordon Bleu status. According to one of the first post-war books on the subject, Diore Lucas' *Cordon Bleu Cook Book* published in 1951, the name was originally used in France for the noblemen who entertained their guests with supreme munificence and so became members of the *Ordre du Saint Esprit*, founded in 1518 by Henry III. It was later associated with cooks who could create vast feasts. But the latter-day use of the term dates from the founding in 1880 of the Parisian *Ecole du Cordon Bleu* by Mlle Martha Distel for daughters of upper- and middle-class French families. It soon became an internationally renowned Mecca for aspiring gastronomes.

Not everybody could afford the genuine Cordon Bleu classes described in the government-produced magazine *Housecraft* in 1954. Pupils flew to Orly and stayed at Chateau de Mont Jean (baths extra, and education in the use of gas, electricity and solid fuel – 'a sensible precaution especially during General Strikes').

Diore Lucas opposed the prevailing trend towards rational recipes and scientific management. She preferred approximations like 'a little of this' and 'just enough of that' which invited the cook 'to express individuality and imagination'. She saw the kitchen as 'the heart of the home … not a scientific laboratory where each ingredient is accurately measured.' She lost the argument. The way ahead lay with the exactitude exemplified perfectly in the astonishingly detailed spelling out of stage-by-stage preparation, cooking, and presentation that is a feature of the classic French cookery book of the 1960s, Simone Beck, Louisette Bertholle and Julia Child's *Mastering the Art of French Cookery* (1961). Women stopped trusting their own judgement and decided to rely upon experts.

COOKING FOR COMPLIMENTS

The contemporary cook-hostess has the best of it, for she sees her efforts appreciated and hears the dishes discussed, which is a pleasant innovation, for talk about food used to be taboo.

CONSTANCE SPRY, *Constance Spry Cookery Book* 1956

Tea could be laid on the low table by the fire, she decided, with the cloth with the wide lace border. Mrs Glaze had eventually been persuaded to make a Victoria sandwich cake, there were little cakes from the Spinning Wheel and chocolate biscuits, and Flora intended to cut some cucumber sandwiches and what she thought of as 'wafer-thin' bread and butter.

BARBARA PYM, *Jane and Prudence* 1953

After the first flush of excitement in recreating food just like (his) mother used to make, women graduated to 'hostess cookery'. Improvements in the quality and availability of ingredients led to new sophistication in methods of preparing dishes. Women rose to the challenge of outdoing anything that could be bought ready-made with astonishing culinary excesses. 'Particular consideration' had to be given to presentation. This was the age of the multi-ingredient garnish, of maraschino cherries and sculpted gherkins, of hardboiled eggs transformed into swans with pipe-cleaners and duchesse potatoes. Food became a fashion – and status – object, changing at the whim of media pundits.

Coffee mornings were occasions to display prowess with shortbread and plum loaf, butterfly cakes and brownies. Tea could be even more formal, especially when guests were present. Doreen Hunt:

> If it was a weekend, and you'd invited people to tea, it was usually the best tablecloth that you chose. Sometimes that used to be an embroidered one, and that would be a talking point, because they would say, 'Ohhh, did you do this yourself?' And you'd say 'Yes', and that was always admired, and then you'd set out the tea. It always had to be cups and saucers, and tea plates for bread and butter. Sometimes we used to do sandwiches, fish paste – sardine and tomato, or bloater, those were the favourites. And then large plates for a salad – hardboiled eggs, or shrimps and winkles, and lettuce, spring onion and radishes from the garden. And beetroot. Spam was still a great favourite. Then we used to have jelly, or trifle. Or blancmange.

A coveted household feature of the 1950s was the serving hatch. First introduced in the 1920s as a butler's pantry convenience for the reduced staffs of middle-class villas, it became extraordinarily popular, a practical way of 'saving steps' that also hid the state of the kitchen from prying, would-be helpful eyes. 'I saw them in the houses my mother worked in, and in the houses I was evacuated to during the war.' says Doreen Hunt. 'They used to fascinate me. I just loved the idea of giving them a "wop", and having the doors fly open. And you could just stick the food through, and the people on the other side took it from you. The convenience of it! I really wanted one.' 'It was a stage everyone went through,' adds her husband Sandy. 'I personally didn't think much of the idea. But then it wasn't my domain, the kitchen.' 'The builders put them in whether women wanted them or not,' says Nora Riddington. 'There were lots of advertisements for them – and on the films you often used to see some film star popping her nose into the space in the hatch.' Hatches solved the problem of the household that had a dining-room separate from the kitchen but no staff to wait at table. They also catered to the growing feeling that it was somehow not quite right for mum to be shut away in the kitchen.

The 1950s also saw the triumphant return of the cocktail party, originally borrowed from America in the 1920s and now made newly acceptable by Constance Spry's championship of it in the very first chapter of her cookery book. 'Perhaps a cookery book should start in a less frivolous fashion than with a chapter headed "The Cocktail Party", and should show in its initial stages a proper seriousness of purpose and general sober-mindedness,' Spry opens, 'but I have an idea that perhaps a lighthearted approach might present more immediate appeal.'

Cocktail party canapés were a visual display of the general glee at the new era of plenty. The weekly ration of 'mousetrap' cheese was forgotten as guests munched into Stilton cheese in celery sticks, and balls of cream cheese rolled in coconut and Parmesan. Citrus fruits, once carefully hoarded, were prodigally wasted in display – half a grapefruit bristling with cocktail sticks holding melon and prawns, segments of orange as garnishes, elaborate little baskets fashoned out of lemons. Exquisitely small and well-flavoured 'cocktail sausages' celebrated the end of anxieties over the mysterious ingredients inside those all-concealing skins. Instead, according to Marguerite Patten, 'butchers all over Britain were taking a pride in their sausages, winning prizes with them, and extolling their virtues'.

Successful vol-au-vents, which were impossible to make out of tough wartime flour, became as much a test of the calibre of a cook-hostess as the pea beneath a real princess's seventh mattress. Patten's *Cookery in Colour* (1960) explains that puff pastry required not only 'cool hands and a light touch' but 'seven rollings and foldings'. Oysters Rockefeller and aubergine caviare were also part of her repertoire. Aspic was essential. 'People were inclined to put anything in aspic,' laughs Patten. 'I used to think when they asked me about it, good heavens, we'll be having kippers in aspic before long. But it was also because the wartime habit of thriftiness was still about. If you put leftovers in aspic, they didn't look like left-overs any more!'

THE DINNER PARTY

It was in the air that if you ran a home, you ran it as well as possible. There was a certain amount of competition between women if you gave dinner parties, as to whether the food was as enterprising as other people's food . . . We took more trouble in the 1950s to dish up things looking attractive – in the war we just dished things up and got on with eating them. Now we wanted things to look nice and taste nice, and that involved doing it intelligently.

JUDITH HUBBACK

I preferred it if we had people first, because then I set the tone. If we went somewhere else first, I knew what competition I was up against, and it was harder work trying to beat them. Because really that was all the wives had to do, to try and make a better dinner than the other wife.

FRANCES STEWART

She put success on the menu in next to no time!

Dinner parties were the highpoint of socializing, the occasion when the wife's domestic prowess won the approval – or disapproval – of the outside world. They could be a very important part of business fixing. Frances Stewart, whose architect husband often used to invite his clients to dinner, remembers that 'the important thing was to impress the wife. I'm sure the husband didn't take a lot of notice of the meal, but if the woman was impressed, then the husband was likely to be impressed as well. It did actually matter. You see, the women would have nothing else to talk about because they wouldn't know each other, where the men had their business in common. The women had to have something to talk about, so it was the food.'

The all-round effect was the thing. The house had to look nice, the table had to look nice and the food had to be good – 'then it would be presumed that the architect was good as well. And plenty of good wine. I must emphasize that there was always plenty of good wine, because that helped an awful lot.'

It was also important for a wife to dress the part. In the autumn of 1958, *Woman* told its readers to 'Make Yourself A Hostess Dress', with 'sophisticated scooped out neckline' in 'the new luxury-feeling chenille tweed' or, for glamour and warmth combined, in 'Jacqlinta, the wool tweed with the gold Lurex glitter thread interwoven'. 'We wanted to look as near as possible like the films,' says Nora Riddington. 'I remember Doris Day coming out, and people suddenly having the very full skirts that she had.'

Frances Stewart remembers that, 'I would probably have my hair done for the occasion, and I would have bought a new dress and put on a little bit of jewellery. You had to look good, make the guests welcome, and of course you'd *never* overrule

Home is a place to bring back the boss to: advertisements stressed the role of the successful cook-hostess in furthering her husband's career

anything your husband said, even if you didn't agree with him. You kept a low profile, in actual fact. The row would come afterwards!'

If the magazines are to be believed, the 'contemporary cook-hostess' had a chameleon quality that reflected a genuine schizophrenia. A capacious frock-protecting kitchen apron would stay over the best dress until the guests arrived. After drinks and a move to the table she would disappear to the kitchen and re-emerge in the tiny flounce of frills known as a 'hostess apron', wheeling that fashonable adjunct of servantless entertaining, the hostess trolley. Some trolleys were electrically heated, with chrome sides and chrome feet and glass doors. Others had several decks and folding out display trays, with serving dishes kept hot by a night-light in a chromium frame underneath.

Electric hotplates on the sideboard and plate-warming ovens also helped the new imperative that food should be served piping hot. But the menu itself was the ultimate test of the evening's success. Frances Stewart again:

> We always had to produce starters. I made my own pâté, mincing up the liver and bacon, or we had soup. The main course was usually something French. Coq au vin, that was quite popular. And boeuf Bourguignon, that was always a good thing to have. I think I got the recipe from Graham Kerr, who was the TV chef of the time. As there were different people, it didn't matter if you repeated your menu. For sweet, I have always made a good apple pie, so I occasionally did that. Or for something that looked attractive, pineapple upside-down cake. You could always guarantee that was going to look nice and colourful, and people would go, 'Ohhh!'. Then we ended with cheese and biscuits. Not petits fours. I don't think I ever got round to making petits fours.

This was, above all, the age of the *flambé*, Marguerite Patten:

> We flambéd meat, we flambéd fruit salad – it was one of the great show-off dishes, a way of creating a great impression. Soufflés were another great show-off, and of course gateaux. We really were into gateaux, and we were beginning to hear about the gateaux of Austria. We were beginning to show off with our knowledge of other countries. I'm sure you must have heard that it was the men of the Eighth Army in Italy who brought the idea of scampi back to Britain, and scampi was on most menus. It couldn't really be scampi, because of course that's a shellfish of the Adriatic, but Dublin Bay prawns were a jolly good substitute. And of course people had heard about America and we had some of their dishes, devil's food cake, that was a great favourite. But no, the real show-off was: set light to it, dear, and your reputation is made.

The greatest compliment to one's hostess was to ask for the recipe for a dish. Before the war, food, the province of the cook, was a taboo subject. Today the tactful guest,

Facing page: The picture
of confidence – the ideal
hostess of the period

aware of the omnipresent usefulness of Marks and Spencer, again avoids the subject of food unless it is quite obviously home-made.

MAN ABOUT THE HOUSE ▐████████████████████████

Pop always felt more passionate in the kitchen. He supposed it was the smell of food.
Ma sometimes told him it was a wonder he ever got any meals at all and that he ought to know at his age what he wanted most, meals or her. 'Both,' he always said. 'Often.'

H. E. BATES, *The Darling Buds of May* 1958

It is difficult for a woman to understand a man's sensitivity to any slur on his virility.
'Next time it will be better' comforts him as little as 'Never mind, we'll open a tin of something' soothes her wounded self-esteem at a spoiled supper.

J. H. WALLIS, *Marriage Observed* 1963

Men want both an intelligent companion, a mother image and a Venus de Milo: a woman for whom they are the sole aim in life and with whom they can be proud of appearing in public.

VIOLA KLEIN, *Working Wives* 1959

How did men fit into the new kitchens of the 1950s? 'There was a lot of pressure on not being tired when the husband came home,' remembers Judith Hubback.

> It was very important to tidy up, take one's apron off, and if possible the younger children should be in bed or have already had supper, so that they weren't making the usual bedtime fuss. Many men took time to read to their children at bedtime, and they wanted to see them, but they did want the younger ones to be out of the away. The older one had supper with us on a trolley in the sitting room, but the others had already had their meal.

The time and energy saved by the new appliances and processed foods affected both sexes. While women were being seduced by white goods and dreams of concocting cheese and anchovy crostini, men were sitting in armchairs on the other side of the service hatch admiring the classic proportions of a sex kitten called Marilyn Monroe, who was flamboyantly featured on the first centre spread of a magazine that was very different from *Good Housekeeping* and *Woman's Own*.

Early in 1953 the second Kinsey report, this time on *Sexual Behaviour in the Human Female*, was published. First British reactions were as defensive as they had been to its 1948 predecessor, *Sexual Behaviour in the Human Male*. 'In spite of our modern novelists and the Kinsey report, feeding plays a major part in the happiness of the family,' remarked Joan Robbins tartly in *Common Sense Cooking and Eating*, published later in 1953. But across the Atlantic, a certain Hugh Hefner read the report. In direct response, he abandoned the thankless task of promoting a magazine called *Children's Activities* and dreamt up another that sounded the same but was distinctly different. *Playboy* – the title was significant – was first published in 1953 and amounted to an invitation to forget responsibility and become one of the lads again.

Ian Fleming's first novel, *Casino Royale*, was also published in 1953. Its 'snobbery with violence' was in marked contrast to the macho but gentlemanly thrillers of John Buchan, Dornford Yates and 'Sapper'. Dining out in restaurants in which he knew exactly which wine to order was very much Bond's thing, and his chosen menus were to have a marked influence on male eating.

> With ceremony, a wide silver dish of crabs, big ones, their shelves and claws broken, was placed in the centre of the table. A silver sauceboat brimming with butter, and a long rack of toast was placed beside each plate. The tankards of champagne frothed pink. Bond proceeded to eat, or rather to devour, the most delicious meal he had had in his life.

In the same way that women were luxuriating in frills and cosmetics, men moved into gallantry. In Bermondsey, 'New Edwardians' donned velvet-collared drape suits, lacy shirts and thick crêpe soles and became 'teddy boys'. Middle-class men went to Moss Bros for single-breasted dinner jackets and pleated dress shirts.

A distinctly male glamour began to be attached not only to eating in restaurants but to cooking for show. The Australian Graham Kerr, ITV's hugely popular 'Galloping Gourmet', was something of a role model to a generation of young men tired to death of grey flannels and baggy tweed jackets and eager to try their hands at flambéd steak *au poivre*. Complete with sharply contemporary tie, immaculate suit and with a glass of wine to hand, to say nothing of his glamorous 'right-hand girl' Treena hovering helpfully in the background, he was as much a performer as a cook.

Graham Kerr took an almost sadistic relish in pseudo-sophistication. His suggestion of 'poached eggs in Chartreuse sauce' as a starter for a Sunday-night supper sounds fine (apart from the Chartreuse), but the recipe actually calls for four 'collops' of lobster, 1.3 kg (3 lb) potatoes, first baked, then mashed, then piped around scallop shells, and 'a garnish of paprika, chopped dill and red pimiento (tinned)'.

The flamboyant art of the flambé is demonstrated by television's 'Galloping Gourmet' Graham Kerr

But programmes like Kerr's did not alter the truth that the new spirit of culinary adventurousness was profoundly mixed with inhibition. The hostesses of the 1950s were not ready to be playmates. Roland Barthes, in a 1972 essay on Ornamental Cookery, drew attention to the post-war tendency to disguise the true nature of foodstuffs with complicated sauces, rather as upwardly mobile middle-class Victorians liked to clothe the limbs of their chairs and tables in decently plush garments. One method is the 'fleeing from nature thanks to a kind of frenzied baroque' (sticking shrimps in a lemon, for example, or making a chicken look pink and serving grapefruit hot), the other is 'trying to reconstitute nature through an incongruous artifice' (such as strewing meringue mushrooms and holly leaves on a traditional log-shaped Christmas cake or replacing the heads of crayfish around the sophisticated béchamel which hides their bodies).

Kinsey had been read, marked and learnt, but not inwardly digested. Certainly, efforts were made. New aspirations in the context of the couple relationship meant much more work behind the scenes. An advertisement for Oxo could feature a glamorous wife lighting candles for the dinner table as her husband comes home, a striking change from the days when women did not even sit down to eat with men. But acting out this script of togetherness meant that a wife would not only have to do the ironing during the day (instead of while hubby ate his meal), but would also have to find time to dress herself up and don make-up in order to fit the part of attentive and stimulating *femme fatale*. And could Oxo really guarantee that when her man came home he would not be righteously tired, wanting only to bury his head in the paper and nod off to sleep?

SUBURBAN NEUROSIS ▬▬▬▬▬▬▬▬▬▬

It was nice in the early 1950s to settle back and be the little woman for a time, and father came back and shouldered the burdens of everything. But then women began to think, 'Do I really want to be a little woman at home always?'

MARGUERITE PATTEN

The question became more urgent: what is the place of women in the second half of the twentieth century? The Fifties gave two answers – the home and the bed. Both were confidently given and both were found wanting.

PETER LEWIS, *The Fifties* 1978

The sentimental cult of the domestic virtues is the cheapest method at society's disposal of keeping women quiet without seriously considering their grievances or improving their position.

HANNAH GAVRON, *The Captive Wife* 1966

The demanding and varied nature of the homemaker's job, even as late as 1957, was clearly shown by a summary of a housewife's day recorded by Mass Observation.

The day of one housewife (a Thursday) followed this pattern:

A.M.
7.15 Got up and washed myself
7.30 Did the grate out
7.45 Prepared the breakfast
8.00 Had breakfast
8.30 Cleared away and got the children ready for school
8.45 Ironed a couple of small things
9.00 Made beds and had a good tidy round
10.30 Went out shopping
11.15 Got back and started to prepare the lunch

P.M.
12.00 Did some washing
12.30 Had lunch
1.15 Sat and read the paper
1.45 Washed up
2.15 Finished the washing and hung it out } While listening
2.45 Washed the floor } to the radio
3.10 Wrote a couple of letters
3.45 Sat and did the crossword in the paper
4.00 Machined a dress for daughter
4.45 Prepared the tea
5.00 Had tea } While watching
5.30 Cleared away the tea things } television
6.00 Did some more dressmaking
7.45 Prepared supper for the children
8.15 Gave the children their supper
8.45 Put son to bed
9.00 Put daughter to bed and gave husband his supper
9.15 Tried on the dress had been making
9.30 Tidied round and washed up
10.00 Put the finishing touches to the dress
10.30 Got some milk for husband
10.45 Did a bit of knitting
11.30 Had a cup of milk
11.45 Went to bed

Although the appliances of the 1950s and early 1960s were a considerable improvement on the laborious methods of earlier days, women soon discovered that the visions of a life of ease sketched in the advertisements were far from easy to fulfil. Housework and cooking still required a lot of effort. Twin tub machines required the washing to be transferred, then put through a wringer garment by garment and hung outside by hand. Nor were they anywhere near as reliable as modern machines. 'Houses weren't as labour-saving as they are today,' says Patten. 'The other thing is, and I'm sure many modern women would like to seize me by the throat when I say this, but our standards were higher. We had starched things, starched tablecloths, starched napkins; our clothes had to be ironed more. Today with drip-dry everything, washing isn't nearly as hard as it was.'

The magazines' message that a professional attitude to domesticity was a fulfilling career in itself was wearing thin. In November 1949, *Good Housekeeping* had attempted to counter the omnipresent hype with a prescient warning of the limitations of the much-heralded age of infinite domestic leisure.

> Nobody has yet invented the machine which will make the beds, lay and clear the table, run to answer the door, take the children to school, or even, in fact, look after itself completely. The most versatile machine requires to be assembled, cleaned, and in many instances taken from a cupboard and replaced after use. This quite often takes a longer time than doing a short job with simple hand tools.

In contrast to the advertisements of the 1940s which showed self-assured women being assiduously courted as independent customers by the banks, the women in those of the 1950s and 1960s were always serving. Aprons on and trays in hands, they carried food from the kitchen to the waiting family or pushed it through the serving hatch. Permanent waves and lipstick topped the pinafores, but the message was unmistakable. This was a slave class.

After saying just this in her shrewd appraisal of the feminine condition, *The Art of Being a Woman* (1951), Amabel Williams Ellis suggested that wives turn to the family for help. 'Most young husbands are only too pleased to help out ... Explain that you need a few hours a week to yourself. Ask if anyone would be prepared to cook supper on Thursdays so that you could take an evening off to go to evening classes ... Or if they mind if the brass is put wrapped up in a cloth in a drawer so that you don't have to clean it every week'.

It was true that the new housing estates and garden cities initially brought husbands and wives closer together in the creation of suburban utopias. 'Only in the last twenty years has the working-class home really become a place that is warm, comfortable, able to provide its own fireside entertainment,' wrote Hannah Gavron in *The Captive Wife* (1966). But once the carpentry and do-it-yourself stage was over, men looked outside for both work and leisure while women ran the house and devoted themselves to giving their children the 'constant, loving care' recommended by childcare experts.

An unlooked-for result of the modernization of household work and cooking was the increasingly private nature of the household at all income levels. Fewer servants and fewer co-operative support systems between housewives led to a generation of women closeted behind net curtains. The communal tap, the public baths, the local wash-house all disappeared. Once the children had gone to school there was not even an excuse for getting together over toddler groups. Matters were made worse by the ideology of privacy, of 'keeping oneself to oneself', which has always been native to the British – perhaps a natural development in an over-crowded little island.

The distance that separated a mere housewife and mother from wider stimulation became painfully evident. Discontent was further intensified by a growing sense that the rat race of keeping up with those imaginary Joneses was a never-ending one. Day by day, year by year, the prettily furnished sitting-rooms and immaculate kitchens on the television screen contrasted more tellingly with the rubbed corners and food-spattered surfaces of home. 'Suburban neurosis is affecting one woman in four,' declared a cinema news feature in 1960. All that doctors could offer were pills – 'mother's little helpers' – or a cup of Horlicks to counter 'night starvation'.

The decline of community contacts increased the importance of the couple relationship. Many could not take the strain. In 1950 there were 32 000 divorces, four times as many as there had been in 1939. Even allowing for the emotional aftermath of the understandable strains of wartime, this was disturbing. By 1951, there was so much concern at the number of marriages falling apart that a Royal Commisson on Marriage and Divorce was appointed. 'I think it was perhaps because people expected too much, and both partners found that they weren't getting quite what they had hoped,' says Hubback. New legislation in 1964 released another flood of petitions. Women did not know exactly what they did want, but Frances Stewart at least was quite sure that it was not another dose of Constance Spry: 'When the children were all off at school, I said I wanted to do evening classes in geology. And he said, "Why don't you do cookery or flower-arranging or some-thing?". And that was the point at which I began to realize that there were cracks in our relationship!'

THE PROBLEM THAT HAD NO NAME

> *In Britain the first generation to enjoy household technology en masse were also the first to have gone through full secondary education en masse . . . these women felt they had good brains going to rust.*
>
> ANGELA HOLDSWORTH, *Out of the Doll's House* 1988

> *We were a bit worried about whether we were being aggressive if we were trying to say, We don't only want to stay in the background'. We hadn't quite got as far as saying 'What about me?' in an aggressive sort of way. But we were beginning to think 'What about me? . . . I was envious of women whose careers had not been interrupted by family life. But then, of course, I knew they were envious of me for having family life*
>
> JUDITH HUBBACK

> *The effect of the post-war economy on home life was uneven, It meant an increase in the standards of a steelworker's wife, and the lowering of those of a solicitor's. The women workers that the middle-class wife lost in the home were gained by her husband in the form of secretaries, waitresses, clerks.*
>
> ELIZABETH WILSON, *Only Halfway to Paradise* 1980

The new emphasis on elaborate entertaining dramatized the conflict between being a successful society hostess and a career woman. 'The college girl who tries to get on in the world and to make a success of her life feels that she is running in two races at the same time,' wrote Viola Klein. 'She is never quite sure whether her advance in one field may not be a handicap in the other. The reputation of a brain could still "kill a girl socially".' Klein suggested that women heading for home management should take up careers in related jobs – nursing, teaching, social work or personnel management, etc.

Judith Hubback came from a tradition of working women – her mother-in-law had been principal of Morley College, and she herself had a degree from Cambridge. Though she wanted to look after her own children ('I'd been brought up by a nanny, and I was very hostile to nannies – I was very influenced by [the paediatrician] John Bowlby's research, and he stressed that you should never leave your children') and valued such domestic arts as cooking, she also hoped to have some sort of career after her children had grown up. 'I felt discontented without knowing quite why – frittered into lots of different occupations. Although my husband was very supportive I felt that he was doing a highly valued job, and that I was the inferior partner. And I began to wonder if other people felt the same.'

She decided to contact 2000 women with degrees, half of whom had graduated before the war, and half afterwards. The response was remarkable. Sixty-five per cent replied and the end result was *Wives Who Went to College* (1957). 'I think I was on a wave of interest … People's ideas on the subject hadn't been formulated before. There was even a second leader in *The Times* when the book came out, which was amazing.' She found that not everybody was discontented by any means, but that most would have liked some sort of part-time work while their children were at school. 'But it was very very difficult to find part-time work in the professions.'

What graduates did not want, she discovered, was to be 'married to their homes':

> Some people didn't continue to be married to their husbands, either – but fewer, on the whole, than now. Many of us did voluntary work – there were many more women available for voluntary work then, that was in fact one of the advantages of the age. I gradually discovered that I wanted to become an analyst, a Jungian analyst, and that was going to be a specific profession, not odds and bits.

Some men tolerated their wives' aspirations to work. But the attitude assumed by a *Good Housekeeping* lecture to businessmen in 1965 was much more typical:

> Money invested in a washing machine will soon be returned in fewer laundry bills (as your wife copes with more washing), in reduced decorating bills (as she does a bit of painting), in income (as she goes back to work, even if only part-time) … She may undertake voluntary work which will boost her morale and yours. On the other hand, she may do nothing at

all in the saved time, but be prettier and sweeter than before – perhaps the best return of all for your investment.

Maureen Nicol started the National Housewives' Register in 1960. Struck by an article in the *Guardian* which called on women to 'sharpen' their minds instead of letting home and childminding blunt them, she wrote to the newspaper asking like-minded women to join her in forming a register of women who were interested in meeting each other. She had over 2000 replies and by the early 1970s members of the National Housewives' Register topped 25 000. Maureen herself made contact with half a dozen who lived nearby and they babysat for each other and organized joint projects: 'painting, discussing, reading, and getting much more out of life.'

Maureen Nicol sees her generation as the first in which a significant number of women failed to find fulfilment in home and family.

We were reasonably well educated. We'd all had reasonably satisfying jobs. We never ever considered – looking back, it's extraordinary how my daughter's generation is so different – leaving the children and going back to work until they were at school at least. But we needed more stimulation. We needed to talk about things. There are so many more things in the world than just in the confines of a home.

Over the next 15 years, a steady stream of books would begin to analyse what Betty Friedan in the United States had christened 'the problem that has no name'. The first was Hannah Gavron's *The Captive Wife* in 1966. Gavron, mother of two small children, was interested in the rupture of family ties caused by new housing estates, and the book aimed to identify the active nature of the way in which a circle of contacts and friends is maintained. Gavron herself committed suicide in the year it was published.

Superficially, however, all was still well. Demure and unthreatening to a generation of men who had had their masculinity on trial for quite long enough during the war, the woman of the day favoured a frilly apron rather than dungarees, resolved her sexual anxieties by reading about what Jayne Mansfield made of motherhood, laughed at the feather-headed *faux pas* of giddily glamorous Lucille Ball in *I Love Lucy* on the family's newly acquired television set, and longed only to bake a Victoria sponge better than her mother-in-law. But times were changing.

'Early in the 1960s the cooking programmes ended, because it was felt that women no longer wanted to be at home cooking – they were more interested in the idea of climbing Everest,' says Marguerite Patten. 'I remember in 1962 receiving the official letter from the BBC saying "Dear Marguerite, we hate to tell you but we have decided that the time has come to end the women's programmes as they have been run. We don't want to involve cookery; although it's been extraordinarily popular. Women are now feeling that they want to spread their wings." I'm sure that they were right, that it was time. But things happen in a circle, don't they? Because there's more cookery on television now than there ever has been before.'

CHAPTER THREE

Rock and Roll and Ratatouille

*Today, youth has money, and teenagers have become a power. In their struggle to impose
their wills upon the adult world, young men and women have always been blessed with energy;
but never, until now, with wealth. After handing a pound or two over to Mum, they are left with more
'spending money' than many of their elders, crushed by adult obligation.*

COLIN MACINNES, *England, Half-English* 1961

*We thought the food in the Wimpy Bar was wonderful – burgers, cokes, milkshakes.
It was so different, it was what we didn't have at home.*

'SUNGLASSES RON' STAPLES, former Teddy boy, Newport

*In London with a beautiful hungry girl one must show her to Mario at the Terrazza. We sat in
the ground floor front under the plastic grapes and Mario brought us Campari-sodas and told Jean how
much he hated me. To do this he practically had to gnaw her ear off. Jean liked it.*

LEN DEIGHTON, *The Ipcress File* 1962

*O scent of the daubes of my childhood! During the holidays, at Gemeaux, in the month
of August, when we arrived in my grandmother's dark kitchen on Sunday after Vespers, it was
lit by a ray of sunshine in which the dust and the flies were dancing, and there was a sound like a
little bubbling spring. It was a daube, which since midday had been murmuring gently on the stove, giving out sweet smells which brought tears to your eyes. Thyme, rosemary, bay leaves, spices, the wine of
the marinade, and the fumet of the meat were becoming transformed under the magic
wand which is the fire into a delicious whole, which was served about seven o'clock in the
evening, so well-cooked and so tender that it was carved with a spoon.*

PIERRE HUGUENIN, *Les Meilleures Recettes de ma Pauvre Mère* 1936,
quoted by ELIZABETH DAVID, *French Provincial Cooking* 1960

While Mum was showing her devotion by garnishing the grapefruit, and Dad was pottering around the vegetable patch, thankful not to be under fire in Normandy, the younger generation had begun to be restlessly aware that its future lay elsewhere. For inspiration they looked to America, where a novel character called a teenager was bopping to rock and roll music, and to Italy for Vespa scooters and the romance of coffee bars, garlic and streetwise style. The cult foods of the age – hamburgers and frothy coffee, pizzas and Coca-Cola – were talismans of new influences, exotic climes and cash.

As the rebellious teenagers became twenty-somethings, they were still affluent, still eagerly informal, but ready for entertainment in a more substantial way. Italy remained the style-setter, offering cars and domestic appliances, sharply-tailored suits and stiletto heels, holidays in the sun and evenings out remembering them beneath the kitsch vines and straw-bound Chianti bottles of the new 'trattorias'.

When couples settled down with their 2.4 children (we were becoming population-conscious), a newly informal domesticity succeeded the aspiration-hungry 1950s. Artificial barriers between the stove and the family were swept away. Serving hatches swelled into archways, archways into 'through rooms'. Table-cloths took early retirement along with hostess trolleys. Fashionable everyday eating took place on pine tables in the kitchen itself and, except on extra-special occasions, the dining-room was given over to children's paints, Play-Doh and recorder lessons.

This was the birth of the age of good, simple food (the first Raymond Postgate *Good Food Guide* came out in 1950). Discriminating middle-class homes abandoned the rigours of Cordon Bleu for the lusty garlic and rosemary hotpots beloved of Southern European peasants. The woman who defined the terms of the love affair with Provence that still characterizes British holiday-making and eating 40 years on was Elizabeth David. Her vision of good food, prepared for friends and family as a labour of love from ingredients redolent with Mediterranean romance, was perfectly suited to the times. Liberated by domestic appliances and much smaller families, women were flexing their muscles, reading avidly and looking outside the household – and beyond Britain itself – for inspiration. But they were still in thrall to the image of the good wife and mother.

Finally, as a coda to this story of teenage hipsters and marinating mums, some account must be given of the developments in food retailing that made the exotic ingredients essential to the new simplicities generally available, and which would in the long run transform the way we ate out of all recognition. Supermarkets and instant frozen foods were the respectable, unexpectedly subversive agents of a social revolution. 'Then, we thought supermarkets were wonderful,' reminisces Frances Stewart. 'Now we're inclined to go back and think, oh, you can't beat the little old shop. But at the time supermarkets were coming in, and they stocked such a great variety of foods that it did make you want to do other things. Elizabeth David brought out this cookery book with Continental things in it and you actually found that your supermarket had got those ingredients, so you had no excuse for not trying. And it livened cooking up. It livened it up for the family, and it livened it up for you to do something different.'

JUST FOR KICKS

If you went out with your parents, to somewhere like the Wedgwood tea-shop or the Durngate bus station café, you had to hold the cup with your little finger up, drink quietly … you felt you were a prisoner. But when we were out on our own, drinking coffee, we could do what we wanted, hold a cup with our elbows on the table. We wanted a new world, where you weren't hidebound by class and etiquette and by having to follow your betters and where you could respond to basic human instincts and have some fun and be free like the Americans were. We wanted to kick the old world of afternoon tea and school dinners and having to sit upright into touch. And we did.

RAY GOSLING

'There's an entirely NEW kind of girl around. Awkward and angular, pouting and petulant, history has seen nothing like her before.

Sunday Express 1958

In the mid-1950s teenagers' real earnings were 50 per cent higher than they had been before the war, and their incomes doubled again between 1958 and 1966. Paid factory wages and working in jobs that treated them as adults rather than domestic menials, they had a new confidence as well as full wallets. With none of the responsibilities of adulthood, they had a golden decade of spending to enjoy before settling down to marriage. This new wealth made them of great interest to Admass. 'The teenage trade cannot be treated as a sideline,' declared the *Draper's Record* at the time. Although teenagers made up only 10 per cent of the population, they accounted for at least 25 per cent of all consumer expenditure on bicycles and motor cycles, records and record-players, cosmetics and toilet preparations, and cinema and other entertainments. Not, let it be noted, alcohol. Less than 40 per cent of 18- to 25-year-old boys and only 10 per cent of girls were drinking as often as once a week.

The teenagers of the 1950s had a new confidence and a new environment to enjoy themselves in: the sharply contemporary coffee bar

The sense of a unique identity was given a helping hand by generous funding of youth clubs and youth centres by the State. In the 1950s, four out of ten 14- to 18-year-olds belonged to some sort of youth organization. Improved nutrition meant children were taller and reached puberty sooner – 11-year-old London girls were reading *Valentine* and *Roxy* as well as Enid Blyton and Noel Streatfeild; 13-year-olds were experimenting with make-up as well as joining the Girl Guides, and 15 was not too soon to be 'going steady'. The milk bar was the place in which to see and be seen, posed on high bar stools, sipping milk shakes through straws, listening to the newly introduced juke-box.

Soon light, unbreakable '45s' and 'LPs' began to replace the heavy old breakable '78s', and wind-up gramophones gave way to moquette-covered Dansette record-players with stacking mechanisms and 'hi fi' sound. Even as Elvis the King warned us not to step on his blue suede shoes, our own Tommy Steele, the Cockney boy wonder, was 'putting on the agony, putting on the style' with a lanky character called Marty Wilde in a Soho coffee bar called the Two I's. In 1961, *Children's Hour* was axed. 'Some children do not like being called children any more,' explained a BBC spokesman. Music programmes like *Ready Steady Go*, *Juke Box Jury* and *6.5 Special* took over. Judith Hubback recalls the envy with which her contemporaries regarded the new generation.

> They were different from us; they weren't so sunk in anxiety that they were not going to emerge. They had rather more career before getting married. Things were more exciting for the young. There was a lot of talk about the word 'teenager' – for a short while they were called bobby-soxers … We rather older people, we were beginning to realize the young were going to have much more fun than we'd had. Make-up was much more available, and they were taking much more trouble to get it really good, and to mind about their clothes. Jolly good for them. But it was a bit rough on us!

Culture rocked and rolled to the rhythm of pirate radio stations. 'Turn that hooliganism off,' growled Ray Gosling's father on finding the family wireless tuned to Radio Luxemburg's legendary 208 waveband. 'Or I'll take the valves out and then you won't be able to play it.'

The generation gap had never been wider. The war, though still endlessly won and rewon in comics, films and television programmes, did not haunt young people born in the late 1940s in the way it haunted the unfortunate juvenile urban generation whose childhood had been punctuated, punctured even, by the Blitz, evacuation and separation from their parents. The shame of Suez in 1956 demoralized only those old enough to remember the glories of empire, as Ray Gosling witnessed when he was training as a relief signal-box boy.

> The men in the signal-box … were completely deflated. Eden had sold them down the river. We'd been beaten by wogs he'd assured us we would beat before breakfast. It didn't mean much to me, but … the effect it had on

them was – astounding … They so deeply believed in British muscle, might and right, to put foreigners in their place. As Suez broke loyalty to mother Britain, so rock 'n' roll between children and parents. The men were bewildered. They'd listen to the news, and we, people like me and Porky, would tune in to pop music.

It was the self-invented categories – Teddy boys, Mods and Rockers, Beatniks – that puzzled the older generation most. 'The youth of today' were discussed with all the earnestness that women's issues were accorded a decade later. In 1954, the psychoanalyst Anna Freud defined the typical adolescent as 'egotistic but capable of extreme self-sacrifice and devotion, enjoying passionate love relations but breaking up as easily. They will throw themselves into the community, but also have a passionate longing to be alone. They are capable of both blind submission to leader and defiant rebellion – selfish yet idealistic, ascetic but indulgent, inconsiderate but touchy, they veer from lighthearted optimism to extreme pessimism.' In the face of a society that tried hard both to understand them and to explain them away, post-war young people were intent on creating their own rites of passage in time-honoured terms of gang confrontation.

Most were more interested in escaping from adults than looking for trouble but there were villains, then as now. Robert Fabian, the legendary Scotland Yard super-intendent who wrote regular newspaper articles and books after his retirement, discussed the problem of 'juvenile delinquency' in *London After Dark* (1954). He described a case involving two 15-year-old 'spivs' in drape jackets, crêpe soles, bright bow ties and red and yellow socks who 'hang around late-night milk bars until they see a drunk.' Then one of their girls 'plays her part by pestering him. Then these two bright beauties jump him with knives and coshes on the pretence he's insulted their girlfriend, cosh him and rob him and run off.' London territories, he wrote, were as clearly demarcated as those of Chicago in the age of Prohibition and the speakeasy barons.

> A milk bar on one side of the street can 'belong' to one gang, while the soft-drinks bar with the juke-box across the way is in the territory of another gang. Let either side trespass and there may be a battle that may take three or four carloads of police officers to stop. Every gang has its team of 'brides' or 'chicks', who are girls of 13 to 17, painted like Jezebels and captivated by the 'glamour' of belonging to a boy gang.

Fish hooks were sewn into the sleeves of jackets, so a gentle graze of the arm could leave an horrific wound. Fabian recalled a 14-year-old Hoxton girl who was leant against in 'a milk-bar gang fight' and 'had half her face stroked away'. He claimed that 'on an average a hundred juvenile gangsters are arrested in London every week, and between them they are responsible for almost exactly half the total of indictable crimes on the City's nine million inhabitants. In every Scotland Yard graph, the 15-year-olds stick out high above every other age group … One robbery in every four is committed by a 14- or 15-year-old. One stolen car in every five is taken by a teenager.'

For Mods and Rockers, mobility was the new excitement. Once they were old enough to drive on two wheels they moved on from youth clubs to rival citadels set up in highway transport cafés such as Jack's Hill on the A1 and the Ace café on the North Circular. From these they sallied forth to fight a private tournament, on scooters and motor bikes in lieu of noble steeds, up and down the streets of seaside towns that had been deserted by holiday-makers in favour of package trips to Spain. Most of the Mods and Rockers did remarkably little damage considering the scale of the moral panic they produced. All in all, they achieved everything they hoped for: notoriety, style and the history books.

The upper classes were more tolerant of the 'young Elizabethans' than were the moral middle majority of Horlicks-quaffing has-beens. 'I think youngsters are splendid,' gushed Lady Lewisham, in accents you could cut with a flick-knife.

I have met many teenagers up and down the country when I have been travelling around and I have always been particularly struck by their enthusiasm about everything. I am always very bored with people who say 'Oh young people aren't what they were in my day'.

PLEASURE FOODS ▪

Our town was surrounded by American Air Force bases ... the long coaches would come in and the Yanks would stand at the top of the steps and throw chewing gum and Hershey bars into the square, and as kids do, we'd grab them ... They were ambassadors for dreams come true.

RAY GOSLING, *Personal Copy, A Memoir of The Sixties* 1980

The girls would come in to the Wimpy Bar, and want their tutti-frutti icecreams and their milkshakes, and looking all ladylike, prim and proper – but showing a bit of ankle – it was great!

RON STAPLES

*Does your chewing gum lose its flavour on the bedpost overnight?
If your mother finds you chewing, do you swallow it in fright?*

Recorded by Lonnie Donegan, 1959

The godlike status of the Americans after the war was reflected in lust for all things American – motor bikes, cult figures like Marlon Brando, James Dean and Elvis Presley, television programmes, music – and teenage rebellion. *Rock Around the Clock* was already a living legend when it was released in Britain in September 1956.

Near riots broke out as Teddy boys raved in the aisles of cinemas. One of them was Ron Staples, who still sports large black sideburns and Brylcreemed hair, and belongs to several societies dedicated to preserving the traditions of the 'Teds'.

> We tuned in to AFN, the American Forces radio network. I told my parents, listen to this. The look of horror that came over their faces! That … music! It made you want to dance, it just had something; there was a beat, the words were crazy, they were singing about teenagers and how they were rebelling against everything. It was so different.

In this context, food was not for nourishment but to be toyed with, for fun. First and foremost the Americans were into oral satisfaction. Coca-Cola and knickerbocker glories sipped through straws, chewing gum continuously masticated, Lucky Strikes hanging from permanently curled lips. And the hamburger, the food of the future, an innovation as historic as the beef wrapped in toasted bread that John Montague, 11th Earl of Sandwich, had devised in the early 1760s as a convenient snack to be eaten during his 24-hour gambling binges.

No ham was ever involved: it was Hamburg seamen who brought the idea of a small grilled or fried cake of minced beef to America and in 1904, when visitors to the St Louis World Fair consumed them by the ton, they became established as America's quintessential fast food. Chain restaurants in the United States began serving them in the 1920s, clamped between two halves of a toasted bun.

Wimpy Bars were the first British attempt at emulating the American hamburger industry. Brian Salmon, General Manager of Lyons' Coventry Street Corner House, hired the franchise idea of 'Wimpy Grills' from an American called Eddie Gold, who had 12 such outlets in Chicago. The name came from a burger-munching character in the Popeye cartoon who had the splendid name of J. Wellington Wimpy. 'Wimpies', sizzling hot burgers topped with tomato ketchup and sandwiched in a toasted bun, were first served at the 1953 Ideal Home Exhibition. Cooked in front of customers by chefs in tall white hats, they were, says Wimpy's former managing director David Acheson, 'a fabulous success. We used forequarter steer beef in those days, cooked to very tight specifications.' That summer Wimpies as well as tennis balls were served at the All-England Wimbledon Championships. 'The square meal in the round bun' sold well, though umpires and players alike complained about the pungent aroma of onions wafting over the tennis courts. David Acheson:

> But we realized that we were attracting an entirely new clientele – young people. So we introduced Wimpies into the Corner Houses with specially designed, well-ventilated areas of their own where the waitresses had Hardy Amies uniforms, and there was also counter service. The visual act of the chefs, raised up a little at the griddles, cooking your own personal order was very attractive. Soon there were permanent queues outside. That made us decide to open them as individual shops, and to set up a company to manage them. We called it Pleasure Foods.

A high-hatted chef pontificated over the newly opened Chiswick High Road Wimpy Bar in 1962

In 1960, Lyons celebrated the success of the new product by suggesting that they serve freshly griddled cocktail-sized hamburgers in cocktail-sized buns at the Buckingham Palace garden parties. 'The equerries were a little doubtful, but the Queen heard about it and thought that it would be fun. And they were a great success!' By 1969, there were 460 Wimpy Bars in the United Kingdom, eight or nine in London's Oxford Street alone. 'They attracted a whole new tranche of customer,' says Acheson. 'People who weren't used to eating out. They liked seeing the food being cooked, and knowing what they were in for. And having the menu in the window made it clear what it was going to cost.' Children were welcomed, too, as a Wimpy Bar was designed to be difficult to damage. It was also one of the first eating-places that girls felt they could go into on their own. It was, David Acheson points out,

> … a social meeting place for boys and girls before or after the cinema with bright lights and no alcohol, so parents were happy about it. Above all it was cheerful – red roof tiles over the griddle area, tomato ketchup in red plastic tomatoes, backlit transparencies of food, lights beaming out into the street, attracting people like moths to a flame. A lot more fun than sitting at home with the parents in front of black-and-white TV.

With those daring young girls sporting wide belts, frou-frou skirts and bouffant hair-dos, feminism was not yet much in evidence. Nice girls had to be home by ten o'clock, and nice boys shook hands with anxious parents when they delivered their charges punctually to the minute. Ties were worn to dance halls, and too much make-up ('war-paint') was frowned on. These were the innocent years when Connie Francis bemoaned 'Lipstick on Your Collar' and Cliff Richard got himself a 'Living Doll'. But by the early 1960s, a distinct British youth culture was emerging, focused on Beatles music, Carnaby Street fashion, miniskirts and Mary Quant. Milkshakes were much too nourishing for young people in the age of Twiggy and drainpipe jeans. Instead, they took to coffee.

GAGGIA-CRAZY

> *Nowhere was Britain's youth revolution more evident than in the coffee bars which sprouted up during the 1950s in every town centre and suburban high street. For the price of a cup of frothy coffee, Teddyboys, Rockers and skiffle fans could sit for hours behind a steamed-up window listening to the latest Elvis or Chuck Berry hit on the juke-box, accompanied by the loud hiss of an espresso machine.*
>
> JUDITH SUMMERS, *Soho* 1989

> *In the new coffee bars, jazz cellars and youth clubs, grammar school and modern school rubbed Italianate shoulders; fish-and-chip girl and Acacia Avenue girl alike embraced the new informality of 'separates' and drove holes into the floor with stiletto heels of approximately the same sharpness.*
>
> HARRY HOPKINS, *The New Look* 1963

> *Our beer used to be frothy*
> *But now it's frothy coffee*
> *And fings ain't wot they used to be*
>
> Title song from the musical, *Fings Ain't Wot They Used to Be* 1959

Coffee has traditionally been associated with exchanging new ideas. The great clubs of Almacks, Whites and Brooks all originated as coffee-houses, as did Lloyd's of London. Money for one of the first post-war coffee-houses, which opened in London's Northumberland Avenue in July 1952, was put up by a group of professional men and women who felt that good coffee in congenial surroundings was a necessity of life. It was an immediate success. 'Long may we enjoy this fine innovation to London's catering services,' wrote Catherine Uttley in the 1957 *Where to Eat in London*. She listed nearly 200 'coffee-houses', most of them somewhat sedate.

The coffee bars designed to attract young people were sharply contemporary in style, with angular chairs, Formica-topped tables and the indispensable juke-box. Futuristic furniture, a multicoloured ceiling and artful subdued lighting were all features of Maurice Blair's Kaleidoscope Coffee House in Gerrard Street in Soho. Outside, coffee bars signalled their status as haunts of the youth tribe with fascias sponsored by Coca-Cola (even then a company with an eye for self-promotion).

Inside, 'each place had a slightly different decor,' recalls Rica Teagno, a dress-maker who worked in Hanover Square in the 1950s. 'I used to go to each one that opened to see how they'd done them up.' The most outrageous was the Macabre. Its inky depths were hung with skulls, skeletons and cobwebs (many of them real). The juke-box offered the 'Danse Macabre' and the 'Dead March' from Saul as well as the current 'hit parade'.

The ritual of making the coffee was very important. The centre of attention, the mark of the genuine coffee bar, was a gleaming, wheezing espresso coffee machine. Invented by Gaggia of Milano in 1946, it was a triumph of Italian style and design. 'Each cup is made individually, with the aid of large heavily chromed machines which splutter and hiss,' explains Terri Colpi, author of *The Italian Factor*.

A little knock-drawer under the machine made of wood and lined with metal paper, conspicuously opened and closed for every cup, held the discarded coffee. The tiny black cups of caffeine-rich espresso that provide day-round pick-me-ups in Italy were less popular in Britain than the more mellow capuccino. Capuccino (the name came from the brown and cream habits of the Italian order of Capuchin friars) was the drink that defined coffee bar culture.

But the presence of a gleaming Gaggia on the counter did not always guarantee a decent cup of coffee. Skiffle-player Chas McDevitt, who ran a Camberley coffee bar called Freight Train (after the hit record), was not the only manager to economize in ways that would have made the machine's Milanese inventor as pale as cheapskate coffee. 'I used to take a full scoop of coffee from the Gaggia machine, froth up powdered Millac under the machine, and make two cups of coffee, which I would then dilute into six cups with hot water,' he admits. 'No one complained except the French and American customers.'

By 1960, there were 2000 coffee bars nationwide, 500 in Greater London alone. Soho was the Mecca of the coffee bar circuit, and catered for every variety of taste. The New Left ran a coffee bar called the Partisan in Carlisle Street. Above it was the *New Left Review*'s editorial office, occupied by Stuart Hall, one of the first journalists to treat the new culture with respect rather than as a fad or hooliganism. Colin Wilson, author of *The Outsider,* the most popular user's guide to the decade, was nicknamed 'the coffee bar philosopher'.

The most famous of all London coffee bars was the Two I's. It took its name from the Irani Brothers who used to own it, but had been taken over by Paul Lincoln, an Australian wrestler whose professional name was Doctor Death, and Tom Littlewood. It was the scene of the launch of Tommy Steele and of a special session of the BBC's *6.5 Special*. Innumerable 'pop stars' appeared in its tiny cellar – Adam Faith, Connie Francis, Little Richard and the Beatles.

The clientele was respectable enough, according to columnist Jeffrey Bernard. 'Tom Littlewood will not stand for any villainy in his place, such as punch-up merchants or purple heart bandits; these people get extremely short shrift.' But

Facing page: The pride of the coffee bars – a hissing, gleaming Gaggia machine

parents were dubious about the form the new culture was taking. The first rumours of drug dealings were in the air and coffee bars were seen as likely 'haunts of vice', places where the illicit pep pills known as 'purple hearts' were peddled. But parental power was on the wane when the option of 'bedsit' life lay ahead of every teenager.

URBAN NOMADS

Cooking a decent meal in a bedsitter is not just a matter of finding something that can be cooked over a single gas ring. It is a problem of finding somewhere to put down the fork while you take off the lid, and then finding somewhere else to put the lid. It is finding a place to keep the butter where it will not get mixed up with your hairpins. It is having your hands covered with flour and a pot boiling over on to your landlady's carpet.

KATHARINE WHITEHORN, *Kitchen in a Corner* 1962

Living in a bedsitter was a sea-change from the usual 1950s custom of taking lodgings with a landlady. Technology made independence easier. Refrigeration, compact electric cookers (classically the 'Baby Belling') and tinned and frozen foods made it possible, if not particularly elegant, to cook for oneself. Coffee spoons and can-openers were the only essential batterie de cuisine.

The wide new horizons that made any job anyone's oyster meant that it was increasingly common for young men and women to live away from home before getting married. As a result of the expansion of the universities effected by Harold Wilson's Labour Government in the 1960s, student numbers increased from 200 000 to 390 000 between 1961 and 1969. The new universities were sited in attractive parts of the country like Norfolk, Brighton, Bath and Warwick, and so the costly practice of sending young people off away from home to get educated continued. It was unique to Britain, and illogical in origin – an extension of the upper-class boarding-school tradition. But in the age of boom, no one in Whitehall was counting the cost. Popular wisdom emphasized that it was an excellent way of learning independence; young people experienced it as another wedge driven between the generations.

After university, big city life was the great draw but it was not easy to serve up the traditional British meal of meat and two veg in a metropolitan bedsit. In 1962, Katharine Whitehorn came to the rescue with the first cookery book for people without a kitchen. Originally titled *Kitchen in a Corner* and addressed as much to young men as to young women, it was perfectly in tune with the new informal spirit of the times. 'As far as I'm concerned, the chefs of the world labour in vain to bring themselves up to the standards of a single cold potato eaten out of the larder in the middle of the night,' she announced anarchically. There could have been no greater contrast between this witty and practical little Penguin book and the substantial bible that was *The Constance Spry Cookery Book,* and Whitehorn knew it.

> The principles of English cooking demand that first-class food should be cooked as simply as possible, and that a number of different foods should be cooked separately and served together. This is impossible on a gas ring. Indeed, bedsitter people have far more natural kinship with nomads brewing up in the desert over a small fire of camel dung, or impoverished Italian peasants eking out three shrimps and a lump of cheese with half a cartload of spaghetti.

Whitehorn was a journalist already noted for plain speaking and lack of affectation. 'If your friends don't like garlic, get some new friends,' she quipped, and one of her most memorable pieces was on sluttishness.

> Have you ever taken anything out of the dirty clothes basket because it had become relatively the cleaner thing? Changed stockings in a taxi? Could you try on clothes in any shop, any time, without worrying about your underclothes? How many things are in the wrong room – cups in the study, boots in the kitchen?

The right answers, she concludes, made you 'one of us; the miserable, optimistic, misunderstood race of sluts.' This sort of informality would be familiar enough after Peg Bracken's *I Hate to Cook Book* (1961) and after Conran's revelations of the true making of Superwoman in the mid-1970s. But in the 1960s, it earned Whitehorn a profile in *Time* magazine. 'This woman,' declared *Time*, 'rewrites the marriage vows. "Dost thou, Algernon, promise to laugh at this woman's jokes, push the car until it starts, and bring her sherry in the bath?"' And it is revealing that Whitehorn saw herself not as a bright young thing heralding a new wave of liberated womanhood, but as a chip off the old block,

> … the last of a breed represented by the mother who says to her daughter: 'You were trained for work, and not necessarily for marriage.' That breed's completely died out, but I'm the last of that lot … Our family was very much the sort that thinks that the career is important and the boyfriend is a frivolity. None of this business about marrying you off.

Born in 1928, she had run away from Roedean as a teenager, appalled by the 'captivity' and the attitude of the other girls. After a Glasgow day school, a sixth-form crammer and an English degree course at Newnham College, Cambridge, she went into publishing. It was a teaching job in America that inspired *Cooking in a Bedsit*. She was sharing a house with five other girls, including a Finn and a Chinese-American. They used to take turns to do a week's shopping and cook in pairs. The origin of the famous 'Dish' was an occasion when Whitehorn bought the wrong sort of steak to fry quicky for a boyfriend. The result was a slowly braised meat and vegetable stew which earned her her first foodie compliment: 'As he wiped his mouth after a second helping and sat back in his chair, he said, "I didn't know Limeys could cook."'

THE DISH (So called because my flat-mate and I cooked almost nothing else for nearly two years. It is absolutely foolproof. We left it on all night once by mistake, and it still made a lovely ragout. For four on its own, six with rice.)

1 lb braising steak	1 pimento
flour, salt and	4 onions
pepper	¼ lb mushrooms
1 aubergine or	olive oil for frying
1 head of celery	bay leaf
2 leeks	tomato paste (essential)

The point is that you can vary the vegetables, so long as you keep in the onions and pimento, and make sure the rest are interesting (i.e. not turnips). Cut the beef into slices and beat the flour (mixed with a little salt and pepper) into it thoroughly. Chop up all the vegetables. Heat 2 tablespoons olive oil in heavy pan, and turn the slices of meat in it till all is brown. Add vegetables, mixing all thoroughly together and putting the tomato paste among the layers – about 1 dessertspoon in all (a little wine or beer makes it, if possible, even nicer.) Add about 2 tablespoons water, and cook over lowest possible gas 1/2 for 2 hours.

Journalist Katharine Whitehorn, pictured in 1956, and her recipe for 'The Dish'

Whitehorn was interested in good results and much influenced by Elizabeth David, but not snobby about tins. 'I think the point is to realize that a baked beans and chips meal is gorgeous and a poulet au gratin savoyard is gorgeous in a quite different way,' she said to food writer Michael Bateman. 'I use stock cubes ... I use gravy mixes ... I use teabags all the time, but I don't particularly like tea. I'm a little fussy about the things I actually like. I think this is the only sensible way to live in the twentieth century.'

Whitehorn recalls a chapter in the early editions of *Cooking in a Bedsit* called 'Cooking to Impress' with a wry laugh. 'These days I don't think there's anything like the same urge to cook the way an older generation cooked. I mean, why would you?' But even in bedsitters, the tyrannies of the age of hostess cookery lingered.

FROM GUNS TO GASTRONOMY

To the old saying that man built the house but woman made of it a 'home' might be added the modern supplement that woman accepted cooking as a chore but man has made of it a recreation.

EMILY POST, *Etiquette* 1956

When I have six or eight authentic recipes I compare them on paper. I look for: one, logical procedure, two, scientific accuracy, three, simplicity and four, does it work?

LEN DEIGHTON quoted in *Cooking People* 1966

By the 1960s, men were beginning to progress from providing an appreciative background to an aproned wife's efforts to making an effort themselves, not least because the new generation of women were less sure that aprons suited their image. In Len Deighton, 'with-it' young men had a thoroughly modern role model. Deighton's pragmatic approach to cookery debunked James Bond's gourmet eating just as his anti-hero in *The Ipcress File* defused the glamour of *From Russia With Love*.

His mother was a cook in a hotel, his father a chauffeur. 'I started cooking very young. My mother let me fool around … the day of triumph was the first day I cooked the Sunday lunch. It was roast beef and Yorkshire.' He served in the RAF during the war (while his mother took up oxy-acetylene welding, Rosie the Riveter fashion), and afterwards he joined BOAC as an air steward. Then he spent six years at the Royal College of Art. Although he loved cooking, and had odd jobs in restaurants, including one in the Royal Festival Hall as assistant pastry cook, his aim was to be an artist or writer, never a cook.

His eye-catching *Observer* cookstrips came about by chance. Deighton did not want to spoil his collection of recipe books by using them in the kitchen, so he copied out recipes that he was using for a meal. A journalist and designer who saw one hanging on his wall, suggested he add numbers and lines to make it a grid, and took it along first to the *Daily Express* and then the *Observer*.

The Action Cookbook was published at the same time as *The Ipcress File* in 1962, and its cover emphasized the connection with a drawing of a gun sprouting parsley: 'Thriller writer and cook extraordinary turns from guns to gastronomy.' Its tone is authoritarian, man to man, with no frills. Deighton was aware that there were still deep-seated doubts about the threat to manliness posed by men taking to the

A strip from Len Deighton's *Où est Le Garlic?*, published in 1965

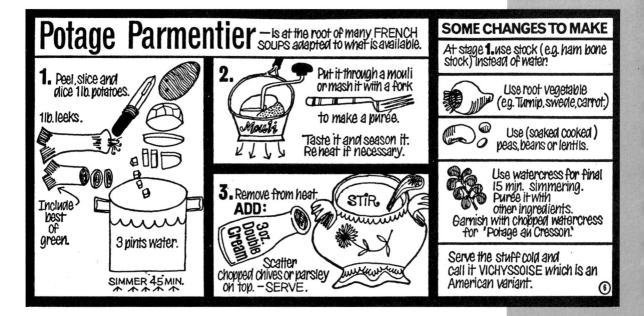

kitchen. 'It's a pity parents discourage children who want to become interested in it; a shame. Frightened they may become queer.'

His confident assertion that the kitchen could be not only male but distinctly masculine territory was taken further in his second cookbook, *Où est Le Garlic?* (1965), an implicit tribute to Elizabeth David's increasing influence. However, his approach to the subject was very different from hers. He saw cookery less as an art than as a set of rules to be followed. 'What was bad in British and American cooking stemmed from a desire to invent instead of a desire to work to tested rules and recipes – which was what made French cooking so good.'

Science and speed, rather than atmosphere, mattered to Deighton. His step-by-step directions assume no knowledge at all, but explain everything carefully: 'Understand the principle involved, and you will handle things right.' Besides demystifying the creation of soufflés, choux pastry and *'galantine de volaille à la gelée'*, he offered such 'bachelor quickies' as a two-minute lobster bisque made from a tin of condensed chicken soup and a tin of lobster. This was cooking to impress at breakneck speed, perfectly suited to the coming age of independent individualists.

LA DOLCE VITA

'This is the kitchen,' he said, waving his hand at it. It was equipped like an American kitchen. 'All the things one needs in a kitchen, I believe. So my wife said. She ran off with someone else last year. No loss. Not really. But I don't use the kitchen. I eat out.'

DORIS LESSING, *In Search of The English* 1960

Pasta has almost become the staple diet of Londoners. Spaghetti, ravioli and lasagne are featured on the menus of many non-Italian restaurants, and even in pubs. Londoners who have never been to Italy are nonchalantly dexterous with a forkful of gleaming spaghetti al pesto. Some have even learnt enough cucina-Italian to convey the impression they know much more. 'Due café nero', one hears them command, 'and may we have another carafe of vino rosso?' 'Vino Rosso!' shouts the waiter, accenting the words and loving the sound they make. 'E due neri!'

ADRIAN BAILEY, in LEN DEIGHTON'S *London Dossier* 1967

Attractive options to cooking in bedsits and bachelor pads were developing. Innovations in public catering, especially those introduced by immigrant cooks, began to make eating out affordable, something to do for convenience and not only on special occasions. The first, and the most enduring, foreign influence to make its mark was Italian. Its acceptability to the notoriously culinarily conservative British was the more rapid because travel was fast broadening our xenophobic minds.

Affluence and improved working conditions – 40-hour weeks, and a fortnight's holiday as a minimum expectation – led to a boom in holidays abroad, and the British began hitting Europe by the coachload. In 1950, 900 000 Britons travelled to the

Continent. Initally, they showed caution. One busload of miners from Wales took their own cook with them to Spain. But his services were rapidly dispensed with when they discovered just how tasty paella and fritto misto could be.

By 1958, over two million tourists set out for the warm south. New jet airliners like the Comet and the Caravelle made possible cut-price 'tourist class' fares that meant a fortnight in Benidorm could be cheaper than two weeks in Bournemouth. Jerry-built skyscrapers began to fringe the Mediterranean like uneven teeth. Suntans were suddenly fashionable, another way of drawing the line between the generations. So too was slimming, to ensure that an itsy bitsy teenie weenie yellow polka dot bikini did not reveal too much solid flesh. In 1962, Cliff Richard starred in a film called *Summer Holiday*, and soon Club Méditerranée was providing a Robinson Crusoe idyll of grass huts and bartering with beads.

Back home again, but still in holiday mood, nothing was more natural than to be attracted by the warmth, hospitality and Mediterranean atmosphere of one of the many little Italian trattorias that had followed hard on the heels of the coffee bar culture. Coffee bars encouraged the clientele to linger, but students measuring out their lives with coffee spoons meant slim pickings for the owners. Two-thirds of the new coffee bars that had sprung up like magic mushrooms all over the country closed down within five years. First light snacks, and then more substantial meals, began to bolster takings in the 'hep joints' that remained. The food was a distinct improvement on the depressing fare typical of public eating in Britain at the time, and mordantly described by P. D. James in *Cover Her Face*, the first of her detective novels.

> Today's mixture of tomato (orange) and oxtail (reddish brown), thick enough to support the spoon unaided, was as startling to the palate as to the eye. Soup had been followed by a couple of mutton chops nestling artistically against a mound of potato and flanked with tinned peas larger and shinier than any peas which had ever seen pod. They tasted of soya flour. A green dye which bore little resemblance to the colour of any known vegetable seeped from them and mingled disagreeably with the gravy. An apple and blackcurrant pie had followed in which neither of the fruits had met each other or the pastry until they had been carefully arranged on the plate by Mr Piggott's careful hand and liberally blanketted with synthetic custard.

Suddenly the most sought after social skill of the day was the art of managing spaghetti. 'In London in those days, mid-fifties, there was a gap!' exclaims Alvaro Maccioni, now padrone of La Famiglia, a stylish Chelsea trattoria. 'You had on the one hand Quo Vadis and places like that. French restaurants with Italian names. Then you had the café and the coffee bar where the spaghetti was always overcooked and with, yukk, ketchup. We wanted to do something in the middle.'

Italianness was traded on – Chianti bottles dangled from the ceiling, and 'Come Back to Sorrento' murmured from the muzack. Nothing like this had ever been seen in Italy, but the romance of all things Latin took off like an expresso train in Britain. The discreetly lit, smoky rooms with their red table-cloths and candles were perfect settings for illicit affairs. Handsome waiters wielded pepper pots suggestively and delivered single red roses with lecherous grins. Len Deighton captures the atmosphere perfectly in *The Ipcress File*.

> We ordered the *Zuppa di Lenticchie* and Jean told how this lentil soup reminded her of visits with her father to Sicily many years ago …
> 'Those days in the hot sun were as perfect as anything I remember,' Jean mused.
> We ate the Calamari and the chicken deep in which the butter and garlic had been artfully hidden to be struck like a vein of aromatic gold. Jean had pancakes and a thimble-full of black coffee without mentioning calories. Mario, deciding I was on the brink of a great and important seduction brought us a bottle of cold sparkling Asti 'on the house'.

Where did the Italian presence in London come from? A late 1950s episode of the popular cinema programme filler *Look at Life* celebrated the ubiquity of Italian style in 'The Roman Invasion', and reminded cinema audiences that there had been a sizeable Italian community in Britain since the end of the nineteenth century. It interviewed the Servini family, fourth-generation owners of delicatessens, and explained that Italians had first settled in Clerkenwell, with a church of their own for weddings Italian-style, and that Giuseppe Mazzini had lived in London for a time during his exile from Italy for his revolutionary activities. The Italian Club was an elegant and comfortable meeting place. Restaurants such as Quo Vadis in Soho were much older than the coffee bar craze. In the Roman Room, customers were served by legionaries and vestal virgins.

When Mussolini entered the war against Britain in 1940, it was the first time since Julius Caesar's invasion in 55 BC that Italians had been at war with the British. Internment either in Britain or in Commonwealth countries was thoroughgoing, and bad treatment of the internees created some bitterness after the war. But in camps like that at High Barnet, which was close to Italian communities who had long worked in the Bedford brickfields, prisoners of war received regular visits from resident British Italians who brought them salami, pasta, pizza and *prosciutto*. POWs working on the land often fell in love with local girls and elected to remain in Britain after hostilities ended. Others stayed because prospects seemed better in Britain than back in war-ravaged Italy. Once their four-year-long agricultural contracts were up, they were free to migrate to towns, and a history of skills in catering coupled with the boom in eating out led many of them to open first coffee bars and then trattorias.

By the mid-1960s, trattorias had become so successful that chains of restaurants developed. Otello Schipioni was one of the earliest and most successful of the Italian catering entrepreneurs. When he came to Britain in 1949, his first job was as a waiter at the Savoy Hotel. His Trattoria Toscana opened in Frith Street in 1954,

Above: Specialist shops provided for the needs of the Italian community in Bedford in the 1950s

Left: The popularity of informal and romantic Italian trattorias increased rapidly in the 1960s

decked with Italian flags, artificial vine leaves and Chianti bottles. 'I wanted to run a restaurant in which people would feel at home.' Disgusted by the cheap cutlery typical of the time, he bought a set of silver from Woolworths for £15 ('everyone thought I was mad, that it would be pinched by the customers'), and introduced his own-label wine in raffia bottles to tempt the novice British drinker.

Garlic and olive oil were introduced only gradually. 'The British knew them only as medicines, and hated the idea of them. But little by little …' Schipioni went from strength to strength, naming his third trattoria La Dolce Vita after the hugely successful Fellini film. A string of other trattorias followed. 'But I began to forget customer's names. I decided that if I couldn't give that personal touch, I should retire. So I did!'

The Fraquelli family carried the group concept much further. They too arrived from Italy just after the war, and opened a coffee shop called The Bamboo Bar under a railway bridge in Golders Green. The area was well-chosen – home to a cosmopolitan and adventurous community who were willing to experiment with food. Building on this success, Lorenzo Fraquelli and Simone Lavarine opened the first of the Spaghetti Houses, in Goodge Street in London's West End, in 1955. 'Spaghetti, but not on toast!' read the sign in the window. Customers were soon queueing outside for tables, just as they do at the Hard Rock Café in the 1990s. The aim was to provide popular Italian cuisine in an informal family atmosphere where a broad range of age-groups would feel at home. They served simple Italian food – spaghetti, minestrone and steaks, all freshly cooked on the premises. Alcohol could be bought at a neighbouring off-licence and drunk at the table.

Next came Zia Teresa in Knightsbridge and the first Pizza House, again in Goodge Street. This was the first time that genuine Italian-style pizza had been put on sale in Britain and its success was rapid. The Villa Carlotta became the flagship of the rapidly growing Spaghetti House group, and the headquarters of the operation is above its dining-rooms and banqueting rooms. Though Lorenzo Fraquelli has died, his son Stefano is now Managing Director of the group and a total of nine members of the two friends' large extended family are directly involved in management.

In the 1960s, Enzo Apicella provided Italy in Britain with a new concept of restaurant design. When he first came to Britain, he was struck by the dark, hidden feel of its Italian restaurants, 'as if people were ashamed to be seen eating and drinking'. Given the opportunity to redesign the famous Terrazza restaurant, he swept away the mural of Vesuvius, the fake vines and real grapes, and substituted white walls, ceramic tiles and spotlights. This was a place to be seen, not to escape into. The new pizzerias took up the theme, especially those of the very successful Pizza Express chain. Italian eating began to move on from second-rate spaghetti served in quasi-bordello conditions. The quality of the food began to matter as much, or even more, than ambience. It became 'authentic', distinctively flavoured with fresh basil and mozzarella flown in daily. That new insistence on authenticity was triggered above all by the one woman culinary revolution set in train by Elizabeth David.

■■■■■■■■■■

She completely opened up the insularity of British cooking. Food was just grey and awful and lifeless and across those awful grey mud flats, Elizabeth David burst like a sunrise, gilding pale Spam with heavenly alchemy. She made it all seem colourful and fun and part of civilization, not something that happened in a room down at the far end of a corridor and that nice people didn't talk about.

KATHARINE WHITEHORN

Auberon Waugh has said that Elizabeth David would get his vote as the single person responsible for most improving British life this century. And I think he is right.

JILL NORMAN, Cookery Editor

Britain's culinary love affair with America after the war had brought instant food of all kinds on to the high street and into the home. A second post-war romance took longer to mature, but was to prove just as enduring. While young people were showing their independence by sipping capuccinos, their mothers began to show theirs by inviting friends to eat in the kitchen, and in cooking new casual, peasant-style meals. They were likely to have been taken from the pages of one or other of the five epoch-making cookery books written by Elizabeth David between 1950 and 1960.

If interest in food now amounts to a kind of new religion, then David was its Messiah. The daughter of Rupert Gwynne, Conservative MP for Eastbourne, she was brought up by a nanny who cooked wild mushrooms on the nursery fire. Nothing prepared her for the horrors of school tapioca and boiled cod. She studied French history and literature in Paris where she lodged with an 'exceptionally greedy and well-fed family' for 18 months, an experience which educated her taste for all time. She also learnt German in Munich. She was travelling in Greece and Italy in the late 1930s when war broke out, and was evacuated first to Alexandria and then to Cairo, where she ran a reference library for the Ministry of Information. It was there that she met Anthony David, the Indian army officer whom she soon married. After the war she went out to India to join him, but returned to Britain in 1946 because she disliked the climate and the troubled end-of-Raj atmosphere.

Her first book, *A Book of Mediterranean Food*, began as an escape from the spartan conditions of post-war Britain. David began writing about food in the notoriously chilly winter of 1946/7 while staying in a hotel in Ross-on-Wye. It was an intense reaction to the abysmal quality of the food served there, 'produced with a kind of bleak triumph which amounted almost to a hatred of humanity and humanity's needs'. The descriptions and notes were not originally meant for publication. They were, she wrote in the introduction to the 1988 edition, just 'memories on paper',

... so that I would not forget about the bright vegetables, the basil, the lemons, the apricots, the rice with lamb and currants and pine nuts, the ripe green figs, the white ewe's milk cheeses of Greece, the thick aromatic Turkish coffee, the herb-scented kebabs, the honey and yoghurt for breakfast, the rose petal jam, the evening ices eaten on an Athenian café terrace in sight of the Parthenon.

Gradually her memories grew into book form, and a literary friend showed the manuscript to publishers. Despite the inauspicious time, John Lehmann had the imagination to publish it, in discreet brown cloth with line drawings by John Minton that sang of the tastes and scents of the South. In 1950, *Mediterranean Food* offered a vision of cooking in an entirely new way, a mouthwatering alternative to the pre-war years of being hostage to cook's good will and sullen suet dumplings.

David was unusual, but not unique, in calling for delicious food every day, cooked with love by the mistress of the house. But she gave to the enterprise a romance and poetry that it had never had before. In *Mediterranean Food* the scene for each chapter is set with a quotation or two from such books as Compton Mackenzie's *Athenian Memories*, Norman Douglas's *South Wind*, Lawrence Durrell's *Prospero's Cell*. It, and all the later books, are rich in reminiscences, recipes acquired in foreign kitchens, local folklore and scholarly comment on contrasting usages in Britain and Europe.

More books followed rapidly. *French Country Cooking* (1953) contained recipes that had not been suited to David's first book, and punctured the myth that all French cooking was necessarily rich and elaborate. *Italian Food* (1954) was the fruit of ten months spent in Italy in the early 1950s, and emphasized the enormous regional variety of Italian cooking. *Summer Cooking*, a delightful reminder of the seasonal nature of food, came out in 1955. But it was ten years or more before the prevailing domestic atmosphere of aspic and aspirations gave way to David's ideal, described in the introduction to *French Provincial Cooking*, of 'sober, well-balanced, middle-class French cookery, carried out with care and skill, with due regard to the quality of the materials, but without extravagance or pretension.'

For the majority of Britons, her books were fantasies and inspirations rather than guides to be taken literally. Their mouthwatering ingredients were unlikely to be obtainable outside Soho. A young Barnsley miner off work with a broken leg picked up one of the books in a public library in 1950. 'I did not even bother to look for olive oil, garlic, or aubergines – I knew they weren't in the shops. Instead I waited until the plaster was off my leg, and travelled to the places Elizabeth David wrote about. I have never been back to Barnsley since.'

There are few good British cooks today who do not admit to learning the grammar of their profession from David. One of the most influential and admired of post-war chefs, George Perry Smith, when he was proprietor of the Hole-in-the-Wall in Bath, declined to supply an editor with recipes because, he said, he had learnt almost everything he knew from Elizabeth David. What exactly had he learnt? 'Real cooking in a white-washed room.' Her distinctive treatment gave the simplest

of dishes new magic, as the cookery articles collected in *An Omelette and a Glass of Wine* show:

Above left: John Minton's illustration for the title page of *French Country Cooking*
Above: Elizabeth David in 1969

> As to the omelette itself, it seems to me to be a confection which demands the most straightforward approach. What one wants is the taste of the fresh eggs and the fresh butter and, visually, a soft bright golden roll plump and spilling out a little at the edges. It should not be a busy, important urban dish, but something gentle and pastoral, with the clean scent of the dairy, the kitchen garden, the basket of early morning mushrooms or the sharp tang of freshly picked herbs, sorrel, chives, tarragon. And although there are

those who maintain that wine and egg dishes don't go together, I must say I do regard a glass or two of wine as not, obviously, essential but at least an enormous enhancement of the enjoyment of a well-cooked omelette.

David was deeply in tune with her times in many ways. Wine was part of the 1960s' revolution in eating and drinking. Consumption rose sharply in the late 1950s and early 1960s, and has continued ever since. The pleasures of the grape are inseparable from David's concept of cooking. She quoted with approval a passage from Douglas's *South Wind* describing a good cook.

> If she drinks a little, why, that is all to the good. It shows that she is fully equipped on the other side of her dual nature. It proves that she possesses the prime requirement of the artist; sensitiveness and a capacity for enthusiasm. Indeed, I often doubt whether you will ever derive well-flavoured victuals from the atelier of an individual who honestly despises or fears – it is the same thing – the choicest gift of God.

She also inspired a quite new way of arranging and equipping the kitchen. Her initial ambition was to be a painter, and she clearly saw herself as an artist as much as a cook. 'The perfect kitchen would really be more like a painter's studio furnished with cooking equipment than anything conventionally accepted as a kitchen,' she wrote in Terence Conran's *The Kitchen Book* (1977). Her dream kitchen was 'very large, very light, very airy, calm and warm', a cool, practical background to the most important element in her profession: the beauty of the food itself.

> I recoil from coloured tiles and beflowered surfaces and I don't want a lot of things coloured avocado and tangerine. I'll just settle for the avocados and tangerines in a bowl on the dresser …Too much equipment is if anything worse than too little. I don't care for the exotic gear dangling from hooks, the riot of clanking ironmongery, the armouries of knives, or the serried ranks of sauté pans and all other carefully chosen symbols of culinary activity I see in so many photographs of chic kitchens. Pseuds' corners, I'm afraid, many of them.

David's writing inspired a fashion for concealing machines in the kitchen, refitting deep 'Belfast' sinks and buying heavy French casseroles and English slipware that could go straight from oven to table. 'Look at the friendly browns and warm terracottas, the ivories and greys and the pebbles-on-the-beach colours of old English earthenware and stoneware,' she wrote in *House and Garden* in 1958. 'You see that utterly plain long white fish dish? On that dish a whole pink and silver salmon trout is unimaginably elegant and lovely.'

Kitchens became places for guests as well as the family, rather than the wife's lonely domain. Jill Norman, her editor for many years, and a close friend, says that 'Elizabeth felt most comfortable in the kitchen. In fact, she hardly used the living-

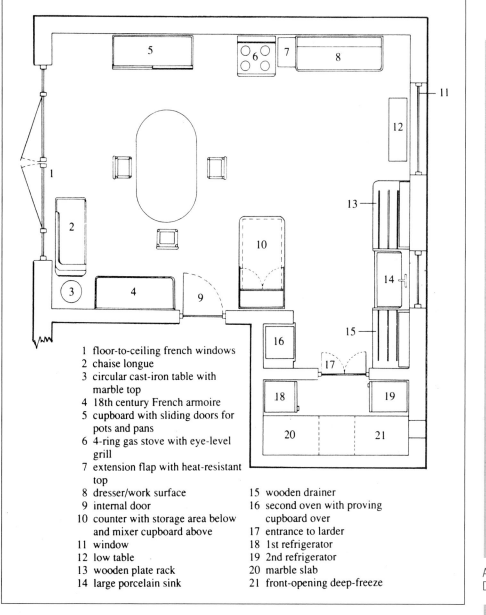

1 floor-to-ceiling french windows
2 chaise longue
3 circular cast-iron table with
  marble top
4 18th century French armoire
5 cupboard with sliding doors for
  pots and pans
6 4-ring gas stove with eye-level
  grill
7 extension flap with heat-resistant
  top
8 dresser/work surface
9 internal door
10 counter with storage area below
   and mixer cupboard above
11 window
12 low table
13 wooden plate rack
14 large porcelain sink
15 wooden drainer
16 second oven with proving
   cupboard over
17 entrance to larder
18 1st refrigerator
19 2nd refrigerator
20 marble slab
21 front-opening deep-freeze

A plan showing Elizabeth
David's dream kitchen

room. And it was her writing that turned the English kitchen from a secret place away from the prying eyes of guests into the primary place where you socialize. Cooking was no longer a chore, but a pleasure, and things were done in a more creative spirit.'

For all her scholarly rigour, David's approach was never doctrinaire, always intuitive and inventive. Jill Norman recalls how they 'would take turns to cook. And it was always done in the spirit of experimentation. This whole notion that everything has to be perfect crept back through the back door in the late seventies and early eighties. But as far as Elizabeth was concerned, you cooked with care and spirit, but you were allowed to make mistakes.'

Her relationship with the women's liberation movement was complex and is still far from being over. 'I think her influence on the way women organized their lives was very profound,' says Jill Norman.

> She made people realize that they could combine cooking, something that had been considered a household chore, with a very easy and pleasant life-style . . . When the feminists came along, they were more rigid, and tended to think of domestic issues as of less importance than women being free to express themselves outside a domestic environment. Chores were relegated to a lower level. But for Elizabeth, there was nothing of a chore about cooking, and I think this is what many women have learned from her: that you may not want to clean your house every day, but that there is a great satisfaction to be had from cooking and eating well, and this was just part of civilized behaviour and civilized life.

In the 1960s, the best kitchen supply shop in Soho, Madame Cadec's, closed down, and David decided to branch out from writing about cooking to providing the right utensils. What was also needed, however, was a source for all those mouth-watering Mediterranean ingredients. Elizabeth David could never have achieved her present popularity without the revolution in food processing and retailing that has now made garlic as easily available in Stranraer as in Soho. But the first stage in turning her Provençal fantasies into everyday British realities was the wave of delicatessens which initially sprang up to service the new trattorias.

DELICATESSENS

> *Olive oil was something we bought in little bottles in Boots the Chemists; lemons were only for gin and tonics or Christmas puddings. And if you saw a red pepper for sale, it was something you treated with enormous reverence, a few little bits in your spag. bol. perhaps ... My father regarded mushrooms as exotic.*
>
> LINDSAY BAREHAM, Food Writer

Interest in European foods led to a demand for the essential basics, olive oil, garlic, spices to suit. In the 1950s, supplies were so short that pizza pioneer Peter Pizet could envisage gaining a monopoly in imported mozzarella for his new pizza restaurants, and finally solved the problem of supplies by opening his own delicatessen, King Bomba, in the King's Road. It rapidly became a fashionable haunt of Sloane Rangers, and a place of pilgrimage from Reigate to St Albans. Although delicatessens were few and far between, they were not only to be found in Soho. The

.. every available piece of land must be cultivated

GROW YOUR OWN FOOD

supply your own cookhouse

Food rationing continued for several years after the end of the war. After nearly seven years of very few treats, sweets finally became more widely available in 1949. In the health conscious 1990s, we look back regretfully to the days when children had no opportunity to over-indulge in sugary foods. People were certainly fitter when sweet and fattening items were not so readily available

Facing page: Sliced, packaged bread was one of the first convenience foods of the 1950s. But there was a great deal more than 'goodness' in each slice. Additives ensured its whiteness and softness

You can't keep him away when there's Sunblest on the table

YOU CAN see by the way he's tucking in that he enjoys a good slice of bread. And it really is good when it's Sunblest bread. Made entirely from the finest ingredients and baked to perfection, Sunblest bread is full of goodness for all the family.

Look out, too, for the Sunblest speciality breads, BROWNIE, FRUITIE and MILKIE — each has its own delicious character and flavour and the American Top Grade loaf has extra rich ingredients. All bear the famous Sunblest symbol—*your* guarantee of top quality.

Sunblest bread is good bread
FRESH TO THE LAST SLICE

ISSUED BY THE QUALITY BAKERS OF BRITAIN

Taking the drudgery out of housework. The new kitchens of the post-war years were brighter and more colourful. Floors were covered in easy-to-clean linoleum or lino-tiles, and work tops clad in the exciting new material Formica. Everything was 'scientifically' thought out to save time and effort, and to accommodate such new appliances as electric cookers, refrigerators and food mixers

The plans on these pages for 'the house women have chosen' appeared in the *Daily Mail Book of Britain's Post-War Homes* published in 1944

VIEW OF LIVING ROOM WITH FOLDING DOORS OPEN TO KITCHEN

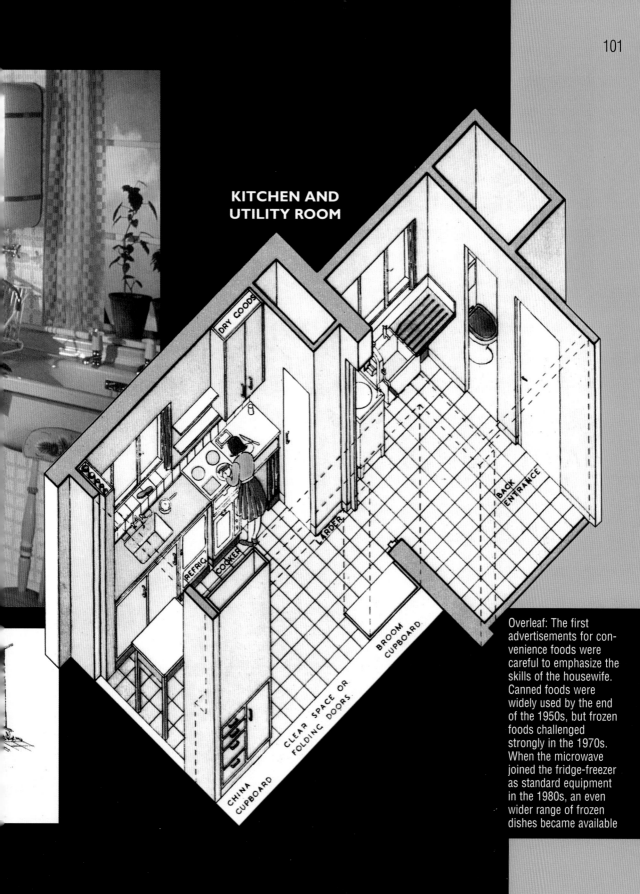

**KITCHEN AND
UTILITY ROOM**

Overleaf: The first
advertisements for con-
venience foods were
careful to emphasize the
skills of the housewife.
Canned foods were
widely used by the end
of the 1950s, but frozen
foods challenged
strongly in the 1970s.
When the microwave
joined the fridge-freezer
as standard equipment
in the 1980s, an even
wider range of frozen
dishes became available

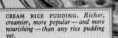

Look! It's the sign of the times

FOR
WONDERFUL EATING,
WONDERFUL VALUE,
AND FULL-FLAVOUR
FRESHNESS . . .

stop at your Birds Eye Shop

SUCH A VARIETY OF VEGETABLES!

Green Peas. Sliced Green Beans. Broad Beans. Green Broccoli. Brussels Sprouts. Sweet Corn. Mixed Vegetables. Peas & Carrots. Spinach. Corn on the Cob. *There's* variety for you! And all so fresh and tender . . . such a delicious change at this time of the year!

YOU'LL ENJOY THE FRESHNESS

Your family gets the *full* flavour—the *full* food value from Birds Eye. Because *all* Birds Eye foods are selected at the peak of perfection, then quick-frozen while they're still morning-fresh.

SHOP AND COOK THE MODERN WAY

Quicker shopping—you'll buy all you want from your Birds Eye Shop, from the frozen-food cabinet—a treasure chest of wonderful eating and wonderful value! All sorts of vegetables. A variety of fish fillets. Poultry. Pies. Fish Fingers. And lots of other good things. All quick-frozen so that you enjoy their natural fresh flavour and every bit of goodness. You'll get on with your cooking quicker, too. For everything is prepared ready for you to cook.

For wonderful eating
Stop at your Birds Eye Shop

Live better—on a budget! Just reach into that cabinet and take home all the flavour, the goodness of really *fresh* food. Real value, too. Never a scrap of waste.

BIRDS EYE FOODS LIMITED, HESKETH HOUSE, PORTMAN SQUARE, LONDON, W.1   BYG 423-9671

'Bonjour. Could you tell us the way to make rilettes de canard aux paysannes?'

Holidays abroad were the start of many people's interest in the cuisine of other countries. The popularity of Italian food was reflected in the appearance of romantic 'trattorias' beside the Chinese and Indian restaurants on the high street

Previous pages: Indian restaurants sprang up rapidly in Britain in the 1960s, first serving the many immigrants from the subcontinent, but soon adapting to attract white customers. Today they vary from the simplest of take-aways selling not only curry but deep-fried fish and chips to the spledidly baroque *Star of India* owned by Azam and Reza Muhammed

Anxieties over diet escalated in the 1970s. Vegetarians, once scoffed at, were treated with new repect. In London's Covent Garden, Neal's Yard became a mecca for macrobiotic and whole-food enthusiasts. David Cantor's Cranks restaurant founded in 1961 used organically grown fruit and vegetables and served them on earthenware crockery, setting the style for the next three decades of vegetarianism

'An excellent meal.
My compliments to
the gardener.'

Food on the move. In the 1990s half of the nation's meals are consumed outside the home and eating is now a round-the-clock event. The comfortingly familiar identikit surroundings of fast food chains like McDonalds, Burger King and Kentucky Fried Chicken are not only places to eat but places to socialize

Overleaf: Food of the future – the incongruous sight of ostriches on a farm in Devon. This experiment is just one of many efforts to cater for the demand for lean 'wild' meat, reared in natural conditions, and thought to be healthier and tastier than battery hens, factory-farmed pigs and additive-filled cattle

Valvona and Crolla in Edinburgh had existed since the 1880s, but before the war had catered mainly for the local Italians. When war was declared Victor Crolla, son of the shop's founder and a pillar of the Edinburgh establishment, was interned as an enemy alien and spent the duration in a prison camp on the Isle of Man.

When he returned to Edinburgh after the war, he rebuilt the business from scratch, and found himself catering to a different clientele. The Scots Guards had spent most of the war in Italy and many had been sheltered by members of the Italian Resistance, living in the mountains with Italian families. They had developed a taste for proper pasta and, back in Scotland, Crolla's was the best place to find it. Crolla's encouraged the new trade by letting people try the strange products, having spaghetti tastings and patiently answering questions like, 'Is it true that tagliatelle grows on trees?' In 1957, on 1 April, an entire episode of the television programme *Panorama* was devoted to the failure of the spaghetti harvest in Ticino, Italy. It was taken seriously by a remarkable number of people.

The late 1950s and 1960s saw delicatessens opening in every town that had any middle-class pretensions or an immigrant community. Crolla's had a van that went around Scotland making small deliveries, and set up mini-delis in many Highland towns. They distributed pasta, Parmesan and olive oil – and vegetables like aubergines, courgettes and peppers. Once wholesalers perceived the new interest, such exotics began to creep into greengrocers but they were still expensive luxuries.

In 1962, Deighton's *Action Cookbook* featured several pages on the gourmet items available from the 10 000 or more delicatessens which had by then opened up in Britain. Avoid British-made noodles, he warned. He also recommended shoppng in health food shops and chemists – good cooking still had all the thrill of the chase. The successive editions of Elizabeth David's books, carefully annotated and footnoted by their scrupulous creator, give an almost shop-by-shop account of the spread of Mediterranean ingredients across Britain. By 1965, she could write proudly in a new introduction to the boxed set of all five paperbacks issued by Penguin that, 'the English are now more creative and inquiring about cooking than they ever have been.'

'Ronald and I have discovered this marvellous little bistro just around the corner. We often mis-pronounce everything and they never seem to mind.'

But although delicatessens have gone from strength to strength in the last 30 years, it is the transformation of our shopping patterns, from high street to super-market, from fresh food to frozen, that has allowed an upper middle-class taste for foreign food to turn into a national commonplace.

TROLLEY SOCIETY

Almost without our realising what has happened, technology has come to influence the basic philosophy by which our behaviour is moulded.

MAGNUS PYKE, *Technological Eating* 1972

You could go down to the shop and buy your food fresh every day and within walking distance. Now we've got to go to Croydon one way or Streatham the other and it's all the same thing when you get there.

SANDY HUNT

I went into a pieshop and bought a picnic dinner. 'Two and ten for the lady', called the pieman over my head. I took my two and ten to the cash desk. A jolly round-faced cashier smiled at me and called me dearie. I shall come here for our rations, I thought.

VERILY ANDERSON, *Spam Tomorrow* 1956

Little did Verity Anderson imagine what was really in store for her in the New Jerusalem of food plenty after the war. A revolution in retailing methods was beginning which not only enormously extended the range of what the British would be eating over the next 50 years, but also governed its character. And it dramatically altered the way that people related to each other in everyday life. The woman in the queue, so vociferous and influential in the first chapter in our story, gradually lost her political muscle and turned into a Stepford wife, hypnotized by the hype of the hypermarkets.

As home cooking and baking declined, shopping habits changed: there was a tendency to shop more frequently and in smaller quantities, and to buy foodstuffs requiring little preparation. But the typical shop in the 1950s was still small and specialized. A 'wants' list meant dropping in first to the dairy, then the baker, then the butcher and the grocer. Shopping involved encounters with a variety of different people, and discussion of the quality of the items purchased. It was an essentially personal experience. As Judith Hubback recalls:

Before the days of self-service shops, shopping actually was quite interest-ing in many ways. There was a girl, usually a girl, behind the counter, and together you would assemble all the things that you needed. It was really quite interesting choosing the joint carefully. We'd been very restricted in the war as to how much meat we could cook, and so we actually enjoyed the variety of foods, mainly fresh foods, that were available. And then there were what I would now call proper greengrocers, where it was quite different from buying in the supermarkets. And there was really good fish. We ate quite a lot of fresh fish off the slab at MacFisheries. I remember being really sad when MacFisheries came to an end.

Chains of grocery shops could take advantage of the economies of scale made possible by new techniques of food processing. Many of the most successful modern supermarkets have very early beginnings. The Maypole Dairy Company, founded in Wolverhampton in 1898, had 500 branches when it was taken over by Home and Colonial, by then an equally large chain, in 1924. John Sainsbury opened his first shop in Drury Lane in 1869. But the most successful of the early chains was Lipton's.

Thomas Lipton was to food shops what Henry Ford was to motor cars. The son of a small Glasgow shopkeeper, he opened his first shop in Glasgow in 1871 at the age of 21 with a capital of only £100, saved while travelling and working around America. The basis of his success was bulk import of a few uniform commodities of good quality which were sold at lower prices, and a talent for vigorous American-style advertising. He began by importing ham, bacon, eggs, butter and cheese from Ireland, then extended his range of proprietary brands to the still famous Lipton's tea and a patent fat known as 'butterine'. Next he substituted a central manufacturing plant to replace the independent bakeries that produced his bread, cakes and biscuits. Jam factories followed. By 1898, when the firm went public, it owned over 400 shops, 70 of them in London, and employed over 10 000 people.

But at the end of the 1920s, only 20 per cent of Britain's 80 000 grocer's shops were part of a chain. Small retailers could still compete effectively by offering customers credit and delivery services, both of which were increasingly highly rated, especially by the hard-pressed middle-class housewife, short on domestic staff and extra cash, who was quite likely to be thinking of going out to work herself.

Jack Cohen, the co-founder of Tesco, was one of the first shop-owners in Britain to imitate the United States' example of the 1930s and launch self-service stores at the end of the 1940s. The use of self-service in works canteens and British restaurants had opened customers' minds to its convenience, and wartime shortages had created a horror of queueing. There was a slowish start, but 20 new Tesco shops opened in 1950 and business continued to grow. The Co-operative Society and other retailers were doing the same, and by 1956 there were over 3000 self-service stores in Britain. The new, larger versions of such shops were christened 'supermarkets' and by 1962 some 12 000 self-service and supermarkets were trading. Five years later, there were 24 000, aided and abetted by the ending of Resale Price Maintenance on food. It was Ted 'Grocer' Heath who pushed for its abolition in the run-up to the 1964 election.

Not everyone was pleased with the idea of 'self-service'. Some disliked the idea of prying eyes seeing the kind of food one was buying; many missed the old friendly, not to say unctuous, attentiveness of shop staff. In the Croydon branch of Sainsbury's, the first of the chain to go 'Q-less' in 1959, a woman threw a basket at the manager's head in protest at the new barbarism. But the petty tyrannies of shop-keepers in the days of rationing still festered in the minds of many customers, and most people welcomed both the lower prices and the opportunity to browse and ponder without the urgency of a queue behind them.

As the range of prepared products extended into infinity up and down the aisles, packets became more assertive and seductive, as well as (in appearance at least) more informative. Trolleys were introduced so that shoppers could be tempted to buy more than they could carry. First child-seats and then cradles were fitted into them – the latter a response to a spate of baby snatching in 1973 from prams left outside supermarkets. Shopping was becoming addictive and took up more and more of the day. But its nature had fundamentally changed. It had become an essentially solitary activity, feeding dreams but never allowing them to be satisfied.

Changes in the opening times of the new stores also affected household management. Shopping could be less of a routine and more of an impulse. Not many people realize that this development was in fact a wheel turning full circle. Before the war there had been few restrictions on shop opening times. At the turn of the century, Sainsbury's first out-of-town store in Croydon was open on Sundays. 'It was not uncommon for a husband to make a stop at the grocer's store on a Sunday

Facing page: The 'corner' shop: personal attention from staff and the opportunity for a chat with friends

Below: Sainsbury's first self-service shop in Croydon, 1959

afternoon while returning home from the pub,' reports the company's historian. Staff had to be at work at 7.30 a.m. every day except Sunday. On Tuesday, Wednesday and Thursday, trading ended at 9.15 p.m., on Friday at 10.45 p.m. and on Saturday at midnight.

A series of legislative measures intended to protect shop assistants from exploitation changed this radically after the end of the Second World War. The Shops Act of 1950 consolidated all previous provisions and gave local authorities the power to enforce specific closing times. All shops had to close for a half-day and employees had to have a half-day's holiday. Late shopping until 9 p.m. was permitted on Saturday, though an alternative day could be agreed, and trading on Sunday was heavily restricted. This Act prevented a return to pre-war conditions of retailing.

By the 1960s, conditions had changed again with the end of rationing and the innovation of self-service. Pay-day was now not necessarily Saturday and there was therefore less demand for late-night Saturday shopping. Instead of responding to their customers, the new shops now dictated both when and how people could buy food. Sainsbury pioneered a five-day trading week among food retailers. Supermarkets closed all day on Monday (giving them time to refill the shelves after the busy buying on Friday and Saturday), stayed open wherever possible on local early closing afternoons (an effective way of weaning customers away from their local shops) and extended shopping hours until 6.30 p.m. on Friday.

By the 1980s, the growing number of women at work meant that customers needed greater flexibility in shopping hours. The chains began to open first for half a day, and then a full day on Monday, and to stay open in the evening on Saturday. Co-ops introduced their daily 12-hour 'eight till late' policy in 1990. Finally, to much outcry from the 'Keep Sunday Special' brigade, many chains have returned to opening on Sunday. There are now all-night stores in every large town, and the range of food available at ever-open garage shops is extending rapidly.

Supermarket shopping has led to the disappearance of the most ancient and important of community forums (the word *forum* itself is, of course, Latin for marketplace). Expressions like 'the man in the street' are becoming meaningless. Neither men nor women spend time in the street any more: they drive in cars to an impersonal hypermarket. Shopping, reported as the activity most enjoyed by house-wives in Ann Oakley's 1974 survey *Housewife!* because of the opportunity it provided for meeting people and finding stimulation outside the home, turned into just another chore to be hurried through.

Supermarkets also contributed to the disappearance of the delivery men who were a useful disincentive to casual burglaries when they informally policed our streets, first in carts, later in vans. A natural Neighbourhood Watch, they tended to know who should be where, and when. Now there are only window cleaners (the most notorious blackmarket industry in Britain) and those mysterious fish vans, all optimism and calamares one week, sold to another naive franchiser the next. We are all less inclined to answer the doorbell. Milkmen, too, are under threat from the 2 litre plastic bottles that massively undercut the cost of the doorstep pint.

The social impact of supermarkets is not limited to their customers. The historian of technology Magnus Pyke points out that supermarkets are 'a nice example of the way that food technology dismembers the body social'. The shop assistant's life as an employee of a large organization like Sainsbury's is qualitatively different from that of the counterhand in a local butcher. Most supermarket staff do not talk to customers at all; they stay behind the scenes packaging and unloading. Even those on checkouts relate directly to customers only for the few seconds it takes to announce the cost of a trolley of goods and deliver the receipt. Time-and-motion study experts stand behind them, calculating how to make checkouts ever faster.

In such circumstances, our social behaviour is altered by anonymity. Pressures to conform are lessened: no one can see the *Guardian* reader economizing by buying a battery chicken. Pilferage increases as establishments become larger. Magnus Pyke points out that in small shops, 'one finds the most significant safeguard against theft: a proper human web of personal relationship'.

One must not exaggerate. Nothing could be more sociable than the small VG grocery store in Hurworth-on-Tees, the village where I happen to be writing this chapter. But, as my neighbour said to me as she fought her way through a throng of acquaintances to the post office counter, 'That's village life for you.' And time of life, she could have added. Seven out of eight of the customers were pensioners.

CONVENIENCE FOODS

The adjective, with its lavatorial connotation, is well-chosen.
RAYMOND POSTGATE, *Good Food Guide* 1969

People were quite secretive about using convenience foods, as it showed a lack of devotion. They would have been horrified if you went and used a sponge mix when they were expecting a cookery demonstration.
NORA RIDDINGTON

For making quick meals, with that extra dash of personality, there is nothing to better canned foods.
Libby's Art of Canned Food Cookery 1969

The food industry has taken on to itself the role of kitchen genie. It has flooded the market with ready-cooked meals of such variety as to dishearten even the most inventive housewife. True, the pastry of those plastic wrapped supermarket pies, life-sized versions of doll's house food, is never burnt; the stews never stick to the bottoms of their polystyrene containers; the powdered soups, poured from their vacuum packs, offer no surprises. It's precisely this mediocrity of sameness, this lack of any surprise in texture or taste, which gradually makes the consumer feel that feeding is nothing but a physiological necessity, something to be got over as quickly as possible.
BENOITE GROULT, *Loaves and Wishes* 1992

Just as important as when and how we shop is what we buy. The 1960s saw the start of a paradox – a dual tradition of authenticity and cutting corners – that has continued ever since: the thorough historical and geographical homework of Elizabeth David contrasted with Len Deighton's bachelor quickies. In March 1979, *Woman's Own* offered 'a cheat's charter for quicker, posher, nosh'. 'Classic fish and shrimp mousse is delicious, but the recipe is a trifle long-winded. However, if you take a pack of frozen cod in shrimp sauce and liquidise it you're half-way there!' Other triumphs were mock *zabaglione* from instant custard mix and beef in red wine pie from tinned red wine sauce.

Cheating started a long time ago. Bird's Custard, the first and most famous ready-mixed kitchen staple, was not in origin a convenience food. It was invented in the 1840s by Alfred Bird, a Birmingham chemist whose wife had an allergy to eggs. Its great advantage was that there was no risk of it turning into scrambled eggs while cooking. Soon demand outran supply to such an extent that Bird devoted the rest of his life to making custard for the nation.

During the inter-war years there was a steady shift towards ready-to-eat manu-factured foods as bulk food producers responded to the challenge of adequately feeding crowded urban populations. Canned foods saved time, effort and money. They also improved the quality of the diet of the majority of the population. Canning was invented in 1804 by a Frenchman, Nicholas Appert, who was duly rewarded by Napoleon, always alive to the importance of food to his armies. However, it was only introduced to Britain on a large scale after the First World War. Between 1920 and 1938, the consumption of canned vegetables (primarily peas) rose from just over 400 g (1lb) a head to 4.4 kg (9.75 lb) per head, that of canned fruits from 1.1 kg (2.5 lb) to 4.4 kg (9.75 lb) and that of fish from 900 g (2 lb) to 1.8 kg (4 lb). In the United States, the industry was established much earlier. 'The modern housewife is no longer a cook – she is a can-opener,' declared Christine Frederick *(Selling Mrs Consumer,* 1929). Although home canning plants, notably Smedleys, Chivers and Hartleys, grew rapidly, Britain imported five-sevenths of the tinned food she consumed. Only peas were domestically produced.

More and more proprietary brands – Kellogg's, Quaker Oats, Horlicks, Ovaltine, John West salmon, Heinz 57 varieties – became household names, heavily promoted by advertisements in newspapers and on street corners. In the columns of a 1949 issue of *Good Housekeeping,* Lin-Can and Batchelor's tinned peas competed for the housewife's favours with that old faithful, the kilner jar. At that time advertisements played down the fact that products like these were likely to appeal to working women and sold them instead in terms of usefulness on such occasions as hubbie telephoning 10 minutes before dinnertime with the news that he was bringing the boss home. Any time that was saved was envisaged as being spent on family and home rather than going out to work.

The domestic frozen food revolution began in 1923 when Clarence Birdseye established his first freezing plant in the United States but the technique was treated with suspicion in Britain until Unilever bought out Birdseye in Britain and put its muscle into establishing a market. Peas and herrings were the first leading lines, but

"So this is love!"

"OF COURSE, George loves me. But sometimes it's very hard to believe. For instance, when he 'phones from the office that he's bringing business friends home to dinner. What to do? I rely on Batchelors canned foods to make the meal a real success and big enough for all. First, Batchelors soup, so rich and satisfying! Delicious Batchelors peas with the meat! Often, too—luscious Batchelors fruit for the sweet course. Our guests are delighted!"

Food News from Batchelors Bee
With so little meat for meals, serve delicious Batchelors Peas as *often* as you can—they are rich in body-building protein!

B for Batchelors

Batchelors
WONDERFUL Foods

English Canned
SOUPS · VEGETABLES · FRUITS

BP 17/818

Sweet and Lovely

It doesn't seem ten years since Diana was married. She's as young and lovely as ever. And clever . . . she saves *so* much time and trouble in the kitchen with LIN-CAN Fruits and Vegetables. Diana says they're good for health too—keep you fit and fresh! And as LIN-CAN Fruits are steeped in sweet syrup, they save the sugar rations as well.

Garden Fresh

LIN-CAN
FRUITS & VEGETABLES

LINCOLNSHIRE CANNERS LTD.
BOSTON, LINCS., and WEST LYNN, KING'S LYNN, NORFOLK

products increased steadily in variety and quality. Sales doubled between 1955 and 1957 and Lyons entered the fray with Froods. By 1961, cheap and (reasonably) palatable frozen food was easily available. There were over 60 Birdseye products alone, including the famous fish finger, first presented on television by the trusty Marguerite Patten.

In the 1950s canned food was sold as a way in which women could stay glamorous despite the domestic demands upon them

Frozen beefburgers, frozen peas and the famous fish fingers were Birdseye's most popular early frozen products

We have come a long way since then. The unholy alliance of the home freezer and the microwave has encouraged an astonishing range of frozen products, from cream and croissants to full-scale party banquets. Caterers have used them to transform the nature of pub food. Vans from Alveston Kitchens deliver identical frozen gourmet dishes all over the country. You can now eat the other half of the chicken you enjoyed *à la Kiev* in Norwich converted into curry in Tooting Bec.

Critics deplore the second-rate sameness of the universal Black Forest gâteaux, but is the success of catering for the masses due to manipulation or a keen awareness of what is most popular? Lord Forte declared that his catering empire 'gives people the food that they like', and that his turnover proves it. From the start of mass catering, the trend was undoubtedly towards increased opportunities for more varied eating experiences and the development of more discriminating tastes. Cooking could change from a daily struggle to make cheap ingredients stretch and look appetizing into a creative and satisfying leisure pursuit, enjoyed by men as well as women. Using convenience foods to make daily economies in time and money made people more prepared to be adventurous on occasion, to experiment with foreign recipes and with new foods.

But such products undoubtedly contributed to the growing sense of dissatisfaction that marred the post-war dreams of domestically fulfilled womanliness. 'The deep freeze appears to have gained over the minds of the English housewife and restaurant keeper a hypnotic power such as never was exercised by the canning factories,' wrote Elizabeth David in *Summer Cooking*. 'Even leaving out of consideration the fact that the pleasure of rediscovering each season's fruit and vegetables at the appropriate time is thereby quite blunted, this method of marketing seems to me to be an extravagant one.'

Writing in such terms was fine if your profession happened to be that of a cook. But for the people who had different occupations, convenience foods were the only things that gave them time to live a life of their own. Particularly women with dependent families. Britain in the 1960s needed American ingenuity with fast food and convenience eating just as much as it required the concept of fine ingredients and well-cooked food offered by Elizabeth David. In 1966, Katharine Whitehorn spelt out a culinary compromise still typical of modern eating.

The admirable Marguerite
Patten demonstrates
microwave cooking.
The advent of the
microwave encouraged
an even greater range of
packaged frozen foods

I think the food here tends to be on two levels. There's proper food, which I suppose is more French than anything else, which is what I basically love to do if I've got time … When I do it, it's good. The stock leads to the soup, and so on. It's all a cycle, the materials are good and fresh and it's fine. And then one tends to go with a terrific bump down to 'short order' stuff. The important thing is to keep in one's own mind the distinction, when it's a hamburger night and when it's a proper food night.

But the revolution effected by the new food technology went considerably deeper than the mere matter of meals tasting good. As foodstuffs moved further and further from their natural sources, the gulf which separated the average citizen from the actual sources of production was emphasized. Shrewd shopping around was substituted for the careful management of a seasonably varied larder. All this served to underline the importance of money, rather than the traditional domestic virtues of thrift, energy and skill. The effect was to increase the status of the family bread-winner, and to make it appear that a sexy wife was a more desirable social companion than an experienced housekeeper. It is noticeable that women's markedly increased preoccupation with their appearance, fuelled by the blandishments of booming fashion and cosmetic industries, ran in exact parallel to the rise of convenience foods. Until they began to earn money of their own to redress the distorted balance of domestic power, they were unhealthily dependent on their husbands. Many advertisements spelt this out quite precisely by showing wives posed behind the instant meal in suggestive *decolleté*.

CHAPTER FOUR

From Curry to Coriander

Food not only reinforces ethnic ties; it is also the most rewarding and easiest bridge across ethnic lines. It is a form of 'internal tourism, … What more accessible and friendly arena of inter-ethnic contact could be devised than the ethnic restaurant?

PIERRE VAN DEN BERGHE, 'Ethnic cuisine, culture in nature', *Ethnic and Racial Studies* 1987

'You can't hurry cooking', my mother-in-law used to say as she let the dal simmer for hours in a stony jar on a tiny fire, the spices permeating the liquid while it simmered, finally becoming a harmony of tastes and smells, 'You have to put your heart into it'.

SHASHI DESHPANDE, 'Of Kitchens and Goddesses', *Loaves and Wishes* 1992

Take a walk downtown. Names like Opium Den, Mongolian Wok House, and Jamal's Tandoori punctuate the newsagents, property dealers, boutiques and off licences. Fifty years ago you would have only had a choice between Betty's Teas (Light Lunches 12.00–2.00) and Atlantic Spray Fish 'n' Chips. This rash of exotic restaurants is more than convenient high street furniture: the way we eat ethnic is an accurate map not only of the nature of the new immigrant groups that have established themselves in Britain, but an indication of the manner in which they live here. A single Hong Kong take-away in John o' Groats, thirty Indian restaurants in a hundred yards of Oxford Road, Manchester: the changing fascias of our high street eateries carry a wealth of social significance.

They mirror the story of how Britain has coped with the fact that since 1900 one in ten of her citizens has emigrated, and that since 1946 almost as many new citizens have arrived. It is often expressed as a depressing tale of man's inhumanity to man, of incomprehension and intolerance. But in the context of food, it is a triumph of ingenuity, creativity and perseverance. And it is clear from the strengthening individual identity of Asian restaurants that the answer to coping in a multicultural society is celebration of difference rather than obsessive integration; informed respect rather than grudging tolerance.

Cultural assimilation and immigration are nothing new in the history of our mongrel race. Since Julius Caesar arrived in AD 55, the British Isles have absorbed successive waves of more or less aggressive and more or less numerous immigrants from Italy, Scandinavia, Denmark and Saxony, Normandy, Flanders and Ireland. Elizabeth I commented on 'the great numbers of black people on the streets of London'. 'There is hardly such a thing as a pure Englishman in this island,' declared *The Times* in 1867. 'In place of the rather vulgarised and very inaccurate phrase Anglo-Saxon, our national denomination, to be strictly correct, would be a composition of a dozen national titles.'

In the twentieth century we have also done our share of emigrating – in the last 100 years more people have quitted Britain than have taken up residence. But after the end of the war in 1945, political events in China and India combined with our own post-war economy's thirst for labour to bring over hundreds of thousands of non-white Commonwealth citizens who, with their descendants, now constitute 1 in 20 of the population. Just as many white immigrants from Ireland, Poland, Italy, the Ukraine and the Mediterranean have moved to Britain this century. The changing use of a 250-year-old building on the corner of Fournier Street and Brick Lane in London's East End neatly reflects the successive waves of newcomers. Since it was built in 1744, it has been a Huguenot church, a Wesleyan chapel and a Jewish synagogue. Today it is the Jamme Masjid Mosque.

Food as a way of life has been adopted in different ways by immigrants as diverse in origin, education and intention as one could imagine. Some, like Kenneth Lo, a diplomat's son turned by political circumstances in China into a renowned British food writer, are the highly sophisticated inheritors of a long-established upper-class Asian tradition of coming to England for an education, either at school (remember 'the cheerfulness is terrific' of Hurree Jamset Ram Singh in Frank Richards' *Billy Bunter* stories), or at university. Two generations of the Nawabs of Patandi came to Oxford, as did the brilliant Cornelia Sorabji from Bombay.

Lo's food-conscious autobiography *The Feast of My Life* (1993) is a short cut to understanding the attitudes of the sort of immigrant who has a profound respect for the British educational tradition, but no sense at all of being a grateful mendicant on an alien shore. He was part of the wave of wealthy and well connected post-war visitors who joined an established 'high society' of South Asian academics, retired civil servants, merchants and traders who had settled in London in the nineteenth century.

Given the central importance of food in the cultures of both China and India, and the impoverished blandness of post-war British cookery, it is not surprising that restaurants sprung up for the benefit of these Asian expatriates. They not only provided the right sort of food; they were social centres, places to meet friends, make plans and pool information.

The novelist Attia Hosain records in an essay, 'Of Memories and Meals', that when she moved to London in 1947 she missed India most of all at mealtimes (particularly after a BBC canteen lunch of powdered eggs and wilted lettuce leaves). At home, 'food and companionship went naturally together. Never in India had I found myself alone at any meal. It would have been unthinkable not to share food with friends and relatives.' She was thankful for the Shafi, a restaurant set up in the 1920s by two North Indian brothers and a popular rendezvous for Indian visitors, students and expatriates. 'It was like being back home. The owner was host, friend and confidant to all who came, whether to eat, or just to relax and talk.'

First opened in the 1920s, London's Shafi restaurant, was a haven for Indian visitors to Britain

But the majority of immigrants were very different from this wealthy and privileged élite. Poor economic conditions at home were the main stimulus that made the enterprising leave to seek their fortunes – a well-established tradition in many regions of India and Pakistan. Britain was a natural choice, 'the mother country' of imperial legend. 'Our generation was born under the Union Jack,' writes Yousuf Choudhury in *The Roots and Tales of the Bangladeshi Settlers* (1993). 'The memories of having been ruled were still fresh on both sides.' A reputation as a politically liberal and highly cultured nation, blessed by a generous welfare state, contributed to her attraction.

Moreover, Britain was crying out for workers. Women had left their wartime work posts to have babies, and migration to Australia, Canada and South Africa had never been higher. The post-war export drive desperately needed the willing hands who came over in such numbers from the West Indies, Pakistan, Bengal and India. British firms also advertised in Indian newspapers for staff. In 1956, London

Transport sent recruiting teams to Barbados and, in 1966, to Trinidad and Jamaica. The British Hotels and Restaurants Association and the Regional Hospital Boards (the latter encouraged by the then Minister of Health, Enoch Powell) did likewise.

ARRIVAL AND SURVIVAL

The Chens had been living in the UK for four years, which was long enough to have lost their place in the society from which they had emigrated, but not long enough to feel comfortable in the new.

TIMOTHY MO, *Sour Sweet* 1982

Ties with 'back home' were kept alive by the yearly exchange organised by my grandfather at Christmas. From the end of the war, we would send a parcel of clothing to his family in the Caribbean and we would get in return the most exciting parcel you could imagine . . .
MANGOES, PAW PAW, BREADFRUIT, A COCONUT, SUGAR CANE and black, black Christmas cake dripping with rum. We were home.

TERRI QUAYE, *Taking it On the Road* 1988

The first tangible sign of the new order was the single boatload of Jamaicans (492 legitimate passengers and 18 stowaways) who hitched a ride to London in the Australian troopship *Empire Windrush* in May 1948. All were taking instant advantage of the British Nationality Act, which was just completing its passage through Parliament. It guaranteed that all Commonwealth citizens shared a common status as British citizens. All that was needed to come to Britain was an affidavit of good character signed by a local Justice of the Peace.

Right: Immigrants from Jamaica on board the Empire Windrush in 1948

Facing page: By 1950 West Indian immigrants were arriving at a rate of 3 000 a month. At Victoria Station, a young girl waits, uncertain of her reception

The British government had not designed the Act as an enablement for immigration, nor as an admission of unlimited liability for the sins of Empire. It was merely a tidying up of Commonwealth policy made necessary by the new Citizenship Act passed by Canada in 1946. When news that the *Empire Windrush* had set sail and reached London 'the first reaction in Whitehall was a furious spate of buck-passing,' writes the historian Peter Hennessy. In a burst of candour, a Colonial Office spokesman told the *Daily Herald* on 9 June that: 'This unorganized rush is a total disaster. We knew nothing about it.'

However, the United Nations was criticizing Britain for not allowing more European refugees access. Faced with either more Europeans or more West Indians, the Labour Government settled for the Commonwealth influx. 'There's nothing to worry about: they won't last one winter in England,' said the Colonial Secretary, Arthur Creech Jones. He had not bargained for the spin-off effect of the restrictions on immigration into the United States imposed by the McCarran-Walter Act of 1952, which left Britain the only option for would-be emigrants.

Temporary quarters were found for the *Empire Windrush*'s passengers in the capacious deep air-raid shelter on Clapham Common, formerly used to house Italian and German prisoners of war. The nearest labour exchange was Coldharbour Lane in Brixton, and Brixton was to remain the heartland of the Jamaican community in London. Its street market along Electric Avenue soon reflected the eating habits of the new settlers: yams, sweet potatoes, chillies and garlic scented the downtown air. Settlers from other islands established their own localities: Trinidadians and Barbadians in Notting Hill, Guyanese in Tottenham and Wood Green and Montserratians in Finsbury Park.

Food never became part of the public face of the Afro-Caribbean community, partly because wives were quick to join the exodus and partly because music rather than eating was the focus for public socializing. But the Mangrove restaurant in Notting Hill was, according to the historian A. Sivanandan 'a meeting place and eating place, a social and welfare club, an advice and resource centre, a black house for black people, a resting place in Babylon.'

Quite the opposite has proved true of the much smaller and far more widely dispersed Chinese community in Britain. 'The Chinese in Britain are the prime example of a community which has mushroomed in response to a restaurant boom,' writes Lynn Pan, author of *Sons of the Yellow Emperors*. 'Had there not been the expansion of opportunities in the catering business in the 1960s and early 1970s, there would not have been the impetus for so much migration from Hong Kong to Britain during that period.'

Nine out of ten Chinese immigrants in the 1950s came from agricultural areas of Hong Kong and the New Territories. Originally the Chinese seamen who jumped ship turned to laundries, but in the 1950s they lost their trade to electric washing machines and coin-operated laundrettes. The obvious alternative was an equally domestic pursuit: cooking. Today, running restaurants and the foodshops that supply them occupies over 95 per cent of first-generation Chinese in Britain: it is effectively their only employment.

Timothy Mo's brilliant novel *Sour Sweet* gives a vivid picture of the world of chop suey and chips. It is the story of how an uneducated Chinese family establish a takeaway restaurant in Croydon to get away from the menacing protection of the Soho branch of the Hong Kong Triad. Family is at the heart of things: money has to be sent back regularly to aged parents, children have to be brought up to be Chinese. Even the Triad organization is modelled, like that of the Mafia, on the autocratic paternalism of a traditional family.

ESTABLISHING COMMUNITIES

> *Communities begin by establishing their kitchen.*
>
> FRENCH PROVERB
>
> *At home, men never cook. When we came over, we had to learn to cook for ourselves. Some things were very difficult, like chapatis – there's a special way to make them. But we learnt.*
>
> ABDUL RAHMAN, owner of the Bradford Sweet Centre
>
> *I found some brown bread in the kitchen. I had not seen brown bread before, and it looked very strange so I was not sure whether it was safe to eat. I found some rice, but I did not know how to cook or use the gas cooker.*
>
> *Munir's arrival in England, 1963, Asian Voices, 1993*

After India's declaration of independence in 1947, and the subsequent partition of the country, eight million people were displaced and thousands of families were left with divided loyalties. One solution to a dilemma that many found impossibly painful was to emigrate, temporarily at least, to Britain. Many were in fact highly qualified professionals – doctors, accountants and lawyers – but discrimination against employing them was so marked that they had no hope of jobs in their own fields. Most were men and, lacking wives to cook for them, they set up their own restaurants. The characteristics of such eating houses – cheap, and operating late at night – echoed the attractions of Asian immigrants as factory workers. They were undoubtedly exploited, but grateful for the work and largely unacquainted with their legal rights, they worked long hours for low pay.

The vast continent of India, once 600 individual kingdoms, is as varied as that of Europe in climate, religion and character. In Britain, the newcomers tended to cohere in regional groups. Punjabis came to Bradford's textile mills because of the demand for workers on the new night shifts established to maximize profits from new machinery – women, who traditionally worked in the textile mills, were barred from working at night and British working men disliked doing what was seen as women's work. The Punjabis who settled in Southall in the 1950s found their base by a local accident: the personnel manager of Woolf's rubber factory had been a policeman in the Punjab. Soon 90 per cent of the unskilled workforce was Punjabi.

Midlands communities of Sikhs developed from a relatively small number of Sikh pedlars who had sold goods from door to door between the wars, but who welcomed the prospect of steady jobs in Midlands factories after 1945. They were joined by families displaced by the partition of Pakistan in 1947, when some four million Muslims from the Indian side crossed into the Pakistani Punjab and a slightly larger number of Sikhs and Hindus moved back to replace them.

Of all the Asian communities, the Bangladeshis have always been the most involved with catering. Until the 1990s, when diversity in Asian eating is increasing remarkably, more than 90 per cent of the Indian restaurants in Britain were run by Bangladeshis, all neighbours and kinsfolk from one small area in the north of the country, Sylhet. This was a region from which young men traditionally went to sea for a few years before settling down on the land, but as conditions of crewing deteriorated in the 1950s, they gravitated to Britain, aware of the small communities of seamen who had long ago jumped ship and found work of one sort or another. Many of these earlier settlers had set up restaurants, and the newcomers naturally gravitated into the catering business, often as waiters, washers-up and kitchen helps in Italian restaurants and ordinary cafés. Others found their way to the textile mills of Bradford, and to the booming new industries of Birmingham.

They spoke little or no English and were debarred from going to pubs by a religious objection to alcohol. Transport costs and the special dietary requirements of the Muslim faith made it natural for such workers to aim to live within walking distance of their workplace if they could. Groups of men lived together in over-crowded rooms in lodging houses, working night shifts, sharing beds (and sometimes obliging landladies) and sending the bulk of their earnings straight back home.

'To go back home for good and to spend the rest of our life with our family, that was the common motto,' writes Yousuf Choudhury in *The Roots and Tales of the Bangladeshi Settlers*, a book which reads like a family history. 'When we saw the newspapers classed us as immigrants, we used to laugh.'

This way of life cut down the Bangladeshis' impact on their host country in the 1950s and early 1960s. 'The native people treated Asians sympathetically,' recalls Choudhury. 'If you lost your way, someone would readily help you. He would not only show you the way, but also, if he had time, he would take you to the place where you wanted to go.'

Icons of success in the shape of formally posed photographs showing smart clothes and such desirable status symbols as watches, cameras and transistor radios were sent home, encouraging the belief that England's streets were paved with gold. 'In Pakistan it was ironic that they thought that we who were in England were literally living the life of Riley, living it up,' recalls Yasmin Khan in *Here To Stay: Bradford's South Asian Communities*.

They thought that we had so much money that we were bathing in milk.
My dad's family didn't realize that we were actually working-class people.

It was only when we got here that we suddenly realized that people had to work hard, twelve-hour shifts, seven days a week. Money was plentiful, jobs were plentiful, but living conditions were bad: no bath, no toilet, a back-to-back house. But in comparison to Mirpur, what we had was luxury.

Running your own business was a good way of avoiding racial tensions with employers and helping to establish one's own community. Grocery shops, restaurants, fabric stores and cinemas with snack bars serving kebabs, samosas and teas were set up to service the growing numbers of Asians working in Midland and northern factories. Once established and thriving, such businesses attracted a steady stream of brothers, cousins, sons and nephews.

Restaurants were at the heart of the self-help movement. The Gathor Café in a Percy Street basement was an important meeting place for out-of-town Bengalis in need of advice or help and the Green Mask in the Brompton Road was a sounding board for such nascent politicians as Aftab Ali, Moulani Bhasani and Sheikh Mujib. In 1946, plans for a Bengali Muslim Burial Society were drawn up in the Jhon Restaurant in Steelhouse Lane, Birmingham; 38 years later it had grown into a purpose-built community centre, mosque and school in Alum Rock Road, Saltley. In the East End, the Ayub Ali Master's seamen's café was used as an emergency help and advice centre.

'We learnt to cook for each other, because our women were not here, and there were no restaurants that made our kind of food,' says Abdul Rahmin, owner of the Bradford Sweet Centre. 'That was the way that Indian cooking started in England, with those few restaurants in the East End. Mine was one of the first in Bradford. We served only five dishes: trotters, brain, lamb, chicken and mince meat. Others learned from our menu and our way of making dishes, and it gradually spread.'

Another incentive was the difficulty of cooking in digs. 'Nobody would let a decent room to Indians or Pakistanis,' recalls Ahmed Tarique Afras, who came to London in 1963. 'Anywhere you went they would ask you, "Are you going to cook?" "Yes." "Oh no, garlic smells, we are not going to give you the room." ' Ahmed ended up renting a whole flat where he could cook his own food using halal meats.

Distaste was not a one-way affair. Scrupulously hygienic, Muslims described the experience of using the six inches of water allotted to each person in the tubs at the public bath-houses as 'washing in our own dirt'. Prafulla Mohanti's lively reminiscences of arriving in Surbiton in 1960, as the guest of a fellow architecture student, reveal how Westerners can unwittingly offend the susceptibilities of Asians. 'I saw dogs sleeping in the kitchen,' he records. 'In my village the kitchen is the most sacred place in the home; it is where the ancestors live. No one is allowed to enter it without having a bath and putting clean clothes on. Dogs are not kept as pets, and when a stray dog came into our kitchen my mother said all the food, including the clay pots, was polluted, and had to be thrown away.'

When his hostess triumphantly bore a full-scale turkey on the bone into the dining-room Prafulla Mohanti's first urge was to run away from the table, but he managed to quell his disgust enough to enjoy the meal. After eating beef accidentally, he 'was not able to sleep for weeks,' imagining the meat entering his bloodstream and making him unclean. Belief in reincarnation made it possible that eating steak was akin to cannibalism.

CURRY AND CHIPS

> *Show almost any Indian family (Bengali, Gujarati, Punjabi or Tamil) a standard restaurant menu and the great majority will tell you that, at home, they don't eat or cook 90 per cent of the dishes listed!*
>
> MANJIT PABLA, Friends Restaurant, Leicester

> *There was something indefinable about Mr Chang's spaghetti bolognese. I believe he made a few minor additions – a dash of soya sauce and a sprinkling of ginger.*
>
> KENNETH LO, *The Feast of My Life* 1993

White faces were at first rare in Asian restaurants. But changes in the laws in the 1960s altered the shape of immigrant culture in Britain. Instead of consisting mainly of men living in all-male lodging houses, the balance shifted in favour of families and owner-occupied housing. The arrival of wives and children who could once again cook for their menfolk meant a decline of Asian custom and a casting about for a new clientele.

Taking note of the appreciation of their cuisine by the cosmopolitan Londoners who made the effort to come to Asian parts of town to eat, enterprising restaurateurs set out to attract more white custom. Charlie Cheung was the first to move from dockland to Soho. Soon others joined him in the Gerrard Street area, now the largest concentration of Chinese in Britain. Dislike of competing against their fellow countrymen led to a rapid diffusion of chop suey restaurants out into the suburbs, and further. A similar diffusion took place in the North from a focus in Liverpool. Britain's second largest Chinese community is now in Manchester.

Bangladeshis were as keen as the Hong Kong Chinese to open restaurants for non-Asians. At a grand level, long-established restaurants such as Veeraswamy's created anglicized though still fiery curries on which nostalgic colonial administrators could sate palates so accustomed to spiced food that they found home cooking insipid. It had been opened in the 1920s by Major Parmers, an ex-Indian Army officer who brought his cook back from India with him, and the decor was calculated to inspire fond memories of the glories of the British Raj. Prafulla Mohanti recalled a visit to Veeraswamy's in the 1950s:

> A tall Indian wearing a turban stood at the door. The interior was Oriental with embossed wallpaper and ornate brass vases, depicting a stereotyped image of India. There seemed nothing authentic about the food. I though it

was specially prepared for the British palate. My host explained that the restaurant catered for people like him who felt nostalgic about India from time to time.

But could such businesses be profitable downmarket? Asian chefs soon realized that the fastest profits lay in introducing their own recipes very gradually. 'I took over this restaurant in 1954 from an Italian,' explains Shamsuddin Khan, owner of the Maharani in Clapham. 'At first I kept the menu the same as the previous owner's, only gradually adding a few curries. So I had to learn to cook English dishes such as roast chicken and omelettes. For many years people used to order curry and chips.'

The Bangladeshi initiative was the more successful in that it coincided with the growing trend towards eating out informally. People had money in their pockets for leisure and entertainment, and were already used to patronizing coffee bars and Italian trattorias. The time was ripe for a new sort of eating experience. Moreover, prices were kept attractively low and meals could be eaten at hours when every other place in town was inhospitably closed.

As the Asian communities in Britain became more established, Indian and Chinese restaurants tailored their dished to suit British palates and patiently educated customers into exotic new ways of eating

Asian restaurants were particularly attractive to the 1960s battalions of new university students, already converted to an appreciation of things Indian by the films of Satyajit Ray and inclined to romanticize the cultural revolution being effected by Mao Tse Tung. It is probably not going too far to say that the habit of eating Indian or Chinese was spearheaded by herds of hungry undergraduates disgusted by the contrast between college food and mum's home cooking. At first there was an exotic sense of adventure in pointing a finger at a mysterious name on a menu, but soon the students' new habit of travelling the world in vacations made them enthusiastic, and increasingly knowledgeable, about Asian food.

Once hooked, they stayed hooked. In 1950 there were only six Indian restaurants in Britain. By 1970, there were 2000. The real growth period came in the 1980s, with 3500 in 1982 and 7500 by 1994. By 1970 there were 4000 Chinese restaurants, 2000 Indian and around 500 French. A national catering survey found that of those who ate out regularly or occasionally, as many as 31 per cent had eaten at Chinese restaurants but only 5 per cent at French ones.

Bir Bahadur's Indian restaurants were the first of many small chains owned by extended families. Beginning with the Roper Street Kohinoor in London, the Bahadur family soon established Taj Mahals in Oxford, Brighton and Northampton, and Kohinoors in Cambridge and Manchester. 'All the Bahadur brothers were kind-hearted; they never took advantage of the poverty of their employees and always treated them well,' writes Yousuf Choudhury. 'Nearly all the first generation of Bangladeshis who owned restaurants in the early days learnt the trade from the Bahadur brothers.'

The standard decor perpetuated the Veeraswamy tradition of nostalgia for the Raj by offering flock-wallpapered high-Victorian crimson plush interiors. Staff expected to deliver the same subservient service that they had offered their former rulers back at home. Even a restaurant like the Star of India, run by Indians from Mysore, originally adopted the anglicized food conventions established in Bengali-run restaurants when it was first opened.

'I don't think any of the food in the restaurant was anything like what we ate at home,' says Azam, remembering the days when he and his brother were growing up. 'In those days garlic was not liked at all; even coriander was frowned on,' adds Reza. 'We learnt more about real Indian cooking from our mother at home – she's a fabulous cook – than we did from the restaurant.'

To keep prices low, but to give the sense of variety expected in Indian restaurants, the 'batch' method of cooking was developed. It was quite unlike traditional Indian ways of preparing food, which involve tuning each sauce to suit the food to be cooked in it. Instead, a standardized basic recipe was converted into a wide range of other dishes by adding different flavours in the final stages of cooking. Conventional names were adopted so that customers knew what they were getting and waiters, most of whom spoke very little English, could communicate table orders to the cook. But all the infinite subtleties of real Asian cuisine were lost. The menus might have looked pages long, but more often than not they were merely a series of more or less unimaginative variations on a single theme.

'Madras' was a cue for a curry served hotter than it ever was in India. The notorious 'vindaloo', a macho challenge for a generation of lager louts, was laced with up to twenty times as much chilli powder as was customary even in Goa, where it originated as a dish made from wine *(vin)* and garlic *(aieul)*. 'It's not a popular dish with Asian people,' says Abdul Rahmin. 'It just blows your brains out. English people order it, the sort who don't really know what a curry is. They get legless in the pub, then come in and say, "chicken vindaloo". They also ask for it as a practical joke sometimes, for people who are having their first curry. Normally, very little chilli, and fresh rather than powdered at that, is used in Indian cookery.'

The word 'curry' has no particular meaning in Indian cooking. The generic use of it to describe any exotically spiced dish is, it seems, a British Raj invention, an elision of several similar sounding words associated with food – the Tamil word *kari* (sauce), the *karahi* (a wok-like frying dish), a spicy curd sauce called *kadhi* (traditionally served with a rice and lentil *khichdi*) and the herb of the same name.

FLASHPOINT

> *Every time the government has tried to keep immigrants out, it has actually managed to pull in . . . a flood of people who would probably have been quite happy to carry on living where they were.*
>
> SAHIB AHLUWALIA, of Sahib Foods

> *We must be mad, literally mad, as a nation to be permitting the annual inflow of some 50 000 dependants, who are for the most part the material of the future growth of the immigrant-descended population. It is like a nation busily engaged in heaping up its own funeral pyre.*
>
> ENOCH POWELL (1968)

> *Incidents used to happen about once a month in those days – people had to fend for themselves. You could phone the police, but they'd take two hours to get to you – there was no support for Asians then.*
>
> REZA MOHAMMED, joint owner of the Star of India

The roots of racial prejudice are complex. 'Economic factors, religious and cultural differences, a history of colonial exploitation, with its pseduo-scientific racism, sexual jealousy and nationalism, are all ingredients,' says Nick Merriman in *The Peopling of London*. But acute antagonism only occurs when there is a 'perception of immigrants and refugees as an immediate competitive threat for society's scarce resources'. A combination of 'push-pull' factors in the 1960s and early 1970s led to a dramatic increase in the numbers of black settlers in Britain at a time when the economic boom of the 1950s was actually slowing down. Jobs, particularly in the unskilled trades favoured by most immigrants, were in decline.

Moreover, as families joined their menfolk, children went to school and whole urban boroughs became majority immigrant areas, the ethnic communities were beginning to show a more public face.

Severe riots on the occasion of the Notting Hill Carnival in 1958 triggered the re-election of the Conservative Government in 1959 on an anti-immigration ticket. The announcement that a new Commonwealth Immigration Act was in preparation led to 'beat the ban' hysteria and a doubling – in some cases a tripling – of the numbers arriving every year. In the first ten months of 1961, 113 000 would-be settlers arrived from different parts of the Commonwealth. Most were single men gaining a toehold: the male/female ratio among Pakistanis was recorded in the 1961 UK census as 40:1.

The Commonwealth Immigration Act of 1962 controlled immigration by introducing a system of employment vouchers. Ironically, it is quite possible that the economic recession of 1962-3 would have led to a natural lowering in numbers. But the prospect of the 1968 Act, which restricted entry of Kenyan Asians to those who had a parent or grandparent born in Britain, caused another immigrant stampede, as did news that the 1971 Act would distinguish between 'patrials' (those with British parents and grandparents, that is, the majority of white Britons) and 'non-patrials' (the majority of black and Asian people).

Dilip Hiro, the author of *Black British, White British* (1991), believes that few South Asians would have stayed in Britain without the imperatives of the immigration laws passed in 1962, 1968 and 1971. British culture was too alien. 'Unlike the West Indians, Pakistanis and Indians never visualized their migration in socio-cultural terms. For them, the economic consideration was the sole motive for migration. [The 1962 Act] compelled them to discard their original plan of a few years' stay in Britain before returning home with their savings.'

In the 1960s, notices for jobs and lodgings began to say quite openly 'No Coloureds'. 'Any job I applied for or telephoned about seemed to have gone overnight' remembers Munir, interviewed for *Asian Voices*. 'Most Asians I came across seemed to be working in a restaurant, factory, hospital or shop as porters, whatever their qualifications were. The Asians who had the best jobs worked in Indian restaurants, garment factories or for the post office.' It was not uncommon for a barrister to find himself working as a bus conductor, or for a teacher to be an office cleaner.

Especially where unemployment and poverty existed in neighbouring white communities, racial violence remained unacceptably common. A White Residents Association was established in Southall in the 1960s, and the skinhead culture which succeeded the 'Teddy boys' in the East End contributed the ugly phrase 'paki-bashing' to the language. In 1967, the National Front was launched, and a year later came Enoch Powell's inflammatory vision of a staggering growth of the non-white population: 'Like the Romans, I seem to see "the River Tiber flowing with much blood".' He was promptly sacked from Edward Heath's Shadow Cabinet, but a Gallup poll showed that 75 per cent of the population were 'broadly sympathetic' to his views.

'The British at the best of times are a xenophobic people,' observes historian Arthur Marwick in *Britain Since 1945*. Faced with ethnic groups with long-standing and deeply felt cultural traditions of their own, many of whom spoke little or no English, they were unlikely to find the idea of integration and assimilation convincing. Nevertheless, shadowing all legislation against immigrants there has been other legislation aimed at reducing racial inequalities. In 1966, the first ever Race Relations Act set up a Race Relations Board aimed at conciliation in cases of proven discrimination. Enoch Powell's speech was a protest against the Race Relations Act in 1968, an important piece of legislation which has since helped to combat discrimination in employment and housing. In 1976, a new Race Relations Act vested the Commission for Racial Equality with more power, and provided massive funds for an Urban Aid programme designed to support black self-help groups.

Restaurants, the most public face of the new communities, received more than their fair share of racially motivated abuse and violence. Bad behaviour in Chinese and Indian restaurants had always been a recurring problem, though never a majority pursuit. Timothy Mo:

> The waiters often held impromptu discussions … about the various idio-syncrasies of their hosts and patrons, the English. Among these … were the strange and widespread habit of not paying bills, a practice so prevalent as to arouse suspicion that it was a national sport … Loud and rowdy behaviour was more comprehensible, including fencing with chopsticks and wearing inverted rice bowls on the head like brittle skullcaps, writing odd things on the lavatory walls, and mixing the food on their plates in a disgusting way before putting soya sauce on everything.

'Things started to get worse in the 1970s,' remembers Moinul Islam, of Sheesh Mahal, Croydon. 'One day a gang of about ten or twelve drunken men barged in through the door and started throwing glass and other things. I was ducking down behind my counter frightened for my life. It was always the worst with the people who come in after pub closing time. They would be loud and abusive, and some-times leave without paying. We didn't like to make a fuss – these people were our hosts. We were guests in their country.'

The first defence of the immigrant communities against racial attack and prejudice was to band together in more and more exclusive networks in order to insulate themselves from offensive behaviour. But there were also more aggressive reactions. In the late 1960s Black Power extremists probably did more harm than good with directives such as the one from Roy Sawh of the Universal Coloured People's Association, which urged 'coloured nurses to give wrong injections to white patients, coloured bus crews not to take the fares of black people … [and] Indian restaurant owners to "put something in the curry".' In 1980, Chinese restau-rateurs in Liverpool were reproved for pouring boiling oil out of upper windows and electrifying protective grills in front of their windows.

Now that immigration has slowed to a trickle, the ethnic communities have consolidated their positions and much more positive assertiveness has been evident, particularly among younger people. A number of radical Asian political organizations regularly lobby local and national government. Self-defence patrols and vigilante groups have proved more effective in reducing racial attacks, than the more conservative attitude of older Asian organizations such as the Indian Workers Association and the Bangladeshi Welfare Association.

As immigrant communities have become well established, racial prejudice has diminished. Asian shopkeepers put as much energy and commitment into running shops for the benefit of both ethnic and white customers as into restaurants. Open conveniently late and on public holidays, they too tend to be family businesses

Dilip Hiro points out that the difference between the generations was well-illustrated by the reaction when a gang of white youths murdered Gurdip Singh Chaggar, a young Sikh, in Southall in June 1976. 'While the traditional community leaders approached the police and government for protection, the young leaders openly expressed their distrust of white authority and called on the community to practise self-defence.' The young Asians marched on the police station, and staged a sitdown until two of their number accused of stoning a police van were released. To build on this success, the Southall Youth Movement came into being.

In the East End, where National Front action was most entrenched, the Anti-Nazi League emerged as a national movement in 1977. The role of anti-racist whites in that movement has been crucial in persuading Asians that whites are not uniformly prejudiced against Asians. Restaurateurs, who have more to do with the white community than any other Asian occupational group, know from experience that violent racial prejudice is a minority aberration. 'There is only one Asian to every ninety-nine English people,' says Shamsuddin Khan.

> Ninety-nine people are for us, and only one is against. How could we live in this country otherwise? Ninety-nine per cent of English people are on our side. There is a very close relationship between me and my customers – like the relationship between India, Pakistan and Bangladesh, so is the relationship between me and my customers. They have the same respect, too. We behave very politely, and so do they. If they are having a function for example, I am invited – I've been to many customers' weddings, and their children's weddings. Our children, who have been brought up here, love this country more than we do. Do you think they would love it if it was a bad place?

Second-generation Asians are more confident than their parents, and they know their rights. 'We don't take things lying down like my father's generation used to,' says Sanaul Islam of the Sheesh Mahel. 'Quite recently, four British lads came in here causing trouble … I went up to one of them and said, "Let's sort this out outside." There were four of us and four of them and we did manage to get rid of them – though one of my mates was hospitalized.'

'Yes, there's racism, and it affects all our lives,' acknowledges Azam Muhammed, co-owner of the Star of India. 'But I think it will always be there, and it doesn't actually solve anything to blame it for everything. We've got to find practical ways of dealing with it, and we've got to be able to open ourselves up as a community and look critically at ourselves, too, and grow out from there.'

AFTER JAFFREY

> *Eating habits are changing, and today's English populace seems to have a great desire to experience the 'real' thing, an authentic taste, a different life style... The word 'curry' is as degrading to India's great cuisine as the term 'chop suey' was to China's.*
>
> MADHUR JAFFREY, *Invitation to Indian Cookery* 1973
>
> *Jane Grigson called Madhur Jaffrey the Elizabeth David of India, and, for many people in Britain, Jaffrey did the same for Indian cuisine as Elizabeth David had done for the Mediterranean.*
>
> HAZEL CASTELL AND KATHLEEN GRIFFIN, *Out of the Frying Pan* 1993

There have always been adventurous British cooks who have experimented with exotic recipes in their own kitchens. Mrs Beeton offered recipes from all over the globe; Lyell and Hartley included a chapter on 'Cookery from the Arabian Nights' in their classic little *Gentle Art of Cookery;* Pearl Adams' *Kitchen Ranging* (1920) and Lesley Blanch's *Round the World in Eighty Dishes* (1956) were similarly imaginative. But none did justice to the astonishingly rich Asian cuisines. For most English cooks, wrote Constance Spry in 1956 just before offering a recipe for Banana and Melon Curry, 'the word curry denotes … a done-up dish, something inevitably hot and, as inevitably, deep yellow in colour.'

Then out of the blue came a spirited onslaught on the public and private presentation of Asian food from a woman much better known as the star of the film *Shakespeare Wallah* than as a cook. Most Indian restaurants were 'second-class establishments that have managed to underplay their own regional uniqueness as well as to underestimate the curiosity and palate of contemporary Britain,' complained Madhur Jaffrey on the first page of her *Invitation to Indian Cookery.* 'They serve a generalized Indian food from no particular area whatsoever.' Their cooks 'are often former seamen or untrained villagers' who copy 'standardized menus from other Indian restaurants and refuse to experiment'.

> A restaurant calling itself 'Delhi' had no karhi, that thick soupy dish with its bobbing flotilla of gram flour dumplings; another, advertising food from the Punjab, was minus those delicious Punjabi mainstays, corn bread and mustard greens; at another called 'Bombay', where were the spongy, cake-like dhoklas or those delicious sweet breads called puranpoli? And at all those new Bengali restaurants I saw no roe fritters, or fish smothered with crushed mustard seeds and cooked gently in mustard oil or bhapa doi, that creamy, steamed yoghurt.

In a few vivid, mouthwatering strokes, Jaffrey restored the individual identities of the great kingdoms of India, just as surely as Elizabeth David had mapped the Mediterranean twenty years before. Women were back in their rightful place in the kitchen.

Where did the new food Messiah come from? Jaffrey, who is as noted an actress as she is a cook, did not learn to cook as a child in Delhi, although like children all through the ages, she found watching the cooks in the kitchen fascinating.

> From childhood onwards, an Indian is exposed to more combinations of flavours and seasonings than perhaps anyone else in the world. Our cuisine is based on this variety, which in flavours encompasses hot-and-sour, hot-and-nutty, sweet-and-hot, bitter-and-hot, bitter-and-sour and sweet-and-salty, and in seasonings stretches from the freshness and sweetness of highly aromatic curry leaves to the dark pungency of the resin asafoetida, whose earthy aroma tends to startle Westerners just as much as the smell of strong ripe cheese does Indians.

Her palate received a more varied education than most in that she inherited the Mogul/Muslim traditions of Persia and the north from her father's family and the

Actress and cook Madhur
Jaffrey has done much to
popularize Indian cuisine

Hindu one of vegetarianism and food purity from her mother's. But it was not until she came to drama school in England in the late 1950s that a hunger for home cooking led her to learn to cook for herself – with the help of long airmail letters in Hindi from her mother.

> I took them to school, and as I ate my roast and two vegetables, I would ponder her advice … put in a pinch of asafoetida – don't let it burn – now put in the cumin and stir for a second or two … add the chopped-up tomatoes and fry … my mouth would water and the cabbage would stick in my throat. At this point, I couldn't even make tea.

She turned to writing a cookery book after an invitation to do so from an American publisher who had read in the publicity interviews at the time of the very successful film *Shakespeare Wallah* that she loved cooking. Its most important single effect was to wage war on the ubiquitous use of curry powders. They were, she explained, 'standard blends of several spices, including cumin, coriander, fenugreek, red peppers, and turmeric – standard blends which the Indians themselves never use.' She likened them to 'taking a tablespoon each of dried thyme, basil, rosemary, tarragon, bay leaves, and allspice, putting them in a jar, shaking it and labelling it "French Spices".'

No doubt readers rushed to their cupboards and tossed not only the curry powder but also the ubiquitous jar of mixed herbs that had been there since they got married into the trash can. Jaffrey did not just demystify and simplify; her writing was so rich in anecdotal, historical and cultural reference that it made people see India differently – no longer as just a part of British history (a slightly embarrassing one at that), but as an exciting source of ideas and inspiration. But Jaffrey believes that it is Britain's past involvement with India that has made Indian eating so much more popular here than it is in the United States. 'There is an historical echo which is deep in the souls of the British as colonizers … a hunger for that fun, that ambience and that food which has somehow trickled down to their children … that link triggers a need and then a love.'

In 1978 she presented a television series on Indian cookery which was a surprise success. The day after she mentioned fresh coriander, greengrocers all over Britain were faced with frantic demands for 'flat parsley that tastes of liquorice'. The book of the series sold out rapidly and sacks of questions about recipes from viewers flooded in.

Since then, television programmes, newspaper articles and cookery books all conspired to spread the new international gospel of authentic food. People began cooking Indian meals at home that were far more like those served in Asian homes than the food offered in restaurants. But there was also a knock-on effect on restaurant food as Jaffrey and the many other excellent food writers who followed in her wake provided food-conscious customers with the vocabulary to ask for what they wanted and enabled them to express the intelligent appreciation that was second nature in a French restaurant.

THE NEW WAVE

All that Raj-style decor was very patronizing. If you stick with it, it just paints people into a category, and I don't want to be categorized as anything – I want to be respected for my individuality. We're independent now: there's no reason why we can't just express our own ideas and creative abilities. I think there is no reason why an Indian restaurant shouldn't be appreciated on the same level as a French or Italian one. Take a tradition like lager for instance. I think that Indian food goes really badly with lager – wine is much better. I'm trying to phase out beer altogether at the Star of India – I've started by getting rid of all the pint glasses. Fifteen years ago, you couldn't have done this – the market couldn't have taken it. But now the English palate is ready. I am able to assert my own identity in this way, through the food I serve, and to throw away all the old stereotypes about Indian cooking and Indians in general.

REZA MUHAMMED

The 1970s introduction of Punjabi tandoori recipes – marinated, mildly spiced meat seared fast on skewers in an extremely hot clay oven - was the first public catering venture towards testing the Western palate with the kind of food that is actually eaten in India – or, rather, Pakistan, where it is sold on street corners fresh from the spit. Because tandoori restaurants required a considerable outlay on the special oven required, they tended to be more upmarket than the ordinary curry house, and the 1970s saw a more discriminating, wealthier clientele choosing to eat in Indian restaurants.

Today, with 7500 Indian restaurants in Britain, competition is intense – recession has hit the catering industry badly, particularly at the poorer end of the market which is most challenged by the new initiatives in supermarket provision of ready-to-eat food. But a new generation of restaurateurs is now emerging, managers who express their own style rather than pandering either to an imperial myth or to inexperienced palates. They know how to make their food 'upwardly mobile'; they are also fierce champions of different regional cuisines.

'Because my mother is such a fabulous cook, what I wanted to create was what we would eat at home if we were having a dinner party – like one of the feasts that were served for princely nabobs,' explains Reza Muhammed, the effervescent front-of-house manager of London's Star of India. 'We use authentic names, and authentic flavourings.' Azam Muhammed reflects on how relations with customers have changed since the Madhur Jaffrey revolution.

Every time we have a new menu, we describe all the ingredients to the boys who are waiting at table, so they know exactly what is in the food, and how it is cooked. The days when you could just say, 'Trust me, sir, it will be to your liking,' have gone. Customers want to know what a dish consists of before they put it into their mouths.

The dramatically original decor of Azam and Reza's Star of India is inspired by Zeffirelli and the Sistine Chapel rather than a Rajah's Mahal. Cod Michelangelo statues flank the walls and a mighty baroque Jehovah stretches a finger down to Adam from the ceiling of the stairwell. As Reza, a born showman, cavorts around the restaurant, there is not a trace of the red flock wallpaper, heavy red carpet and subservient waiters of 40 years ago.

CHINATOWN LTD

The Chinese cooking tradition makes for a greater harmony of living ... we all gather together round a table and partake of all the dishes which are placed on the table in communal style. Nobody is served just an individual portion in the western way, and chopsticks are used not just as eating implements, but to help others to a choice piece.

DEH-TA HSIUNG, *Chinese Cookery* 1987

In the past, Chinese cuisine lacked capital, organization and recognition. Now it has some recognition and, before long, the Chinese resources from the Pacific Rim will flood forth to promote Chinese food in all corners of the West.

KENNETH LO, *The Feast of My Life*

Chinese food writers like Kenneth Lo and Ken Hom did for Chinese gourmet eating what Jaffrey had achieved for Indian food, although they never swept to stardom in quite the same way. 'I have had a difficult time convincing the serious aficionado that he didn't have to make a beeline for those dubious establishments which serve up pig's stomach, congealed chicken blood, ox's penis, fish lips or fresh monkey brains, opened at table, in order to taste authentic ethnic Chinese cuisine,' jokes Kenneth Lo in his autobiography. 'The best is usually produced from run-of-the-mill materials, cooked in the simplest manner.' A chance encounter with the assistant food editor of Penguin over dinner gave Lo the opportunity to write a new handbook on Chinese cookery. It was this book, edited by Jill Norman, that introduced thousands of people to the classic Chinese 'trinity' of garlic, ginger and spring onions.

The two Chinese vegetable dishes distilled in my memory are very ordinary dishes. The first is Braised Chinese Cabbage, simmered in the finest stock and the best soya sauce with a trace of dried shrimps and a little sugar. The second is Plain Stir Fried Spinach. The spinach is cooked with nothing more than half a dozen cloves of roughly chopped garlic, a teaspoon of fermented bean curd, two tablespoons of soya sauce and four of hot vegetable oil. The stir fry is conducted over a medium heat so that the vegetable neither dries nor burns but becomes very tender and juicy. The result is a dish of deep green glistening leaves, chunky enough to be a main dish and flexible enough to complement any combination of dishes.

There is fine Chinese eating in Britain, especially in the substantial Chinatowns established in London and Manchester – in 1983, Yang Sing in Manchester won the coveted *Good Food Guide* restaurant of the year award, the first ethnic restaurant ever to do so.

The four great regions of China are now clearly delineated in Western minds. The Peking cuisine of the north, with its dumplings and garlic, sweet bean sauce and sesame seeds, tends to shun pork because of its many Muslims. The eastern school, focused on Shanghai and dominated by the great Yangtze River, is noted for

The pride of Chinatown, Manchester: some of the staff of the award-winning Yang Sing restaurant

Facing page: Chinese food writer Kenneth Lo demonstrates the art of the stir-fry

its vegetarian cuisine and its fresh fish and shellfish. The mountainous western school, including the provinces of Szechuan and Hunan (birthplace of Chairman Mao), is distinguished by strong flavourings and hot spices, especially red chillies, peppercorns and ginger. Best known outside China, because of the many emigrants to Europe and America, is the Canton cuisine of the south. It is famous for its sweet-and-sour dishes, delicacies such as dog, snake, frogs' legs and turtle, and the use of soy, hoisin and oyster sauces. Stir-frying in a wok and steaming are the most popular methods of cooking.

The *Good Food Guide* for 1988 registered the coming of age of ethnic cuisine with a special section called 'Notes on eating ethnic'. It gave hints on what to look out for, and the meaning of the menu, in Japanese, Korean, Lebanese and Indonesian eateries. By 1994 a substantial proportion – certainly over half – of the London restaurants mentioned by the guide served food from east of Aden. But the old Hobson's choice between curry and chop suey has become a many-headed hydra of gastronomic variety, an accurate reflection of the multitude of eager developing countries now touting for a slice of action from the prosperous economies of the West.

Space forbids more than a brief mention of the rapid recent growth of Pacific Rim restaurants. Their owners tend to be articulate, well educated, friendly and eager to communicate. They are presenting a local challenge to the older established ethnic restaurants which is as real as the challenge their vibrant economies are presenting to the world as a whole. Not for their women a retired existence behind veils. The owner of the Cottage Thai in Darlington, county Durham, no mean hand with gingered lobster and shredded beef with limes and coriander, set up the restaurant to keep herself occupied while her husband works near Darlington as a freelance draughtsman.

SILVER FOOD COFFINS

They served from a stereotyped menu, similar to those outside countless other establishments in the UK ... 'Sweet-and-sour pork' was their staple. ... 'Spare ribs' (whatever they were) also seemed popular. So were spring rolls, basically a northerner's snack, which Lily parsimoniously filled mostly with beansprouts. All to be packed in those rectangular silver boxes, food coffins, to be removed and consumed statutorily off premises.

TIMOTHY MO, *Sour Sweet*

We're catering to their needs, but we're also educating their palates. If you look at the way Indian food has developed in this country from the early 1950s to now, you'll find a gradual improvement in authenticity ... now there are some very, very authentic meals available in the market.

SAHIB AHLUWALIA

The take-away was born almost by accident. 'People would come in and ask if there was any way they could take some food home,' recalls Shamshuddin Khan. 'We used to supply it in the cans that the tinned mangoes had come from. Now that side of the business has expanded so much that we offer a home delivery service.'

After the imposition of VAT on food eaten in restaurants, many Chinese restaurants retreated alto-gether from serving seated customers in order to avoid the hated official paperwork. Profit margins were already slim, what with regular payments sent to dependants in Asia and the possible need to pay protection money to such powerful mafiosi as the Triads, and take-aways became increasingly popular. In many towns Hong Kong Chinese took over the fish and chip shop itself, using their considerable skills in deep-fat frying to make rather better fish and chips than the British had ever done. It is now not unusual to see sweet-and-sour pork and spring rolls being sold alongside haddock and chips.

Rival cheap and fast take-away services were offered by Mediterranean immigrants from Greece, Cyprus and Turkey. Moussaka, *kleftiko*, taramasalata, hummous and *tsatsiki* were further popularized by the boom in tourism to Greece. In the 1980s the rapidly increasing country-wide shift towards more eating out and snacking provided custom for all.

In the 1990s, however, a real challenge is being presented to the ethnic take-aways by the super-markets' recent expansion into ready-to-eat meals. Vesta Curries ('just add water!'), conservatively created by the very English firm of Batchelor's, were the first to hit the shelves in 1961, but the growing Asian food industry soon moved on to the scene with some authority. Asian companies like G. K. Noon and Sahib Foods now supply all the major supermarkets with such dishes as chicken korma and *rogan gosht*. Factory-made Indian food is a substantial industry worth millions of pounds a year.

The Ahluwalias' first break was the day they became purveyors of samosas to Harrods (of course) in 1987. It was almost an accident – they were not even in the food trade when a friend suggested that Sahib

Here's a new curry from VESTA...

Lavish Chicken Curry in 20 minutes – prepared by Vesta for you to cook!

A lavish new addition to the famous range of VESTA curries: Chicken Curry—complete with an authentic curry sauce for the chicken, and plenty of long-grained Patna rice. And everything's ready-prepared and brought to you by VESTA!

Expert chefs have done the hard work for you: they've cut the onions, apples, tomatoes (just the right proportions of each!)—carved the tender chicken—created the spicy curry sauce. Your turn now . . . to make the meal (in only 20 minutes!)—and take the credit that's due to you!

Serves One 2/3   Serves Two 3/9

Ahluwalia's wife's samosas were so good that she should send in some samples when Harrods lost its original supplier. There was a domestic panic when they were judged the best. Six years later the Ahluwalias were making 200 000 ready-made meals a year under the 'Sahib' label.

Their plans for the future carry the food offensive right into the heart of the enemy's camp and reflect the new internationalist eating of today. They have started selling Italian pasta dishes and even shepherd's pie. 'We also tried Caribbean food, which was quite successful for a while, and we are now developing American Cajun Creole dishes and Thai recipes.'

Shazad Hussein was a cookery teacher from a family proud of the quality of its food who found herself a whole new career quite by accident.

> Food is a central part of our lives. We used to buy the odd thing from Marks and Spencer and my mother said to me, 'I don't like the Indian food they sell; why don't you tell them that you can do better?' ... So I gave them a ring and explained what I did, and that the Indian food they were selling was not very authentic, and that I would show them the right way. They asked me to come and see them. So I brought a few examples of good home cooking, which they liked. I didn't realize what it would lead to, in all honesty!

Shazad has now been food consultant to Marks and Spencer for ten years. She is impressed with the trouble they take to talk to people in restaurants, select appropriate dishes, try them out and fine tune them to their – and the customers' – satisfaction. But she emphasizes that it is the restaurants who actually introduce the new dishes. 'People have a big influence, and the restaurant process is a way of testing public opinion. If we'd put balti on our counters before anyone had eaten it in restaurants, it wouldn't have sold.' Enthusiasm for 'balti' cookery is now general enough for Sharwoods to be advertising balti pastes on television. However, fashions are constantly changing. From the wilderness years in second-rate high street restaurants, and take-aways, through supermarkets and gourmet Indian restaurants in Clapham and Croydon, Manchester and Bradford, the Asian food culture has at last come of age in British kitchens. Buying Indian food in supermarkets has increased interest in cooking it at home (or at least buying a cookery book on the subject). The new technology of food processing, packing and fast transport by air made significant differences to the availability and cost of 'authentic' ethnic food ingredients. Fresh ginger and coriander can be bought today in even very small supermarkets. Arrays of spices, pastes and powders have extended from their humble slot next to the Oxo cubes into a shopping category in their own right. Almost as important is the new availability of the right cooking pans and utensils. Chimtas, tavas, chakhapaelnas and karahis are now imported not only for the benefit of restaurants, but for use in the home.

Kenneth Lo acts as a consultant for mass market foods. 'When making plans to market it on such a scale, I really feel as if I am systematically pumping the essence of one culture into the veins of another,' he writes in his autobiography. Unlikely as it may seem, reading the small print on packets of supermarket chicken masala and *rogan gosht* could be the first step towards countering racial prejudice with understanding. To share a little of our food is to share a little of ourselves.

IDENTITY AND SUCCESS

> *The Asian community is emerging as an economic and political force in Britain today . . .*
> *Our food, once despised, is a gourmet's paradise and has relegated French and other international cuisines to the sidelines.*
>
> BALRAJ PUREWAL, *Asian Voices*

> *Any immigrant community has to go through a period of adjustment to its new environment before it can feel secure enough to start thriving. Now we have been in this country for a generation, we can stop behaving as if we will accept anything because we are so grateful for being here.*
>
> SAHIB AHLUWALIA

There is now a substantial Asian subculture in Britain, with its own banks and mortgage companies, press, films and cinemas, television companies and schools. A huge annual festival of the arts is held annually in Lister Park, Bradford. Over one hundred thousand visitors converge on the city from all over the country for the weekend. 'You can go out and socialize in Bradford now', points out a Pakistani woman interviewed for *Here to Stay*.

> In Pakistan we did that sort of thing all the time. We went to restaurants as a family. But when we came to England there was nothing like that. There was nowhere we could go and eat. I remember we went to an Asian restaurant and the man said that the women had to sit separately, and they were shocked that my dad had taken his wife and daughters out. That's what's nice now, that I can go with my mum and my brother and sit in a public place and enjoy a meal, and say hello to people I know.

Restaurants are no longer the only social and cultural centres for immigrants. They were succeeded in the first instance by cinemas, but now that videos are so popular a way of watching Asian films, and because women also need places to meet each other, the most important focus for ethnic communities is their place of worship, be it mosque, *gurdwara*, temple or madrassa.

Religious gatherings were local at first, a group of connected families using a house adapted for the purpose, eating and worshipping together. But as the communities have become prosperous, and as links with religious kindred abroad

In a Sikh temple, the women prepare the langar, food supplied to the hungry free of charge

have grown stronger (the Saudi Arabians have been particularly generous to British Muslim communities), substantial purpose-built places of worship have come into being. Food is at the heart of the matter. The *langar*, food which is offered free to anyone who happens to be hungry, is a feature of the Sikh religion. The free kitchen attached to a Sikh temple is a popular meeting place.

The children of the post-war settlers are now themselves grandparents, watching new generations grow up who see themselves as distinctly British, and regard their parents' countries of origin as places for holiday visits rather than dream objectives. 'About half of the second-generation Bangladeshis, even some of those born there, I doubt if they would be able to go by themselves to Bangladesh and find the way to their own homes without someone's help', writes Yousuf Choudhury.

'We are bringing up our children in England,' says one of the older immigrants he interviewed. 'They go to state schools and have a liberal religious education, a sense of identity and tolerance for other races. We go to Bangladesh every so many years. It completely drains our savings, but we think that every penny is worth it.

We have now settled in England with our own house, but my wife and I will always love Bangladesh … I do not think our children will ever go back to live in Bangladesh. Salmon go back to their place of origin to spawn and die. Maybe one day when our children become independent and we are too old and frail we will also go back to Bangladesh.'

This older generation are loth to lose touch with their roots. 'I want my children to learn Punjabi because I think language and culture are interrelated' said a first-generation Sikh interviewed for the Bradford Oral History Project.

> I think if you lose a language, you're well on the way to losing a culture. When people first came here, there were very few of us, and we had to mix in. But now we have made our own communities, and people can live happily as though they're in Pakistan. The older generation especially will speak their own language, cherish their own beliefs, eat halal food, and they are more and more impervious to outside influences. They are in contact with white people only on the fringes, and in a way they are very isolated. The culture has become more consolidated, not weaker or more diluted.

But it is well known that Pakistani communities in Britain are noticeably old-fashioned in comparison with Pakistan itself, where the students are 'very trendy, very Americanized'. The next generation looks at life in Britain differently. 'Culinary insularity is really nothing more than a set of stubborn taste habits,' points out Jaffrey. 'And the best way to break these habits is through enlightened exposure at an early age.'

Many of the children of the post-war settlers now prefer to describe themselves as 'Black British' rather than Caribbean, African or Indian. Pizza Huts and McDonalds are as popular with young Asians as they are with young whites. Dress is becoming as muddled as eating habits. There is increasing conflict between the family's need for help from children, especially in shops and restaurants, and demands for homework from schools.

Nor is popping rice into foil boxes any longer the summit of Chinese ambitions. A survey in 1978 showed that 80 per cent of the young Chinese between the ages of 16 and 24 aspired to something quite unassociated with catering. Like young Asians, they have adopted new aspirations.

'Over time, third-generation Indians may well want to break free of the ties of Indianism', says Reza Muhammed. 'Their culture has evolved. You can't make Britain into India, after all. You have to fit in with the rest of the public. On the other hand, many Westerners now visit India, and are finding opportunities out there. They're trying to find out about Indian mysticism, and understand Indian culture.'

'There's a new generation of Asians around, but not many of them are running restaurants', points out his brother. 'And if they do, they don't necessarily go for Indian food if they themselves prefer Chinese, Thai or Italian.'

CHAPTER FIVE

Green Cuisine to Lean Cuisine

I don't touch meat largely because of what Wagner says on the subject, and says, I think, absolutely rightly. So much of the decay of our civilization had its origin in the abdomen – chronic constipation, poisoning of the juices, and the results of drinking to excess.

ADOLF HITLER to Hermann Rausching 1933

During the course of a Sunday lunch we happened to look out of the window at our young lambs gambolling happily in the fields. Glancing down at our plates we suddenly realised that we were eating the leg of an animal that had until recently been gambolling in a field itself. We looked at each other, and said, 'Wait a minute. We love these sheep – they're such gentle creatures, so why are we eating them?' It was the last time we ever did.

LINDA MCCARTNEY'S *Home Cooking* 1990

When I was a boy, being a vegetarian was as weird as someone with two heads.

BRIG OUBRIDGE, Tepee Valley dweller

'Real men don't eat quiche,' said Flex Crush, ordering a breakfast of steak, prime rib, six eggs, and a loaf of toast … 'There was a time when this was a nation of Ernest Hemingway's Real Men. The kind of guys who could defoliate an entire forest to make a breakfast fire – and then go on to wipe out an endangered species hunting for lunch. But not anymore. We've become a nation of wimps. Pansies. Quiche-eaters.'

BRUCE FEIRSTEIN, *Real Men Don't Eat Quiche* 1982

'Anyway,' said Scarlett, remembering, 'broad-leafed veg retain radioactive … becquerels, or something, for a long time, so even if they're good for you, they're bad for you.'
'It's the case with most things, isn't it?' said Constance. 'Nuts are full of goodness, but they make you fat, and there was a bloke once died of drinking too much carrot juice.'
'You can take it to extremes,' said Scarlett, 'this healthy-eating business.' She scraped a little butter substitute on to her daughter's toast.

ALICE THOMAS ELLIS, *Pillars of Gold* 1992

Food can be intensely pleasurable, a sign of sophistication or cultural identity – but it can also be a taboo, a source of fear. The 1970s were marked by a growing unease about the way society was going. On the one hand, factory farming and food processing methods seemed to be banishing the spectre of famine for ever and giving women an unprecedented opportunity to extend their activities outside the home. On the other hand, there were widespread fears that the planet's supplies of fossil fuels simply could not keep up with demand and it seemed essential to consider ways of surviving without them.

Although technology was producing food in greater variety, more conveniently packaged and more cheaply than ever before, some consumers were beginning to feel that there was an unacceptable price to be paid for local plenty in a world of want. A meat-eating society meant the distortion of the Third World economies that grew animal feeds or coped with the hamburger herds. How moral was it to allow living creatures to be cooped up in unspeakably awful conditions so that we could glut ourselves on snowy white veal, chubby chickens and hormone-tenderized beef steaks? Was meat even good for us any longer? Should pharmaceutical companies continue to search for wonder drugs to cure disease when a more natural diet could be the key to health?

In *The Food Factor* (1986), Barbara Griggs pointed out the irony of the fact that, 'nearly fifty years ago we knew enough about nutrition to plan the high-fibre, low-fat wholegrain diet which enabled Britain to survive six years of war in fine physical shape'. But public interest in healthy eating had withered away after the war. In 1945, to Lord Woolton's bitter disappointment, Oxford University turned down an offer by the Wellcome Trust to fund an Institute of Human Nutrition. 'Nutrition is totally uninteresting; we've solved the main problem and there is nothing left to study,' said the Professor of Pathology, Howard Florey, who had played a notable role in the discovery of penicillin. Vitamins were seen as the answer to everything; the food industry was coping marvellously. Research money backed the discovery of more wonder drugs, quests for cures rather than preventatives.

For all the consumer boom and the prosperous surface gloss on society, the biggest, most unalterable shadow over us was the threat of nuclear war. No one could do much about missiles trained on Manchester and Salisbury Cathedral, but when it came to scientists 'murdering bread', as Doris Grant put it, or turning children's orange squash into a cocktail of additives, they could, and did, protest.

In the 1970s, healthy eating once more became highly fashionable, this time with a counter-culture which asserted a reverence for nature in opposition to the nuclear shadow which lay so threateningly across the future. Hippies grew their hair and turned cool, seeing Lucy in the sky with diamonds and dreaming of a world run by love, not power. Retreating into the extremities and byways of our island and working smallholdings was also a resort from helplessness for ordinary people who resented their inability to influence the decision-makers in Red Square or the Pentagon. Armed with John Seymour's *Self-Sufficiency*, a second-hand tractor and not much else, many men and women decided to make a new start in remote rural areas, digging and delving as energetically as Adam and Eve in Eden. These were the

Facing page, top: Back to all things natural was the mood of the pine and earthenware kitchens of the 'Brown Decade'

Bottom: An enthusiastic convert, Linda McCartney launched her own range of vegetarian foods in 1991

days of hiring water-diviners to rediscover long-lost wells; of reading *The Lord of the Rings* and *The Little House on the Prairie* to your children by candlelight; of wholewheat pasta, real ale and brown rice – one commentator called it the Brown Decade. Environmentalism and vegetarianism were yoked together – and what you consumed was a crucial statement about your politics.

High on the hippie agenda was the idea of recreating real communities. The legacy of mass rehousing of the 1950s and 1960s was beginning to be felt; the tower block, that conveniently rapid and economical way of providing battery housing for people, was especially under fire. Even in the smartly renovated Victorian suburbs and new housing estates, the effect of putting heat, light, water, education, welfare payments and medical advice on tap was to cut down the interdependencies of neighbourhoods and to sap individual initiative. With extraordinary contrariness, a remarkable number of people took one look at a society in which everything was done for them, calculated intuitively rather than scientifically the cost to the environment of the urban West's lifestyle, and decided to reject it.

Religious metaphors lard this chapter like currants in a Christmas cake. Hippies adopted Eastern prohibitions on meat along with the lotus position and quantities of hallucinogens. The New Age vegetarians were stamped with all the hallmarks of the spiritual convert from the initial awakening vision on the road to Damascus ('We happened to look out of the window at our young lambs …') to miracle-working cures ('I would have died if it had not been for grapes/yeast extract/grated apple'), the daily affirmation of observing food laws as rigorous as anything laid down by Judaism or Islam (no meat, no jam, no butter, no fun) and, finally, the missionary zeal for spreading the good food gospel.

The most recent example of the last is Peter Cox's *Realeat Encyclopaedia of Vegetarian Living* published in 1994. In its opening lines Cox takes pains to declare that 'eating a vegetarian or vegan

diet is not like taking holy orders [or] running for sainthood', but in fact his book is as comprehensive as the Old Testament in laying down the right true way. His account of detoxification, a recognized technique for 'making a commitment' to vegetarianism, is closely akin to a religious fast: a trial followed by nirvana. It means eating no cooked food at all for a week to 10 days, besides completely cutting out meat, alcohol and caffeine.

You may feel wonderfully elated or (very rarely) rather depressed. Your body may start to feel lighter and younger. On the other hand you may very well have some kind of deferred reaction – you may get spots and pimples and a bad headache is quite common as your body detoxifies … in this short, intense period, your food tastes will have changed for good. You will have developed an appreciation for fresh food, and a lasting desire to eat something fresh at least once a day. And then you won't look back! You will have made the break, given your body a thorough detoxification, and started to set the pattern for a better, healthier life!

THE ORIGINAL VEGETARIANS

I had no idea that the issues which agitate so many today – a hatred of unnecessary slaughter, the concept of animal welfare, our own physical health, the earth's balance and hence its ecology – would have been perfectly understood in the ancient world, certainly as early as 600 BC.

COLIN SPENCER, *The Heretic's Feast* 1993

*Never again may blood of bird or beast
Stain with its venomous stream a human feast,
To the pure skies in accusation steaming*

PERCY BYSSHE SHELLEY, *'The Revolt of Islam'* 1818

*One sometimes gets the impression that the mere words 'Socialism' and 'Communism'
draw towards them with magnetic force every fruit-juice drinker, nudist, sandal-wearer, sex-maniac,
Quaker, 'Nature-cure' quack, pacifist and feminist in England.*

GEORGE ORWELL, *The Road to Wigan Pier* 1938

Vegetarianism has a fascinating history that stretches back through Shelley and Leonardo da Vinci to Pythagoras. But until the 1970s, it was a fringe movement in the United Kingdom. At the turn of the century, its most noted disciples were Leo Tolstoy, George Bernard Shaw (who was converted by reading Shelley and died in 1950, aged 94, a fine advertisement for his dietary principles) and the English freethinkers Henry Salt and Edward Carpenter. It was also associated, as George Orwell so rudely observed, with socialism, communism and a good deal else. Orwell saw it as an essentially selfish movement. 'The food crank is by definition a person willing to cut himself off from human society in hopes of adding five years on to the life of his carcase; that is, a person out of touch with common humanity.' Although Colin Spencer, author of *The Heretic's Feast*, the definitive history of the movement, is very definitely one of the converted, he also notes 'a pattern common to many vegetarians of individuals setting themselves outside society, to examine, find fault, and attempt to rectify these moral lapses within society by the example of their own lives.' His own choice of title is a deliberate echo of the quasi-religious dissent that has been, until recently, so characteristic of the food reform movement.

Spencer serves up a motley collection of thin sickly boys who discovered that a vegetarian diet spelt the difference between wasting away and blooming with health. Among them were Max Bircher-Benner of muesli fame and Gayelord Hauser, the galloping gourmet of the beanfeast, who was sent to Switzerland with a tubercular hip and no great prospects. But the most unexpected apologist for the delights of nutcake and wholemeal bread was a pale unhealthy lad with a lung complaint called Adolf Schickelgruber. 'I am pleased to inform you,' this young man wrote to a friend in 1911, 'that I feel altogether well … I am trying to cure myself through a diet of fruit and vegetables.' It was an idea he acquired from his hero Richard Wagner, 'who did not touch meat or alcohol, or indulge in the dirty habit of smoking.'

In later life, when Schickelgruber had changed his name to the crisper sounding Hitler, he claimed that being a vegetarian increased his working and intellectual capacities. According to Goebbels, he planned a complete dietary reform of Europe. 'He believes more than ever that meat-eating is harmful to humanity. Of course, he knows that during the war we cannot completely upset our food system. After the war, however, he intends to tackle this problem also.'

Ironically enough, vegetarians were persecuted under Hitler, who was aware that they did not have the most martial of reputations and did not want any dissent except his own. Walter Fliess and his wife, proprietors of the Vega restaurant in Cologne, were doubly under threat as vegetarian Jews and fled to Britain in 1933. Here, vegetarianism was gaining a little more respect from food nutritionists, and the Fliesses set up another Vega restaurant in London, close to Leicester Square. But prejudices remained. *Cookery and Nutrition*, a standard textbook by J. M. Holt published in 1939, defined vegetarians as, 'Those who have conscientious, religious or aesthetic objections to using animal flesh as food.' Notice that she made no mention of health reasons. On the contrary; she warned that if dairy products and eggs were also avoided, 'serious difficulties in proper nutrition may occur', and that even if dairy products and eggs were eaten, 'it will be found difficult at first to arrange menus that seem satisfying or sufficiently varied'.

Although she conceded that nuts were 'of great value', Holt declared that pulses were 'indigestible' and cereals 'insipid'. 'Few vegetables contain protein in appreciable quantities, and where it is present, it is frequently very indigestible.' Vegetable proteins were also 'poorer in the number of amino-acids they contain'.

Many who attempt a vegetarian diet find that the 'meals give a sensation of great bulk without being satisfying'; moreover, 'Vegetarian cookery makes a greater demand on the skill and time and patience of the cook than a non-vegetarian diet.' The two recipes she grudgingly provided – Vegetable Pie (haricot beans, tin of tomatoes, ¾ pint of brown sauce) and Stuffed Onions – were not calculated to inspire much enthusiasm.

Wartime rationing and the mania for growing one's own vegetables appeared to be a golden opportunity to convert people to vegetarianism. But making do in an emergency was not enough to alter the habits of a lifetime. Even snoek, whale meat or horse were preferable to lentil purée. Nevertheless, rationing records in 1945 show that there were 100 000 registered vegetarians. There could well have been others, of course, growing their own vegetables and passing on their meat rations.

EAT AND GROW BEAUTIFUL

Opportunity keeps on knocking and its doors are everywhere. You are opening one right now, as you read this book, a door to new health, new youthfulness, new and adventurous living.

GAYELORD HAUSER, *Look Younger, Live Longer* 1951

It has been fully proved that if we are to have the vitality necessary to make our lives richly rewarding, we must obtain some forty nutrients daily; and that a lack of one or more of these nutrients results first in a below-par drag and eventually in serious illness.

ADELLE DAVIS, *Let's Cook it Right* 1947

American dietician Gayelord Hauser, seen here at a party given in his honour at the Dorchester, promised the rich and famous youth-fulness and vitality if they followed his rules for healthy eating

Glamour hit food reform for the first time in the 1950s when it was taken up in Hollywood and in the smart drawing-rooms of London, New York and Paris. The man most responsible for the smart set's interest was Gayelord Hauser, as dashing as Graham Kerr, but with rather more sense of mission. His first book was *Eat and Grow Beautiful,* but his most famous, shrewdly calculated to take the hearts and stomachs of 40-somethings by storm, was *Look Younger, Live Longer* (1951). The inspiring new angle he offered was to associate healthy eating less with the high moral ground and more with good looks and youthfulness. 'The stuff of which we are made is potentially immortal,' he declared. Living to a hundred was easy, for 'the fountain of youth is good nutrition.'

'When Hauser lectured, even the carriage trade turned up,' writes Barbara Griggs in *The Food Factor.* 'He was positive, inspiring, upbeat. Instead of the grim denunciations of the Hygienists – the near-biblical warnings of dire retribution for gastronomic self-indulgence – Hauser told them that they too could be happy and healthy, full of dynamic vitality, eating a new kind of food.'

Hauser soon became physician extraordinary to the Beverly Hills set. He was introduced by Fred Astaire's sister, Adèle, to the Duke and Duchess of Kent, Lady Diana Cooper and the Windsors. He could offer his readers recipes for 'grilled grapefruit as served by me to Greta Garbo' and for a Hollywood Liquid Diet guaranteed 'to make you as beautiful as the stars'. Healthy food was his watchword, not health food 'from those dreary little ill-health food places'. 'Do not try to substitute vitamin pills for food vitamins,' he warned. 'Without a sound basic diet, vitamin and mineral pills can do you no good.'

His food writing was unashamedly sybaritic. 'There must be pleasure in eating: Americans eat with their eyes,' he insisted. Every ingredient had an exultant adjective. 'Dark California carrots make the most delicious juice … Peel tender young rhubarb, wash fresh ripe strawberries and put through a vegetable juicer'. There were to be no nut cutlets and dandelion coffee for the gourmet health fiend. Hauser allowed meat, though preferably as under-done as possible, as well as tea and coffee in moderation. His five 'wonder foods' were brewer's yeast, powdered skimmed milk, yoghurt, wheatgerm and black treacle.

His contemporary, Adelle Davis, who also ran a Hollywood health clinic, was equally determined not to be typecast as a kitchen kill-joy. Canned juice, tinned fruit and white sugar all featured in her recipes. She had no time for the food faddists who claimed that white flour and sugar poisoned people, and she giggled with the husband who likened his wife's breakfast of wholegrain cereal, hand-ground immediately before it was cooked, topped with powdered whey, bone meal, sunflower seeds, powdered milk, yeast, rice-polish, cream and raw sugar to 'compiling a compost heap'. Her famous cookbook, *Let's Cook it Right,* was first published in America in 1947 (complete with a barbed dedication to her daughter Barbara, 'in the hope that her husband and children will not have to eat TV dinners').

The rationale for her theories was provided in her best-selling *Let's Eat Right to Keep Fit,* published in 1954. The time was ripe for such a book. Thinking Americans were wondering whether their diet was associated with the new killer diseases of the twentieth century – the 'epidemics of affluence' – cancer, heart disease, arthritis and diabetes. Moreover, thanks to the omnipresent domestic appliances, housewives had plenty of time to calculate calories and construct vitamin-rich vegetable cocktails.

Davis quoted nutritionists such as Weston Price (*Nutrition and Physical Degeneration*, 1938) who had studied the simple diets of nutritional primitives such as Swiss peasants, Scottish crofters, Eskimos and Polynesians and the impact on them of a Western diet. It was not just a matter of decayed teeth. Such people, according to Price, had 'no physicians, surgeons, psychiatrists, no crime, no prisons; no mental illness and no institutions for the insane, feeble-minded, alcoholics, or drug addicts; no child delinquency, no homosexuality. Every mother nursed her baby, a non-functional breast was unheard of. Mental, moral and emotional health accompanied physical health.'

The ideas of Hauser and Davis, along with those of our own Doris Grant of breadmaking fame, were very influential among the middle-class intelligentsia in Britain in the 1950s. And it was reading Gayelord Hauser that brought about the conversion of David and Kay Cantor, founders of Cranks, the famous London vegetarian restaurant. David explains in *The Story of Cranks* (1982) how he slipped a disc in 1950. After the failure of hospital treatment with traction and drugs, he visited a distinguished osteopath who 'spent our sessions of back manipulation re-educating me about health, including giving me several books to read'.

> One of them was Gayelord Hauser's *Look Younger, Live Longer*. The effect was dramatic – an exciting and fascinating reversal of all Kay's and my ideas of health and disease . . . We were completely convinced by the obvious sense of a philosophy which stresses that nature knows best, and so the food we eat should be as near as possible to the form in which it is harvested.

Ten years later, a bakery became vacant in the small London backstreet where Cantor was setting up a showroom for the Craftsmen Potters Association. It was pure accident that this was Carnaby Street, then still a place of low rents and small shops and cafés with a saddlery, an ironmonger and a few tailors. Kay and David Cantor, together with Daphne Swann, a close friend and colleague, decided to tilt at the venture of a restaurant that would 'reject the trend towards lifeless, devitalised, refined and chemicalised foods' and offer instead Gayelord Hauser's invigorating salads, soups and juices and Doris Grant's wholemeal bread.

Cranks (the name was a deliberate challenge to sceptics) opened in London on 21 June 1961 and the takings amounted to a respectable £11 17s 1d (£8 a week would be a starting wage for an 18-year-old at the time). Supplies were as pure as possible – free-range eggs, organically grown fruit and vegetables, Loseley yoghurts and ice-creams. It was also important to the Cantors that the restaurant's furniture, fittings and utensils should be made from natural materials. There were pine tables and pottery. 'The pleasure of eating from hand-thrown stoneware, in our view, outweighs the thousands of pounds spent a year replacing it,' writes David Cantor.

'Our customers must like it – they have always tended to take some home with them!'

Cranks set the style for the next three decades of vegetarianism – hominy pie, celery, nut and carrot salad and courgette and cheese wedges eaten to a background of Bach and Vivaldi. Its location made it impossible to dismiss, as the food critic Quentin Crewe did Vega's in 1965, as a haunt of 'cropped-haired ladies with fingers crooked crying in genteel voices sundry pronunciations of yoghurt'. Instead Crewe complained about its crowds – and the crowds were young and fashionable. For by the mid-1960s Carnaby Street had become the internationally renowned style capital of the counter-culture, the haunt of such pop heroes as the Beatles and the Rolling Stones.

LENTILS IN THE SKY WITH DIAMONDS

Peter's father actually brought his own chop down with him, he just thought he wouldn't be able to eat our food. I remember preparing brown rice and seaweed for Peter's mother, and she just refused to eat it – looking back, I'm not surprised. They thought we were weird, and we thought what they ate was awful. There was a huge generation gap. There we were, tripping out on LSD, and they just stood by wondering what the hell was going on.

JENNY DEDMAN, of Infinity Foods wholefood co-op, Brighton

A lot of the children thought their parents had gone off in the wrong direction, that they had fallen for false gods. Families were actually falling apart over issues like the length of their children's hair. And I think that made it easy for the children to just chuck up the whole lot and opt for a very different life style. And I think that their parents have come to understand rather late that their pursuit of money and success was actually a false dream, and that they could get their redundancy notice on a Friday, just like that, after having given their whole life and energy to the firm.

KATE HENNINGS, Herefordshire

When the kids stopped twisting and shouting and took to flower power and pot, they also turned macrobiotic. America had begun it with a seismic mood of discontent among young people doomed to be drafted into the remote and foreign hell of Vietnam. After their tour of the United States, the Beatles also grew their hair, turned cool, and disappeared to find wise men in the East who could help to them to fulfil their dreams of a world run by love, not power. Everyone who could afford a passage to India followed in their footsteps; the rest set to making their own fantasy world from joss sticks, ethnic textiles, brown rice and, of course, hashish fudge, from the famous recipe in the *Alice B. Toklas Cookbook* (1960).

In a mortar grind coarsely 1 tsp black peppercorns, a grated whole nutmeg, 1 tsp coriander and 4 sticks of cinnamon, then chop finely with a knife

8-12 stoned fresh dates, the same of dried figs, plus 24 almonds and a dozen Brazil bits. Pulverize as much hash as you like and mix it, plus the spices, fruit and nuts into 115 grams of unsalted butter, kneaded with 225 grams of brown sugar. Roll into a cake or make into walnut-sized pieces. Two pieces are quite sufficient.

'All right, children, start looking for your own wholefoods ...'

It was a movement that returned to nature to find spirituality. There was talk of absorbing energy, of being in touch with Gaia, the sentient whole of the universe. The best possible diet was a living one, raw food, wholefood, in which nutrients would literally revitalize the consumer. Spencer likens the hippies to the heretical medieval free spirits known as the Beghards and Beguines: 'Often itinerant, refusing work, surviving by anti-social methods like manufacturing and selling drugs, or by music, fringe entertainment activities and street entertaining.'

Jenny Dedman was a flower child of the 1960s. 'I was on the front cover of the *News of The World*, with no clothes on at the concert in Hyde Park. I painted my face, put flowers in my hair … We were very tribal, really. It was an age of experimentation. I remember being told you could use charred corn instead of baking powder, and get high by scraping the insides of bananas. None of it was true!'

Her husband Peter co-founded Infinity Wholefoods in Brighton with a vegetarian Norwegian when Jenny was a student as Sussex University, and the Dedmans found themselves catering for the first Glastonbury Festival, England's own Woodstock. 'It was all brown rice and vegetables. The main thing was that it had to be cheap, and you had to be able to churn out huge quantities of cheap and healthy food.'

Eddie Cahil was a steward on a transatlantic liner in the 1960s. He used to pick up books by Jack Kerouac and records by Bob Dylan in New York's Greenwich Village, as well as sacks of brown rice. 'I made Zen burgers on the ship – a mixture of brown rice and brown rice flour made into patties.' He and two other stewards followed a macrobiotic diet 'because it was hip – but it was also about spirituality. We tried fasting for three days, denying ourselves, because it was a spiritual experience. And drugs helped us get high so we could meditate and get really spiritual. We thought, "This is the way to world peace!"'

Such food was also cheap and very healthy. 'We didn't go in for anything complicated. It was all about simplicity'. This attitude was linked to the 'disillusion with technology' which tepee-dweller Brig Oubridge says was at the heart of the alternative life style that developed in the 1970s. 'Technology has always been a two-edged sword – the same rockets that can put a man on the moon could wipe out the whole of the planet in half an hour. That double-edged sword was hanging over the people of my generation – it's a severe psychosis that the whole of humanity has been under for the past half-century.'

Eddie and his friends had no interest in established vegetarian organizations such as the Vegetarian Society and they, like the Dedmans, thought Cranks and Vega were 'really phoney – they ate a lot of cheese and white bread and sweet things'. His favourite eating-house was Greg Sams's Seeds, in London's Bishop's Bridge Road.

> You went down steps into a basement, as if it was someone's house. There were cushions all over the floor and low tables, always a whiff of pot in the background. It was lit with candles on the tables – you couldn't see what you were eating at all. It was the place to go in London.

Eddie, now 55, is no longer 100 per cent vegetarian. He quit the macrobiotic scene 'when it got taken over by a more puritanical set – a load of people who came over from Boston'. Though he still calls himself a Buddhist, he's 'the Tina Turner and Sandie Shaw sort – not extreme'.

Greg Sams, however, who patented the vegeburger, now runs a wholefood business, Harmony Foods. He himself had been a vegetarian by inclination since the age of ten. He set up Seeds in 1967 with his brother Craig. Craig had been converted while at college in America, attracted by the heady whiff of heresy that arose when the US Food and Drug Administration ordered some books on macrobiotics to be burnt. Greg remembers:

> Seeds was great. We offered free meals to people who didn't have any money. Marc Bolan, before T-Rex made it, used to walk across London every day for the free meal. Later on, people used to abuse it – we'd see them arriving in a taxi and then ask for a free meal. Or they'd ask for a pudding, and we'd say that isn't free, and they'd say, 'Oh, I'll pay for that then.' But most of the time it was really idealistic. We were trying to build a better world.

Marti Feldman, John Lennon, Jefferson Airplane and the Grateful Dead all ate at Seeds when they were in London. 'On a macrobiotic diet it was much easier to live life to the full,' says Greg. 'One guy who used to dance at the Roundhouse said it was the only food that kept him going all night – though he admitted he didn't actually like it much.' There were so many requests for recipes that the Sams brothers set up a shop, Ceres, in All Saints Road. 'People used to drive from Wales and Scotland to stock up on supplies. It was specifically macrobiotic: we had a long debate about whether to sell dried fruits, but we decided they were too Yin. Honey was a sticky subject too!'

LIVING LIGHTLY ON THE PLANET ▬▬▬▬▬▬

If we want a more civilized, organic, decentralized, human scale, less boring, and less dangerous society nearly everyone must start working for it quietly, slowly, patiently and knowing what he is doing ... If the great power shortage does come . . . then we shall be forced into a more decentralized and self-sufficient society whether we like it or not. It is better, in that event to like it and be prepared for it and to move towards it.

JOHN SEYMOUR, *Self-Sufficiency* 1973

The Morris Traveller with the moss on the woodwork was definitely the car. I couldn't aspire to one; they were too expensive by that time, but I had a Morris Minor. And there were books – so many books – on alternative sources of power: waterwheels, windmills and so on. And the Whole Earth catalogue, and books on weeds you could eat for free.

KATE HENNINGS

One of the reasons I live up here is so I can shit in a bucket and compost it and put it back into the garden and grow my food, which is a simple and natural cycle that keeps the earth fed as well as keeping the humans fed.

BRIG OUBRIDGE

A parallel road towards green cuisine was being followed by a rather different group of people. The 1970s saw an extraordinary exit of middle-class idealists to the furthest reaches of the British Isles: the foothills of Wales, the Scottish Highlands, obscure corners of Devon and Cornwall. These enthusiasts who decided to run self-sufficient smallholdings were more often 30-somethings in search of a change of direction than fantasizing flower children and work was very much on their agenda. The overt motive was again to get back to nature, restore a sense of comunity and enhance a sense of spirituality. But for some there were also practical considerations. The soaring price of houses was creating a split in the middle class, between those who had struck lucky by getting their feet firmly on what became known as 'the property ladder' (escalator would have been a more appropriate description) before the take-off, and those who had not done so. The only way that the latter could afford to own property was to move to the outer extremities of Britain.

The extremities had another advantage. In the 1970s, there were very real fears of a nuclear war. It seemed quite possible that, through bad luck as much as malevolent intent, the nuclear warheads known to be trained on strategic targets all over Britain could be unleashed. I can remember going to a course run by the Ministry of Defence in Marlborough in 1976 which told us how to construct domestic nuclear shelters and stock them with tinned food and bottled water, allotted us Geiger counters to test the atmosphere for radioactivity, arranged alarm signals of clashing dustbin lids and suggested that farmers with shotguns would 'escort' refugees from bombed conurbations like London and Birmingham into church halls. There was a distinct sense of unreality, like coming out blinking from a cinema, as we left the horrors anticipated in that sedate little town hall and walked back home along the ancient high street. This was the decade in which the Government sent every household that ludicrous leaflet (parodied heartbreakingly by Raymond Briggs in *Where The Wind Blows*) telling us to whitewash our windows and pile chairs around our dining-tables.

Finally, until the North Sea bonanza in 1977, there were genuine fears that oil might run out or be wielded as a weapon by the Middle East. Cans of petrol were discreetly stockpiled all over the country at the news in 1972 that the price would be doubling to (don't laugh) £1 a gallon. Wind and water were regarded with new interest – and there were few places with more wind or water than Wales. The principality, once quietly depopulating, suddenly began to find its remote, supposedly uneconomic farms in demand.

Those with a successful stake in society made the token gesture of the weekend cottage; those without went the whole hog and began to dream of self-sufficiency. There was no more popular guide to the practical whys and wherefores of coping on your own than John and Sally Seymour's *Self-Sufficiency: The Science and Art of Producing and Preserving Your Own Food*. First published in 1973, it ran through editions almost as fast as the Seymours' pet pig ploughed up their vegetable patch. The Seymours had been living on smallholdings, first in Suffolk and then in Wales, for 18 years and John's role model was not hippie romanticism but the pragmatic approach of William Cobbett, the radical yeoman whose *Cottage Economy* had taught him a good deal. *Self-Sufficiency* provided a script for what Seymour saw as the 'post-industrial future', not a backward-looking rural idyll.

Seymour was not a vegetarian. Although he respected the right of anyone to be one, he pointed out that if cows were to be kept for milk they had to have a calf each year, and that every other calf on average would be a bull. Do you let it starve to death, or waste pasture feeding it until it dies of old age?

> You can't hatch eggs to provide yourself with hens without hatching out as many cocks as hens. What do you do with the cocks? If you keep sheep to shear your sheep will breed, unless you are very careful – or would you allow castration, vegetarian?

Seymour's style of self-sufficiency had its roots in the principles of the Soil Association, founded by Lady Eve Balfour in 1946. Lady Eve had been deeply influenced by the agriculturist Sir Albert Howard's thinking on the value of compost, and Sir Robert McCarrison's ground-breaking work on nutrition in the 1930s. Her book *The Living Soil* (1943) put the ideas of both across to form 'two parts of a connected whole'. Her central thesis was that 'the health of man, beast, plant and soil is one indivisible whole; that the health of the soil depends on maintaining its biological balance, and that starting with a truly fertile soil, the crops grown on it, the livestock fed on those crops, and the humans fed on both, have a standard of

Sandals, corn dollies
and home-made bread:
Sally Seymour's vision
of the self-sufficient
kitchen of the 1970s

health and a power of resisting disease, from whatever cause, greatly in advance of anything ordinarily found in this country.'

Within three months, it was sold out. Nine more editions went the way of the first. So much interest and correspondence was generated that a clearing-house for information was set up in the shape of the Soil Association. Its aims were to increase understanding, initiate research and inform. 'In an important sense,' writes Barbara Griggs, 'it was the first public expression of a new environmental awareness that had been quietly growing alongside – and in opposition to – modern civilization.'

Self-sufficiency was about much more than merely keeping oneself alive by growing food, spinning and knitting wool, making tallow dips and learning to use herbs as medicines. It was about 'living lightly on the planet earth'; a rejection of money values, a deliberate assertion that the quality of life is not necessarily enhanced by material wealth. It was also, as Seymour made clear in *Bring me my Bow* (1977), a very English protest at the individual's loss of control.

> The extended meaning [of] … the words self-sufficiency is: an arrangement of society which allows every one of us to have more control over more of the things which affect us, which enable more of us to see the beginning, the middle and the end, of more things that we do, and which enables more of us to know, personally, the people with whom we deal in trade, for whom we have to do things and who have to do things for us. I think it is a fine thing if, when a man bites into a piece of bread, he can think to himself that he knows the name of the farmer who grew the wheat, the name of the miller who milled it, and the name of the baker who baked it.

MEAT IS MURDER

> *Veal in England now tastes of blotting paper – why? Because the calves live in Turkish baths.*
> NANCY MITFORD, *Portrait of a French Country House* 1962

> *Today the feeling gains ground that three birds in each 'nest' of a hen battery is inhumane. Tomorrow it may be technically feasible to use decerebrate hens (that is, hens with their brains removed) which lay eggs just as well and with less fuss.*
> MAGNUS PYKE, *Technological Eating* 1972

> *Charlotte weaves words into her web to prevent the butchering of Wilbur the pig. Rather than accede to the false naming of Wilbur the pig as pork bacon, and ham, Charlotte effects new naming; Wilbur is 'some pig', not a meat-bearing animal, but 'terrific'. Charlotte's words are a form of vegetarian protest literature.*
> CAROL J. ADAMS, *The Sexual Politics of Meat* 1990

Besides health and independence, two larger issues lay behind the move to organic eating and self-sufficiency. Feelings against eating meat were becoming intensified by lurid newspaper, radio and television features that revealed the increasingly horrific way in which it was being produced. The 1950s had seen the growth of factory farming as new technology and the drive for high production introduced battery hens, broiler chicken coops and veal pens. In 1954, 20 million broiler chickens were reared each year; by 1960, annual throughput (dangling upside-down by the feet) was 142 million.

'Thanks to the efforts of Britain's chicken farmers, the population of Britain has become a nation of chicken eaters,' said Mr Ron Mayes, an executive of the British Chicken Association, in 1968. 'Last year we produced 230 million chickens … this means the people of Britain ate 359 375 tons of chicken, about 12 lb [5.4 kg] a head of population. Compare this with 12 years ago, when chicken consumption was 1 lb [450 grams] per head.'

Cattle were being pumped full of hormones and antibiotics and fed on recycled material. Moreover, the giant agribusinesses were using fertilizers and chemicals that many people were uneasy about. The two seminal texts on the subject, both best-sellers, were Ruth Harrison's *Animal Machines* published in 1964 and Rachel Carson's *Silent Spring* (1963).

It was a leaflet on veal production that triggered the investigations of Ruth Harrison, a Quaker, into the new mass-production methods of breeding and slaughtering animals. *Animal Machines* opened the eyes of a hitherto blissfully ignorant public to the gruesome realities that lay behind the neatly dressed meat and poultry they were buying from butchers. Wholefood shops were thronged with new customers and meat sales dropped by 30 per cent overnight. They soon recovered. In one of the opening shots of a war that rages to this day between food reformists and defenders of the food industry, the Ministry of Agriculture's chief scientific adviser said at a press conference on the day that *Animal Machines* was published that, 'Merely to deprive animals of light, freedom and exercise does not constitute an offence … nor, in my opinion, does it cause suffering.'

But the impact of the book endured. 'The word "merely" stuck in a good many gullets,' Harrison remembers. Nauseated by its revelations, many people began to avoid, or at least eat less, meat and to ask for assurances that it was being humanely reared. 'How big a step is it from the broilerhouse to Auschwitz?' asked *The Guardian*, 'The fact is that an increasing contempt for lower forms of life may be leading us, especially in an agnostic age, to a contempt for man himself.'

Peter and Anna Roberts were dairy farmers in Hampshire in the early 1960s who had became increasingly uneasy about the new intensive methods of farming. A letter to a local paper questioning the practices produced such a large response that they decided to dedicate their lives to changing the way things were going. They formed Compassion in World Farming in the mid-1960s. From the start, the organization made the connection between world hunger and the foodstuffs required for the intensive animal-rearing methods that provided the First World with its cheap meat. CWF has led opposition to battery cages for chickens, tiny stalls in which sows were chained, veal crates and cruel practices connected with the export of livestock. In a remarkable publicity stunt that symbolized the backing given by smart young things to the new movement, top model Celia Hammond was suspended in a scaled-up battery cage hung high above Piccadilly Circus. A CWF leaflet on veal calves was featured in *The Archers*, and the Editor waved the same leaflet at television news cameras during an interview after the programme.

In May 1970, top model Celia Hammond demonstrated how it felt to be cooped up like a battery hen. It was part of an exhibition organized by the Compassion in World Farming Trust, aimed against factory farming

In recent years, television documentaries and media publicity showing farming practices bordering on the obscene have succeeded in switching some 15–20 per cent of children away from meat in their teenage years. Not all of them persist with their convictions once they are catering for themselves, but the combination of such concerns with anxieties over the inherent healthiness of red meat has led to plummeting sales of meat and widespread closures of butchers' shops. Squeamish moderns prefer buying meat in neat anonymous packets in supermarkets rather than watching it being hacked off carcasses before their eyes. The butchers who remain keep pigs' heads, liver and lights from view and do their dismembering out back.

Anti-meat-eaters are no longer timid about declaring their position; they too have come out. 'There's one thing you must never do, and that's apologize,' says Peter Cox in *The Realeat Encyclopaedia of Vegetarian Living*. 'Saying, "I'm sorry, I don't eat meat" is demeaning to you, to other vegetarians and to vegans . . . Subconsciously it reinforces prejudice … Turn it around, and say, "If you're going to eat animal flesh today, count me out."'

TOMORROW WE DIE

Slowly we are learning to understand the role in our body's chemistry of every single one of the nutrients so cavalierly discarded in the refining of wheat, sugar and rice, and dismissed as insignificant by a dozen official committees stuffed with nutrition 'experts'. We are learning how disastrous for our health has been the mishandling and mistreatment of natural foodstuffs in the factories of the packaged-food industry. We are beginning to appreciate the damage we are inflicting on human ecology with our unrestrained use of food additives, pesticides and fertilizers.

BARBARA GRIGGS, *The Food Factor* 1986

We no longer take a pride in being great trenchermen, or even hearty eaters. We fear food in a way that would have amazed our ancestors.

ELIZABETH AYRTON, *The Cookery of England* 1974

When we talk about good food, we no longer mean food that tastes good, we mean that dwindling list of ingredients that are not going to kill us.

A. A. GILL, *The Sunday Times* 1994

Rachel Carson's *Silent Spring*, published in 1962, is remembered by many people as the book that changed their thinking about the way large-scale agriculture was developing. Her warnings, backed up with irrefutable evidence, of the effect of DDT and other herbicides eventually struck home. In 1969 the Swann Committee was set up to examine such hazards. It was decided that antibiotics in food, DDT and other herbicides should be banned. This was just the beginning of the horror stories that began to emerge once critics started to look more closely at the sickening distortion of nature performed in the interests of increasing yields of crops and herds. Hormones in meat were suspected of causing cancer and reducing male sperm counts, salmonella was found to be rife in battery chicken farms. Coronary thrombosis began to be associated with the consumption of the saturated fat that was a hallmark of factory-farmed animals.

It was fears of such things, coupled with compassion, that led Kate Hennings to become a vegetarian in 1973.

I'd heard about factory farming, and I think Rachel Carson's *Silent Spring* had been around for a while, but the thing that brought it all together was a programme that described how Marks and Spencer had discovered that the chickens they were selling had had hormone tablets implanted in their necks, and that the tablets hadn't dissolved, so people who were using the chicken necks to make gravy were getting a nice broth of dissolved hormone tablet. And I just thought, God, it's just not safe to eat meat.

The hormone tablet was calculated to make the chickens retain water, which would increase their apparent weight. 'Fitting that together with what I knew of the arms race, it was really the same,' Kate concluded. 'There isn't much that people won't do for profit. It was hard to withdraw from the arms race, because you had no control over that, but at least in the case of eating meat one could say, well, no, I don't want to be poisoned by chemicals and all these things.'

Scares over pesticides in food rose to a crescendo in 1984, when a coalition of environmental groups – the Soil Association, Friends of the Earth and Oxfam – launched PAN UK: the Pesticide Action Network. Their report revealed that the five main crops grown in Britain received an average of 2.3 sprayings in 1979, which had risen to 3.3 by 1982. The record was held by a crop of lettuce which received 46 different sprayings.

Growing alongside the fear that additives were poisoning food was the fear of food itself. In 1977, a United States report warned that excess consumption of fat, sugar and salt was directly linked to heart disease, cancer, obesity and strokes. In Britain, the National Advisory Committee on Nutritional Education recommended an increase in the cereal content of diet (by which they presumably did not mean Frosties), and advised people to eat bread baked from high-extraction flour. The long-term goals were to reduce average consumption of fats by a quarter, saturated fats by half, alcohol by a third, and salt and sugar by half. The proportion of vegetable protein in relation to that of meat was to rise, and the consumption of fibre in the form of fruit, cereals and vegetables was to increase by half. Interim goals were set at one-third of these targets.

The food manufacturers hastened both to defend themselves and to supply new products that met all the new criteria of health and ethical probity. Free-range chickens and Real Meat conjured up visions of happy days down on the farm. Fat-free cream, 'slimmers' chocolate' and diet Coke intimated that their relatively

low calorie count might even get you thinner than if you didn't consume them at all. Surveys and counter-surveys were hurled across a battlefield of scientific obfuscation that left ordinary eaters bemused and insecure camp followers. They struggled to make sense of the algebraic mysteries of the new food value labels (a recent straw poll of 40 customers in Tesco's failed to find anyone who could translate them into meaningful statements about diet) and remained plagued with fears – of anorexia and obesity, of additives and insufficiencies.

Even water, symbol of all things pure, became unsafe. What was chlorine really doing to our insides? Hunches rather than rational reasons led millions of us to switch to bottled water, especially if it came from France in plump green bottles. Then Perrier itself came under fire and there was a renewed purity panic. Consumption of bottled water continues to rise although, at 30 per cent, market penetration in Britain still has some way to go before it reaches France and Germany's 87 per cent or Belgium's 94 per cent. (One reason for that disparity is that Britain has a longer tradition of safe tapwater; the other is that supermarkets here take a 30 per cent profit on each bottle, compared to 2 per cent in France where bottled water is considered a necessity.) In 1994, Michael Rouse, head of the drinking water inspectorate, was reported as saying that water in the tap was purer and safer than mineral water. Of taste, he said nothing. But at blind tastings, said *The Times*, most people cannot tell the difference, and (the final irony) an increasing amount of bottled water served in restaurants is just tapwater filtered through a water-purification plant to remove everything the water companies have put in to make it 'pure'.

The prophecies of doom that began to surround the process of eating in the 1980s have thickened in the 1990s into a very blizzard of vilification. Every month there is something else: additives in white bread, irradiated fruit, mad cow disease in cat food, salmonella in chicken and eggs. In 1994, Esther Rantzen destroyed the credibility of 'barn chickens' on *That's Life* by showing thousands of little scrawny bald-pated heads, beaks clipped, eyes frantic, cooped up by their own body mass rather than wires in supposedly idyllic 'farm' conditions in Northern Ireland. 'Organic milk, what does it mean?' asks Kate Hennings. 'It usually means that the pasture has not had any artificial fertilizers or herbicides put on it. But it doesn't mean that the cows themselves have not been treated, as they are legally obliged to be, with antibiotics against mastitis.'

'Feeding anybody today is a minefield of fear and worry,' wrote A. A. Gill in *The Sunday Times* in 1994.

> Giving a dinner party is a nightmare, with everyone leaving their own favourite poisons on the side of their plate, or, worse, bringing their own life-saving medicaments with them . . . Ingredients move from the blacklist to the three times-a-day menu with the cynical rapidity of Stalin's cabinet ministers – non-food today, hero of the people's alimentary canal tomorrow.

There is a very real danger of overkill. Marguerite Patten, who has witnessed so many changing fashions in her long and productive life as a celebrity cook, criticizes what she calls 'an epidemic of finger wagging'. And she says, 'It frightens me to death because I feel that sooner or later people will say, "Oh no, not another warning, not another scare." And there could be a really serious warning and a lot of people would say, "Oh, another one, I'm not going to listen to that."'

Why are we panicking? There is every excuse for saying that we have never eaten so good. In the late 1980s, statistics recorded the first fall in consumption of sugar, red meat and snack foods since the end of rationing. Most of us are staying fitter and living longer than we have ever done in human history. A dazzling array of desirable and delicious food is on offer, and only a hundred people died of food poisoning in Britain last year, compared with 4000 on the roads, 8000 deaths from cervical cancer and 7000 from AIDS. Half-jokingly, Gill offers an interestingly subtle reason for the frenzied activity of the self-elected food police. In it there is yet again an echo of religion:

> Our tribal unconscious memory associates food with hard work, worry and pain, but our real lives are one long convenience harvest. We have all chosen to invent a new fear and mystique about food; somehow, chucking ready-washed, topped and tailed pre-packaged mange tout into the supermarket trolley doesn't fulfil a deep-seated need to reverence the ultimate life-and-death power of our daily bread.

But the real new frontier is genetics. One reason for the current confusion is that doors have been opened to a whole new landscape of nutritional understanding for which we have as yet no proper maps. At the moment, there are so many gaps in biochemical knowledge that it is impossible to know which anxieties we need to take seriously. Many of the across-the-board recommendations that are made by nutritionists are beginning to look like hammers squashing gnats. 'One of the problems is to be able to predict whether the diet of any one person is going to make a difference to his health,' writes the microbiologist Richard W. Lacey in *Hard to Swallow: A Brief History of Food* (1994). 'The reason for this is that there is a variable and unpredictable capacity of some people to "handle" and eliminate food components that might be damaging in other people. Because these bodily functions are the result of the quota of genes inherited at birth, an important clue is the state of

Facing page: The switch to bottled water. Despite Britain's reputation for safe tap water, more and more homes and offices opt for bottled water in the 1990s

health and longevity of one's parents and grandparents. If only we could choose our parents!'

Work on allergies is steadily ascertaining that individuals may need to tailor what they eat to their own needs. The next stage, no doubt, will be the issue of designer diets to suit our genetic make-up and personal allergy profiles along with our birth certificates.

THE INCH WAR

'The nice thing about diet,' said Dr Hill, 'is that it needs no fancy preparation – and costs nothing. Anybody can do it . . . To get rid of fat, you simply eat less.'
IRIS ASHLEY, 'Beauty is not Magic', *Daily Mail Book of the Home* 1952

I have a theory that the reason that most slimming methods don't work is that they involve eating.
RICHARD W. LACEY, *Hard to Swallow* 1994

Dieting today has become not so much a daily habit as a daily topic of discussion, preferably at table.
MASSIMO MONTINARI, *The Culture of Food* 1994

Plenty edged towards excess in the 1960s and for the first time obesity began to be regarded as more of a problem than undernourishment. René Short raised the issue in Parliament in November 1965. 'Is the Parliamentary Secretary aware that about two-thirds of the people in this country are overweight and that this leads to heart disease, arthritis, posterial backache and flat feet?' she asked. 'Does he not think that it would pay dividends if Parliament were to undertake a campaign to relieve the National Health Service of a good deal of the problems which are caused by over-weight?' As her roll-call of those problems grew more substantial, the impatient Speaker interrupted to ask her to 'slim her questions', but an impact had been made.

In 1967 the Obesity Society held its first meeting and Weight Watchers was introduced from the United States. In the age of Twiggy and the miniskirt, slimming became a lucrative industry. A diet became what you shouldn't eat instead of what you did eat, and patent formulas of every imaginable kind were seized upon. In Sweden they slimmed by eating nothing but potato water, in France they fined down by limiting themselves to red meat and wine. Some diets were so expensive and prolonged that they were paid for on the instalment plan, rather as if one was joining an exclusive club. Most diets involved a shift towards fruit and vegetables and away from carbohydrates and fats; they also involved taking careful note of the nature of the food that was being consumed. The overall effect was to increase critical consciousness about food, although for a substantial number of substantial people the tempting option of buying a much-advertised wonder pack from the

Facing page: The biggest and most successful of the slimming clubs - Weight Watchers and Twiggy, the underweight model whose distinctly unvoluptuous statistics (32-22-32) were the envy of miniskirt-wearers everywhere

chemist's shelf seemed an easier out than taking the short degree in nutrition that so many of the books demanded.

But why are we all so fat these days? In 1970, Phillipa Pullar wrote in her informative history of food and appetite, *Consuming Passions*, that 'The reasons for this epidemic of obesity are more complicated than greed and persuasion. Despite our urbanized affluence, our equality of women, there is evidence of increasing neuroses, anxieties and boredom … Food is being employed as a distraction from the inner emptiness of people's lives. Cases are also noted when food replaces sex. An American psychiatrist recorded the case of a patient who was impotent; whenever he had a strong sexual urge he went, not to his wife, but to the refrigerator.'

On a more prosaic level, the more sedentary our working lives, and the more modern technology eliminates the need for physical effort, the less easy it is to stay slim. Domestically, electricity has replaced elbow grease and in leisure hours television has tempted us to a habit of apathy, an audience mentality that begins with *Playbus* and ends with *One Foot in the Grave*. Demoralized perhaps by the professionalism of *Match of the Day* and Wimbledon, most of us watch other people play games instead of playing them ourselves. The market for our physical energy is so small that we have to dispose of it artificially in fitness gyms or through tedious jogging routines. Finally, a note of comfort: most people on diets to get slim are not in fact overweight.

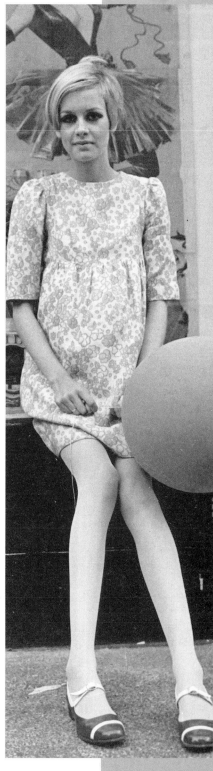

WOMAN THE GATHERER

The counter-culture started out being fairly repressive of women ... there were male hippies and female hippy-chicks – it was a very male-dominated culture, just like the rest of society. They were expected to be earth mother figures, and ended up doing all the cooking and cleaning.

BRIGG OUBRIDGE

It was hard learning to live together. We had a meeting every week, but the rows were usually about the women doing all the work. The men were artists and photographers; they thought they were on a great big holiday.

MARIA DAVIS, 1970s commune-dweller

To compare Spare Rib with commercial magazines is like evaluating the appeal of a spartan wholefood diet by reference to the rich diet of junk food. It is found, inevitably, to be lacking: no layers of sugary icing between the editorial cake and no thick milk chocolate as palliative to the 'hard nuts'. Instead, a heavy textured pudding, somewhat dingy in colour, and somewhat hard work on the jaws.

JANICE WINSHIP, *Inside Women's Magazines* 1987

In the early days feminists had the term vegetarian hurled at them like an insult (Orwell included them in his list of cranks quoted earlier in this chapter); in the 1970s they claimed vegetarianism's messes of pottage as their birthright. Amazon Wholefoods of Digbeth, Birmingham, was just one of many co-ops 'run by women, for women'. Its logo was a double-edged axe.

To an interesting extent, the counter-culture experience of dropping out and returning to a tribal existence, in which life was sustained by eating grains and vegetables rather than the metaphorical 'hunting' that was breadwinning, may have done much to encourage feminism. The patent uselessness of men high on drugs and self-importance when meat and wage-earning were alike off the menu led to a rapid disillusion with the role of 'hippie-chick' and a steady strengthening of women's sense of their own competence. To cap it all, the traditional vision of an early society dominated by man the hunter began to be turned on its head by new research into the origins of civilization. Desmond Morris in *The Naked Ape* (1967):

> We were driven to become flesh eaters only by environmental circum-
> stances, and now that we have the environment under control, with
> elaborately cultivated crops at our disposal, we might be expected to return
> to our ancient primate feeding patterns.

In 1981, the anthropologist Adrienne Zihlman went further, pointing out in *Woman the Gatherer* that, 'An obsession with hunting has long prevented anthropologists from taking a proper look at the role of women in shaping the human adaptation.' As there is inevitably more evidence of meat-eating (bones, tools) than of vegetable and grain consumption, hunting has been given a disproportionate importance, projecting the cultural stereotype of the dominant male into pre-history. Peter Cox agrees that horticulture is far more socially significant than hunting, feeding as it does far more people far more economically than meat-eating.

Whole foods were also the home territory of the earth mother, closely connected with her desire to preserve the health of her children, to say nothing of that of her man. It is no accident that so many of the seminal books that inspired and influenced the direction of food reform were by women such as Lady Eve Balfour, Rachel Carson and Ruth Harrison. In the 1940s, the Housewives League had failed to make a convincing political cause of domesticity because the sources of their discontent lacked a focus. But the obscene idea in the 1960s that woman the provider could also be woman the poisoner, that children might be dying from leukaemia as a result of radiation, possibly from Strontium 90 imbibed through milk, was enough to rally women of all ages and occupations into a protest force of real moment.

In the context of fears of nuclear war, the most memorable image of the 1980s is that of the Greenham Women bent over their cooking fires, encamped for years outside the American missile bases in a vigil that brought them first contumely (the local Little Chef banned them) and finally ungrudging respect. Some, but by no means all, were feminists. Others were ordinary housewives turning up for as long as they could to show solidarity.

Greenham was kept as female territory because the war toys it sought to banish were male territory. The spirit of feminine protest to nuclear war was perfectly defined in a poem written for *The New Statesman* by the archaeologist Jacquetta Hawkes as early as 1958. Notice that the playboy theme resurfaces, but this time women are cast in a maternal role, rather than that of sexual playmate:

> Women have seldom been the great creators
> Rather we have been the continuers, the protectors, the lovers of life, …
> A few men seem to have been possessed of a devil …
> But many more have remained as boys, just boys
> Heedlessly playing. But the spring of the toys they are winding is death.
> We must take power from these madmen, these prisoners, these perilous children.

As more and more women became too busy with their own domestic work and child-rearing, or used any spare time on their hands to go out to work rather than contribute to the community, women lost a great deal of their traditional grass-roots power. Such local organizations as the Women's Institutes and Townswomen's Guild had always been run voluntarily. New organizations with different agendas developed. Some, under the umbrella of the National Council for Women, were specifically aimed at extending equal opportunities and women's political influence, others were concerned with establishing mutual support networks (the Housewives Register, the Pre-School Playgroups Association) and yet others with feminism. But none provided the cradle to grave mutual support of the old Guilds and Institutes.

The only place that almost every woman in the country now goes to regularly once a week is her local supermarket.

Susie Orbach, of *Fat is a Feminist Issue* fame, criticizes the extent to which women sacrifice themselves for the sake of their family.

> While food is something women routinely prepare and give to others, and in that context experience themselves as providing love, nourishment, nurture and care, for themselves, food is dangerous, virtually off limits, or at the very least, to be feared. This is tragically analogous to their position in Western culture where a woman has been designated a midwife to others' activities – her husband's, her children's – to be the person who makes it possible for those around her to function and partake of the world, to nurture them emotionally, to serve them domestically, support them in their needs and desires, while not expecting reciprocal support. The world, like food, is scarcely for her.

But to a degree deplorable to the hardline feminist, many of the survivors of the counter-culture are not ashamed to enjoy just this role. Kate Hennings likes the idea of the earth mother and accepts its constraints: 'I don't think you can be an earth mother and give your child to a childminder … Breast-feeding, home confinement and food are very important parts of the family, of not just the family but of making people feel comfortable.' Nor does she see it as a life sentence, although, she jokes, 'I often say that now, having had 30 years of mothering, I'd like to go off and be a punk rocker or something really outrageous!' But for her, to be 'a midwife to others' activities' is not a tragedy, but a position of power. As she reaps the love that she has sown through the years, providing food remains at the heart of the matter.

> I still feel that in sitting down to a meal and giving food, there's a lot of connections between food and love. And I love the fact that when I go and stay with my older children, they cook for me, and I know that they've given it a lot of thought. There's a lovely dynamic that a lot of people miss when they just see cooking food as being another of those things that is part of a traditional female role. I would never feel in agreement with the feminist view on that, because I think that it's a very powerful role, actually.

SIMPLY DELICIOUS ■■■■■■■■■■■■■

The popularity of vegetarianism really came home to me when I was being interviewed for my latest book, and I realized that instead of my having to defend and justify my views, the journalists interviewing me were themselves vegetarians and users of my books!

Rose Elliot, *Complete Vegetarian Cookbook* 1985

Once vegetarians stopped being cranky figures in sandals and turned into saviours of the planet, to say nothing of the waistline, the stage was set for vegetarian eating to become a mass movement. Exit polenta puritans. Enter the vegetarian gourmet. The career of cookery writer Rose Elliot perfectly reflects the steady growth of interest in food that was not just good for you but good to eat. She first started cooking at the age of 16, when the vegetarian cook at the retreat centre which her parents ran in Sussex suddenly left.

> I'd met and fallen in love with Robert, a man 12 years older than me, and couldn't get away from school fast enough ... To everyone's surprise, including my own, I really enjoyed the cooking ... I started by using family recipes and an old recipe book called *Household Non-Flesh Cookery*, but as I got into my stride I discovered that ideas started to flow.

So many people asked her for recipes that she put them together as a book (by then she had married Robert and had two daughters in quick succession). Called *Simply Delicious* and published in 1967 by the retreat, it was reviewed so enthusiastically by Katie Stewart in *The Times* and by *Woman's Hour* that orders flowed in from all over the country. Rose was asked to give demonstrations, first at Marshall and Snelgrove then on television. Next came a collection of recipes for family cookery and entertaining with the memorable title of *Not Just A Load of Old Lentils*.

Reactions from readers, many of whom treated her like an old friend when they met her at cookery demonstrations or book launches, confirmed Rose's belief that food had a miraculous effect on health. 'Your books changed my life,' said a woman who had been told by a doctor that a chronic digestive condition would mean that she had to stay on drugs for life. There were other similar stories of people who had lost weight or cured arthritis, heart problems, high blood pressure and eczema.

Elliot's approach differs from that of the 'food Leninists' so loathed by the Real Men who don't eat quiche in that she believes in balance rather than elimination. Reducing the fat intake is important, but 'that doesn't mean giving up delicious things like quiches, chocolate, chips, strawberries and cream; it just means you have to plan for them.'

In the greed-ridden 1980s, the decade of infinite choice, vegetarian eating made steady, occasionally exotic, progress. Besides the sense of self-preservation that was daily making more and more people give up meat and experiment with tofu and quorn, the rise of such delights as rocket salad, grilled peppers, olive oil, ciabatta and mozzarella made it harder and harder to see what one was actually missing in giving up meat.

The fashionable nouvelle cuisine added power to vegetarian elbows by making it difficult to see the meat on one's plate. In *All Manners of Food*, Stephen Mennell pins the origins of this most pretentious of all styles of eating to the spring of 1978, when *Elle* reported on two new restaurants in Paris which offered 'a fine, light cuisine, in which flour is banned and vinegar is king instead'. Nouvelle cuisinistes extolled the virtues of steam cooking (something Ur-veggies had been doing for decades), avoided cream as primly as a vegan and made use of the new year-round imports of colourful and exotic fruits and vegetables. The microscopic but exquisitely presented portions on white octagonal plates were initially greeted with enthusiasm by a cohort of gourmets who had been over-eating ever since meat came off the ration, and who were becoming increasingly frightened by scare stories of cholesterol-clogged arteries, septic colons and secretly rotting livers.

Nouvelle cuisine soon got its come-uppance, laughed out of court by such articles as Evelyn Daube's in *The Spectator* in 1984.

> Nouvelle cuisine means dining in a dragged, ragged room full of Fulham anorexics … It is a chef arranging five smears of fish pâté on a plate ah so because the food is like a haiku. It is a gherkin spread out like a flower with a dot of mango gloop in it … It means five blobs of puréed veg on your side-plate and a bill for £72 for three plus VAT. It means you need your head examined.

'Chicken nouvelle cuisine is the same as roast chicken but we get a graphic designer to lay out the veg.'

Above right: Nouvelle cuisine Steak and veg. In this fashion of the 1980s food was beautifully presented but almost inevitably overpriced

But nouvelle cuisine proved once and for all that vegetables and culinary chic were highly compatible. Influences from international cooking styles, many of them traditionally dominated by vegetables, also did wonders to make vegetarian food positively attractive rather than merely good for you. Who could resist the prospect of Coconut Potato Patties from Papua New Guinea, Chestnut Cream from Austria, Plantain Pudding from Jamaica?

Between 1984 and 1994 the number of vegetarians in Britain doubled to 2.5 million adults (4.3 per cent of the population), and the number of people avoiding red meat has tripled. Forty per cent of the population are self-consciously cutting down on the amount of meat they eat. There are almost twice as many female vegetarians as male. One in four of 16- to 70-year-old women are reducing their consumption of red meat and 15 per cent eat little or none.

Supermarkets of the 1990s reflect the desire for healthy food. The bread in this Safeway bakery counter is made with 'Unbleached flour, No animal fats, No preservatives'

Supermarkets have responded to the new trends by providing an impressive range of vegetarian and wholefood products. 'A lifestyle that was once perceived as being dangerously radical is now commonplace,' writes Cox. At current rates of growth – in December 1994 BBC Radio 4 reported that 2000 people a week were becoming vegetarian – there will be 5 million vegetarians, and half the population will have reduced the amount of meat they eat,

Today, vegetarianism may be becoming commonplace, but the messianic zeal of such moving spirits as Peter Cox remains: 'The irresistible logic of a kinder, saner way of living has already touched the lives of millions of people; in the next century it will inspire many millions more ... One day, sooner than you think, we will all be vegetarian ... the logic of vegetarianism is inexorable and inescapable; economically, nutritionally, environmentally and morally.' But, he warns, rising to a climax that takes us straight back to Woodstock and the summer of love,

There is no magic vitamin, no wondrous moral constituent in our food which will generate compassion, consideration and respect. Go vegetarian for selfish reasons, and only you will benefit. Do it for love, and you will change the world.

CHAPTER SIX

The Way We Eat Now

Life's so busy now, there's that much going on, whereas years ago there wasn't and there was more time to sit down and have that family meal. Plus you've got an awful lot of mums working now. I don't think it makes a difference to a family to sit down and have that meal, so long as you all get to see each other and you all know where you're going. It's more important that, at that specific time of day, you all know where you are.

MARGI, housewife and mother of four, Liverpool

It's a matter of juggling around schedules during the week, but we try to eat together if we can. We made a decision that you have to eat, we love food, and so let's make a time together to sit around the table and talk. We'll always have wine, but to be honest, we often have the telly on.

ROSIE, journalist, mother of two, Surrey

Obviously, two is more fun, there's no doubt about that. But there is something tremendously important about the gift of good food, and I think it needs some sort of reverence, so that even if you are alone, you should treat the meal as something special, not walk around the house eating a chicken drumstick.

DELIA SMITH, cookery writer

Food is an opportunity to recreate your identity, to re-make who you might be. And because we've got greater choices, in terms of what products we can buy from supermarkets, the choices are almost infinite.

KATHRYN DODD, co-author of *Young People, Health, and Family Life*, 1994

It's in the kitchen that confidences are exchanged, that family life takes place; it's among the remains of a meal or when you're elbow-deep in peelings that you ask yourself what life is about, rather than when you are sunk in an armchair in the sitting room.

BENOITE GROULT, in *Loaves and Wishes*, 1992

Delia Smith, the nation's favourite cook, produced her first book for the BBC, *Family Fare,* in 1973. But in 1980, she found herself with an unexpected best-seller on her hands in the shape of the book of the television series *One is Fun!* Today's supermarket cabinets certainly endorse Margaret Thatcher's notorious dictum: 'There is no such thing as Society. There are individual men and women, and there are families'. Frozen gourmet meals for one jostle – indeed, rather out-number – the family packs of mince and chicken thighs.

We live in an age of culinary paradoxes; of contrasts between generations, regions, classes, income groups and different stages in the family's own life cycle. Weekday lunches may be in terminal decline for dual-career couples, but they are generally the main meal of the day for pensioners. And though some senior citizens positively enjoy surviving on a sardine, others are booking places on gastronomic coach tours to Alsace-Lorraine. Regular evening meals around the table often fall away in families of young adults, but most small children receive a healthy dose of instruction in table manners. Teenagers eat little and often; their parents stick to the old pattern of three meals a day.

Women may be swopping shopping baskets for briefcases, but that does not mean that this is the end of home-made food: cooking is classed as an art, not a chore, and men and children are starting to take a pride in creating their own kitchen specials. And four of those lonely-looking ready-to-eat individual meals are just as likely to be served up for a weekday family supper as a home-made Lancashire hotpot. What the shifts in eating patterns, some gradual, some sudden, do illuminate are changes in the balance of domestic power, and new ways of organizing family life.

Much is made of the unholy alliance between the microwave and the freezer, but there was none of this dark talk of social breakdown when that equally potent agent of change, the sewing machine, was invented in the 1850s. There are instructive parallels to be drawn between the advance of ready-to-wear clothes and that of ready-to-eat food. Like the food revolution, the clothes revolution liberated and de-skilled women in equal measure. One hundred and fifty years ago, samplers stitched by ten-year-old girls set them on course for the lifetime of sewing that took up much more of women's time than food preparation. Every stitch that was put into sheets, table-cloths and curtains, dresses, suits, shirts and underwear was done by hand, sometimes cursorily, sometimes with a degree of skill every bit as ambitiously elaborate as Cordon Bleu cuisine.

It is significant that the most popular clothes store of our times, Marks and Spencer, began to experiment with modest 'food halls' in selected stores in the late 1950s. Now chilled meals are as important a component of sales (and as imaginatively various in style) as socks and knickers. Last year the company's autumn statement revealed that its £1.2 billion a year turnover in food was almost as large as the £1.4 billion turnover in clothes.

Some foods, like some clothes, are universal. 'Just as blue jeans are worn by both rich and poor, burgers and Coke are available to everyone, from royalty to single-parent families supported on government assistance', writes Gill Corbishley

Facing page: Britain's
best-selling cookery
author, Delia Smith

in *Appetite for Change* 1993. But differences in eating habits can be made as socially or politically aggressive as a red tie or a top hat. 'If I had the choice between smoked salmon and tinned salmon, I'd have it tinned. With vinegar', boasted former Prime Minister Harold Wilson in 1962. 'Foodies are typically an aspiring professional couple to whom food is a fashion', wrote Ann Barr and Paul Levy in *The Official Foodie Handbook* 1984. 'A fashion? The fashion. Couture has ceded the centre ground to food.'

Today the way we eat is, like the way we dress, a means of showing our social identity, an accessory to a lifestyle. We select our diet as carefully as we select our clothes, aware of how both will make us look in the eyes of society, subject to the whims of changing fashions. In fact, we can probably tell more about the person in front of us in the supermarket queue by scanning the contents of their trolley than by looking at the way they are dressed.

INTRODUCING ...

I think people eat what they can afford, basically. If they can afford to have different meals and eat whatever is in the fridge and freezer, they'll eat that. But if money is limited, they've got to put a meal on the table and make the best of it.

MARGI

I'm a terrible housewife. If I didn't enjoy cooking, I would spend a great deal of money in Waitrose ... But I do enjoy it. There is such a pleasure in cooking something nice and everybody sitting down to enjoy it.

ROSIE

I do feel guilty if I eat out of a pan too often – I have to keep proving I've broken away from the stereotype of the grubby, domestically incompetent man on his own. It's about self-respect.

North London bachelor

The everyday voices in this chapter compare and contrast the experiences of two families and two bachelors. Fifty years ago, their differences would have been more noticeable than their similarities; today the opposite is the case. Margi was one of ten children, and her family is still close, with a huge extended family of brothers and sisters, grandparents and cousins. John, her husband, works in the building trade, as does their second son, Carl (18). Their daughter, Tracy (21) also works and their oldest son, Paul, is a university graduate who lives away from the family home in Liverpool. Rosie's family lives in Sunbury-on-Thames, two hundred miles south east of Margi's and is altogether smaller, with only two children and fewer close relations. Rosie is a journalist who works from home and can – and does – flex her working time to suit her family's needs. Her husband Paul, who is a marketing consultant specialising in interactive multimedia technology, is more likely to be away from home than she is. They have two sons Ian (11) and Neil (13) at school.

Both sets of parents value fresh, home-cooked food, and are conscious of the need for healthy eating, but Margi concedes freedom of choice to her young wage-earners and accepts Mathew's predilection for junk food with resignation. Rosie is intenser about avoiding salts, full-fat products and fizzy drinks with meals, but admits that she doesn't always suceed. All members of both families express a sense of the symbolic value of food in the family, and recognize and enjoy certain personal family traditions of eating.

There are also differences. It would be too extreme to say that one family eats to live and the other lives to eat, but the Liverpool family see food more as essential fuel at the end of an exhausting day of physical labour. 'I'd like to see someone come home after a full day's work and eat a salad and not faint afterwards,' says John derisively of government advice on healthy feeding. For them it is the background to relaxing together in front of the television, or at least in the same house. The Surrey family keep food in the foreground. For them, choosing, preparing and discussing the meal is in itself a form of relaxation, and they will eat together at a table although they, too, may sometimes watch television while they eat. Food is an important component of their social identity. 'We live in rampant suburbia,' says Rosie. 'We've got a couple of dozen very good friends, and we often invite them and their families to eat with us.' Eating is a purely private matter for John and Margi – 'People don't usually come round to our house, unless it's family.' But when the extended family does come round for a meal, all three generations - grandmother, sisters, and daughters, help to prepare it.

Families no longer dominate Britain's ten million households, one-third of which consist of couples and one quarter of people who live alone, double the proportion who did so in 1961. Twelve per cent of women over 65 are on their own, compared to only 4 per cent of men, but under 65 the story is reversed: 10 per cent of men live alone (compared with just over 4 per cent 20 years ago). This is a qualitatively new domestic development. Women are more gregarious: only 6 per cent of those under 65 are alone.

But the statistics of loneliness are in part illusion. The figures tell us only the numbers of people who live alone at any one time; not how many do so all their lives. In fact, marriage is as popular as it ever has been. What is changing is when people get married, and how long the marriage lasts. Couples are settling down later, more often than not after a failed experiment or two. A third of all marriages involve at least one second-timer. All this serial monogamy is inevitably punctuated by the periods of solitary 'resting' that are recorded by the census as single households. Life today tends to go through at least three distinct stages: a period of independence, living alone or with friends; a period of marriage or cohabitation (uninterrupted for two out of three couples), and a period of widowhood spent either alone, with friends, or with family.

One influential cause of the increased number of single households is that people are living for much longer. There are now four times as many over-sixties as there were in 1901. They formed 21 per cent of the population in 1990 (one-sixth of them over 80), a proportion calculated to rise to 24 per cent by 2020 (one-fifth over 80). Sixty per cent of those over 80 live alone, most of them widows, as compared with 15 per cent of the 60-64 age group. It is government policy, as well as personal choice, for older people to remain in their own homes for as long as they are able. Cars and telephones make it more possible to keep in touch with families – 70 per cent of those over 60 see a member of their family at least once a week. Vacuum cleaners and washing machines, microwaves and freezers, help out with practicalities.

The same technological easements may well have contributed to the marked increase in the number of bachelor households. A wife to provide home comforts was once seen as a necessity of life for a man (it certainly added years to male life expectancy, though detracting from a woman's). Since feminism altered the terms of the domestic contract, and chilled 'ready meals' solved the cooking problem, far more men are going it alone.

Barry Dainty, who lives in Oldham, has lived on his own since his mother died 15 years ago. He has a good network of friends built around his local church, and positively enjoys his independence.

It's very much more acceptable to live on your own now. Fifteen or twenty years ago I think you were looked on as being rather odd if you lived by yourself. But now it seems to be fashionable to live on your own. It certainly seems to be increasing among single men.

Cookery expert Nigel Slater identifies a '1980s generation of Thatcher's bachelors'; proud-to-be-single young men who lived in smart apartments, drove fast cars and spent a lot of time in restaurants.

Cook-chill meals for one were a real yuppy symbol; it was even fashionable to discuss them at dinner parties. They were about status, a good job, money and being too busy to cook. Now cooking has become about caring again, part of the new 1990s ethos, and people are cooking a lot more. It's not just about families. Cooking is about not cheating yourself of pleasure. Giving someone food you've made is like giving them a present; it's the greatest way of saying, "I love you, I care about you."'

Gratification by eating, be it instant or teasingly postponed in a miasma of marinades, is as much the mood of the 1990s as caring and sharing. Some have even asserted that, post-AIDS, the dangerous delights of free love have been sublimated in promiscuous eating. 'Junk food … has acquired intimations of pleasurable naughtiness – of daring to be unhealthy for the sake of speed and the assuaging of an addiction', writes Margaret Visser in *The Rituals of Dinner* (1991). Certainly, while the rest of British industry has been ailing and wailing, the food giants have been laughing all the way to the bank.

THE FOODIE BOOM

Food is, delightfully, an area of licensed sensuality, of physical delight which will, with luck and enduring tastebuds, last our life long. Taste, texture, sensuous combinations, do not have to be conjured with expensive ingredients. The smell of newly baked bread is almost a cliché for wholesome pleasure, the eggplant or aubergine dip for which Rani Kabbani gives us the recipe is, even in countries where the vegetable has to be imported, a far from extravagant dish, yet its tenderly verdant smokiness is Lucullan in its luxury.

ANTONIA TILL, introduction to *Loaves and Wishes* 1992

Foodism being fashion, you don't live with the same menu for years – you discover, embrace, explore minutely, get bored, and move on tomorrow to fresh meals and pastas new.

ANN BARR AND PAUL LEVY, *The Official Foodie Handbook* 1984

I'd love to be a chef and have my own restaurant.

IAN aged 11

In a 1948 essay, T. S. Eliot wrote that one symptom of the decline of culture in Britain was an 'indifference to the art of preparing food'. There is a line in *The Waste Land* that runs: 'The typist home at teatime, clears her breakfast, lights her stove, and lays out food in tins.' He would be heartened by the British eating scene today. Élitist foodies, first christened with malevolent wit by Ann Barr in *Harpers and Queen* in 1982, have widened their horizons in the last decade, thanks to television food programmes, sophisticated new food technology and the rise and rise of supermarket culture. Cooking is now a widely popular leisure activity in Britain, and television cooks have enticed many people into the kitchen who would have stayed well away a generation or two ago. John remembers his own conversion well:

Just before the big picture on Saturday afternoon there was a brilliant half hour programme on cooking on BBC2 ... It was dead easy to follow, you know, idiot's guide to cooking. Margi was out shopping at the time and there was this programme on spaghetti bolognese, which I'd never eaten till that day – the only spaghetti we got was in tins. They showed you going round the supermarket, picking up the stuff ... how to brown the mince and put the onions in ... And I thought, instead of watching the picture, I'll go and get the stuff. And I went out and got it and cooked this meal, and when Margi came in, she found I'd done it all. And from then on I started to take a bit of interest.

Supermarkets, once criticized as alienating, are now seen as temples to gastronomic ingenuity. Even tins of food for cats, dogs and babies come in gourmet versions. 'The supermarkets have done an awful lot to bring in the unusual things that we're seeing on television and discovering on holidays,' says Nigel Slater. 'The food is now there, the ingredients are now there, and the whole thing has just exploded. You can cook something from anywhere in the world tonight for supper.'

Contrasting the zombies moving down the aisles in the cult 1970s film *Stepford Wives* with the 1990s television game show *Supermarket Sweep* emphasizes the extent to which supermarkets are now felt to be a fun part of everyday life for men, women and children alike. We are learning a new sort of loyalty: a commitment to the type of supermarket we patronize rather than to any one particular shop. The Lords of the Aisles are tightening their grip on us by voluntarily taking over the nanny image that government is so keen to be rid of. Sainsbury's knows best. Posters, labels, recipe leaflets and television advertisements guide us around the new wonderlands of choice, telling us what is good for us, how we should cook it, even what we should eat. It also seems to break down the traditional British reserve, and make the supermarkets altogether more friendly places. Barry:

> When I've been wandering around Sainsbury's with one of their recipe leaflets in my hand trying to remember what I want, the number of people who've said to me, 'You want to try that, it is good, you know, I've done it, but try this in it, and have you tried the other one?'

Such meetings are taken a stage further by experiments in deliberately encouraging close encounters of a romantic kind. The well-established Californian fashion for using supermarkets as contact agencies for single people has now arrived in Europe, reported Herdis Skov in *The Guardian* in 1994.

> Every Thursday between 6 and 9 p.m. you can hunt free-ranging quarry in Quinnsworth at the Merrion Centre in one of Dublin's more exclusive residential areas. Every customer who arrives unaccompanied – and who can confirm that he or she is single – is offered a glass of wine. Gentlemen are provided with a red rose and ladies with a packet of Rolos . . . Customers can inspect each other as they roll their shopping trolleys along the aisles. The idea is that you offer your rose or your chocolate to an irresistible customer before you leave the premises.

The innovation has altered the ratio of men and women customers from the store's usual 25:75 to 50:50, and increased the number of singles to over 400 on Thursday nights. Most are 25-35 years old and in good jobs. A survey revealed that the new customers were tired of having to go to nightclubs or pubs to find companions, and found it easier to judge what people were like from their shopping baskets than from their cars or their clothes.

But supermarkets are not the whole story. Without the even more powerful agency of television, the democratization of gourmandizing could never have happened so fast. All through the post-war period, television cooks of the times have accurately represented, perhaps even in part created, the mood of the nation's kitchens. In the 1980s and 1990s they have burgeoned as never before, driving viewers ever more swiftly towards Barr and Levy's 'fresh meals and pastas new'. From the step-by-step guidance of the famously infallible and reassuringly ordinary Delia Smith, we graduated to the exoticisms of Keith Floyd and Sophie Grigson. Now we have a daily diet of foodie viewing: quizzes such as *Ready Steady Cook*, magazine programmes such as *The Food Programme*, hugely popular sitcoms based on food like Lenny Henry's *Chef* and even historical documentaries.

Above: Keith Floyd demonstrates his art for native Australians in the television series *Floyd on Oz*

Left: The popular sitcom *Chef*. Lennie Henry with co-stars Claire Skinner and Roger Griffiths

Television is responsible for presenting cooking as a glamorous hobby for men, women and children alike
Below left: Junior Masterchef of 1994, Camilla Askaroff.
Below right: Raymond Blanc training chefs

Facing page: Boys are becoming as interested in cooking as girls now that the status of careers in catering is soaring

Twinned with books that enable viewers to make real meals from the screen fantasies – or at least to signal culinary aspirations from coffee tables – the soup operas are set fair to become even more popular than soap operas. The status of the cook is changing rapidly. Children brought up on *Junior Masterchef* are as likely to want to be chefs as lead guitarists, and a new, quite classless career path to fame is taking would-be Floyds and Grigsons off to catering colleges instead of universities. Eleven-year-old Ian:

> It's the one living I want to do. I like finding new recipes and trying them out. I usually cook at weekends, Sunday dinner, or when I have friends round ... Some people call me a cissy for cooking, but I don't think so, and they're going to be the ones who get stuck when they're older!

Television's transformation of cookery from an essentially feminine chore to a glamorous hobby for men, women and children alike has probably done more to make women's liberation domestically acceptable than any number of furious feminist tracts. Carrots, especially sautéd in butter and sprinkled with coriander by the likes of Raymond Blanc and Robert Carrier, are always more efficacious than sticks. It is no longer regarded as patronizing to give women cookery books for Christmas, and in seriously foodie families it will be the man who receives *A Winter's Tale* – Elizabeth David's last word on the history of ice and ices - and the woman who has her nose in Malcolm Gluck's *Superplonk*.

But *Masterchef* menus are not for everybody. 'They're fantastic, but they're not our type of meal,' says John. 'I defy anyone to fill me up with one of those meals. I say to myself, "Could I dig a big trench the next day after eating that, because that's what it means, if you're going to eat, get your energy. It's like charging a battery overnight. If the meter runs out half-way through the night, you know you're not going to have enough energy for the next day.'

As yet, sons Carl and Mathew are unconvinced by the brave nouvelle order. Mathew, aged eight, told interviewers that 'My mum does most of the cooking, and I don't think boys should cook, because my dad doesn't cook that often.' Asked who'd cook if he got married, he said, 'probably my wife – not because I'm lazy; I'd do things for her, but I'm not a very good cook. When we do cookery at school, the teachers help us on every single thing.' And at the end of a hard day's work, Carl likes to find a meal ready for him. 'It's mum's job to cook. She wants us to be fed properly, so she'll cook for us. … What will I do when I leave home? I'll get a slave to cook for me.' But despite the joke, Carl is more than capable of cooking a meal.

Their older brother, Paul can also now cook for himself, although when he left home, says his father, 'I felt terrible – how was he going to survive, he'd never cooked an egg in his life. Then it hit me that it's wrong to do everything for them; you should teach your kids to cook.' But at university, Paul shared digs with a Thai student who taught him to cook very well indeed. And when he comes home now, he treats the family to a taste of Asia.

FOOD ON THE MOVE

It is now a requirement for modern youth that on the few occasions he is required to walk he also has to eat. Munching between outlets of microwaved burgers provides the means. Moreover he has the pure unmitigated pleasure of dropping the polystyrene box onto the ground, giving it a kick as if it were a football and seeing it come to rest in the gutter. He has, like a dog lifting his leg to a tree, left his mark on the environment.

RICHARD W. LACEY, *Hard to Swallow: A Brief History of Food*, 1994

Surveys can no longer keep up with the rate at which meals are being consumed out of the home. Including take-aways and pizza home delivery services, they now account for almost half of the average household's meal occasions. By the end of the century, two out of three meals will be purchased and consumed outside the home, says the sociologist Joanne Finkelstein. The inexpensive local restaurant is viewed as 'a benign forum in which to meet others, pass the time, alter the daily routines, begin a love affair or observe the latest trends. In all instances it is thought to be a pleasurable way of participating in the ebb and flow of public life.' It also emphasizes individualism rather than the co-operation that is typical of a family meal.

Dining out is an opportunity for the individual to express private preferences, tastes and desires. Even though the practice of dining takes place at the heart of the busy public domain, it is still, paradoxically, thought to be an activity expressly for individualistic pleasure … The anonymity of the restaurant allows roles and fantasies to be played out – whether in the familial fantasy of fast food chains or the luxury and romance of the fashionable bistro.

Again, technology has hastened the trend and improved quality. Institutional canteens and restaurants alike have taken advantage of pre-prepared products. From the nutty brown bread and freshly made fruit salads of the Granary Restaurants in motorway service stations to the microwaved dishes created by Clement Freud for sale in Intercity buffet cars, never have so many been fed so fast by so few. Spotlessly clean vans full of chilled and frozen delicacies speed to restaurants all over the country from factory food processing centres.

In the cities and suburbs, shopping centres will soon be as accurately described as eating centres. Everywhere in the land, McDonald's rather than the youth club is

From a very early age McDonald's is the eating and meeting place to see and be seen

Shopping centres such
as London's Brent Cross
now provide a day long
service of meals formal
and informal

the place for the younger set to see and be seen. Where else, after all, is there to go? Chain restaurants have a special appeal for anyone unused to eating out. Their identical architecture, decor and menus provide familiarity, and the protocol to be observed is always the same and clearly signed. 'Queue here', 'Pay here', 'Please wait to be seated', 'Would you like a drink before your meal?', 'Can I take your order?'

This is an international urban phenomenon, not a British aberration. Even in France, birthplace of the gourmet, the popularity of the formal restaurant is declining as canteens, fast food outlets and casual bistros increase. Finkelstein is not happy about the changes. She argues that eating out is 'a constraint on our moral development and, subsequently, a rich source of incivility'. Dining out is 'stylized and overburdened by social prescriptions', so the act protects the individual from real human contact. We dine among strangers and, in what is essentially a financial transaction, 'a degree of impersonality and trivialization of human relationships takes place. Money engenders a callous and calculative orientation which heightens individual self-interest or egocentricity.'

Set against this thought-provoking but perhaps pessimistic analysis are the evident virtues of the new rituals of eating. Sunday lunch in a local pub, or a quick evening meal together in an Indian or Chinese restaurant, can offer gatherings of friends or family groups an environment in which they enjoy each other's company with none of those ignoble anxieties about 'keeping up with the Joneses', battles for parental control or the physical and mental exhaustion of the cook which accompanies the preparation of elaborate meals at home. And when the cook's time, as well as the ingredients, is properly costed, eating out may well be more economic than eating in. But what is the new trend doing to families?

EATING AT HOME

Even if you only take 30 minutes over it, the daily meal does shape your life. It's a focus of the day. But because families eat so differently now, because the daughter's a vegetarian, the son only wants pizza, dad wants meat and two veg, and because getting everyone, with all the different things they do, together at the same time is so complicated, I think the old eating rituals are changing … And I think it's rather a good thing, this break-up of the family meal. Everyone going off, doing their own things. I'm all for it.

NIGEL SLATER, food writer

What goes on at mealtimes doesn't shape or create relationships; it only reflects and dramatizes pre-existing relationships.

ANNE MURCOTT, social anthropologist, 'The Decline of the Family Meal', talk for *The Food Programme*, ABC Radio National, 1993

Towards the end of the 1980s, rumours of a nation eating on the streets led to many panic-stricken claims that the family meal was on the way out, taking family values with it. Recent surveys tell a different story. Mintel research into eating habits in June 1993 revealed that a very high proportion of adults eat with their partners or other members of their households on a very regular basis. Eating a meal together is still the most important social event of the day for most families. But 'together' is a relative term, nor is everyone eating the same thing. And the bigger the family, the less often everyone meets up. 'Some 91 per cent of two-person households ate together every day or most days, compared with 74 per cent of households with five or more members,' says the report. 'This was largely because of the logistics of co-ordinating the varied commitments of different members of the family.'

Frequency of households eating together, June 1993	
Base 932 adults	*%*
Every day/almost every day	57
Most days	16
Only at the weekend	9
Rarely	7
Never	1
Only one person in household	10

Source: *BRMB Mintel*

The most marked shift since the war in British domestic eating has been an absolute decline in the number of 'proper meals' consumed at home. The cooked breakfast is fading fast. In 1958 the cookery writer Evelyn Cowie could say in a little book devoted entirely to breakfast that 'the English breakfast, whatever its merits or faults, is without parallel. It has become a national institution, and like all such institutions attracts both the support of native traditionalists and the critical amazement of foreigners.' Today it is only an occasional Sunday special for four households out of five.

Shelves upon shelves of cereal packets reveal the fact that the traditional English breakfast is a thing of the past

It is ironic, considering that classic image of the 'cornflake packet family', that few products have accelerated the decline of eating breakfast together more than packaged cereals. 'A bowl of porridge is something a housewife serves to a family at a shared meal,' points out Magnus Pyke. 'A packet of cornflakes is suited to an individual alone.'

But cereals have not been the only substitute for a nourishing first meal of the day. A 1988 survey by Kellogg's discovered that 25 per cent of Britons ate only bread or a roll for breakfast, and a staggering 17 per cent of adults and 9 per cent of children ate nothing at all. (That breaks down as 7.5 million adults, 500 000 children under the age of 12, and a million teenagers.) Only 11 per cent of us ate fresh fruit and a mere 3 per cent yoghurt. 'The opportunity exists for a quick (microwaveable) healthy, cooked breakfast product,' noted a Taylor Nelson market research survey in 1988.

Some nutritionists believe that breakfast should supply one-quarter of the body's daily needs for energy and protein, and that children in particular cannot adapt successfully to the complete omission of the first meal of the day. Considering the remarkable success of the Oslo breakfast introduced by the Peckham Experiment in the 1930s (see Chapter 1), the decline of breakfast is perhaps the most dispiriting of any modern trend in eating. Its absence sets in train the need for snack foods at short intervals throughout the day, an eating habit which both encourages any tendency to obesity and makes it less likely that a properly balanced nutritional evening meal will be eaten at all. Ironically, there is evidence that skipping breakfast is regarded as a way of getting slimmer. Most of the non-breakfasters are young women.

On the other hand, the Kellogg's survey, like all the other national food surveys, does not cover food eaten outside the home. Many of those missing breakfasts were eaten in a café on the way to work, either to avoid the rush hour or, indeed, familial stresses. For some, breakfast has become part of work itself. 'In the 1980s a new type of working – "macho working" – became increasingly prevalent,' *The Times* reported in 1990. 'An urge to perform seemed to overtake people, perhaps most notably in the City … It became *de rigueur* to arrive at the office before everyone else and to be the last to leave. The "power breakfast" was born, the better to get meetings out of the way before the rest of the day started.' According to Margaret Visser in *The Rituals of Dinner*:

> Feeling rushed is an important component of our economy … We eat out or buy ready-prepared food to eat at home in order to save time, but also – more insidiously – because we feel that we have no time to do otherwise. Many of us never really learn to cook, and therefore cooking remains not only time-consuming but unrewarding.

The food historian John Burnett believes that urbanization and rising real incomes have encouraged the use of 'stress foods' with high sucrose contents and 'snack foods' eaten between meals. 'The latter have seen a spectacular growth recently to total sales of £1000 million in 1986, of which potato crisps alone were valued at £585 million and savoury snacks at £242 million; the biscuit market added a further £930 million.' The Taylor Nelson survey found that snacks and light meals accounted for 40 per cent of in-home eating occasions. In this context, food is not so much a source of nutrition as a means of immediate oral gratification, of comfort, even entertainment. 'When I go home, I eat loads of times, and after I've eaten, I'll wait for an hour or so, and then eat again. I eat while I'm watching television,' says Mathew.

But there have been other potent influences on the slow murder of the nutritious lunch. The problem of skimped breakfasts was exacerbated by cuts in school meals and milk programmes. 'Maggie Thatcher, the milk monitor, robbing the milk off the kids: that was a disgrace,' says John. The assurance that children were all getting at least one square meal a day during term was ended by the policy changes in 1980 which removed responsibility for school meals from central government and passed it to local authorities.

Forced to look to costs, most schools have installed cafeteria services, many run by private caterers who are much more concerned to tempt children to spend than to ensure that they all eat healthy meals. Even though nutritionally desirable

Below: Food on tap. Fizzy drinks, crisps and chocolate instantly available from a swimming-pool vending machine

Facing page: lunch means a bag of chips for a great many of today's schoolchildren

products are available, too often they are little more than window dressing to veil the fact that sales are dominated by crisps, fizzy drinks and chocolate. Self-service snacks and the vending machine, blind to bad behaviour and emotionally neutral, have replaced the discipline of a hot lunch with a prefect sitting at the head of the table to monitor manners.

A considerable number of children eat nothing at all, but disappear into the boundary hedges with a packet of cigarettes acquired with their lunch money on the way to school. In the East End of London in the late 1980s, a survey quoted by Burnett revealed that 20 per cent of 10- to 11-year-old boys and 30 per cent of girls were regularly fasting for 18 hours. 'There was strong evidence that this was tending to loss of scholastic performance.'

Is the government right to be concerned at the quality of the diet eaten by some families? A study undertaken by Manchester Polytechnic showed that the unemployed eat the least well of any social group, and that the best food is reserved for men and children. Nutritionists point to a downturn in the quality of the nation's eating since the mid-1970s. 'In 1976 the average energy intake for the first time stood at 95 per cent of recommended value,' points out John Burnett. In the last 20 years, the downward trend has continued. But food surveys also show that the poor

Casual eating and obesity
are part of everyday life in
Britain in the 1990s

generally buy food very effectively, obtaining a third as much energy and protein
and twice as much vitamins A and D per penny spent as wealthy families.

It is possible to argue that a sedentary population with a high rate of unemployment requires less energy than a physically busy one. The average working
man probably ought to eat much more food, and possibly different food, from his
officebound counterpart. Nor is it easy to keep up with the constant stream of
contradictory nutritional diktats that are rapped out in the media. In the long run,
how much difference does following an ideal diet make? Richard W. Lacey can come
up with nothing more specific in a chapter on the subject in *Hard to Swallow* than
'an increased life expectancy of 1–2 years, perhaps as much as 10'.

FADS AND FUSSINESS

*Why do so many children eat poorly? Most commonly because so many parents are conscientious
about trying to make them eat well. You don't see many feeding problems in puppies, or among young
humans in places where mothers don't know enough about diet to worry.*

Dr Spock's Baby and Childcare for the Nineties, 1992

*Most families see teaching children how to handle knives and forks and so on as part of their task
of socializing children. But as they get older, there seems to be a loosening of that kind of control.*

KATHRYN DODD, social anthropologist

In a well-run Victorian kitchen, every single item of food was accounted for. Larders, and the first refrigerators, were actually locked in between mealtimes to prevent depredations. There were heavy penalties for 'raiding the larder', a nursery crime carried out by tearaways like Richmal Crompton's William in defiance of the ordered passage of the day's mealtimes. Today, there are fears that anarchy rules in the kitchen. Grazing is not just what cows do. Juvenile likes and dislikes are religiously catered for although they may defy all logic and the nutritional food Leninists to boot. Like many children of his age, eight-year-old Mathew is 'just not into vegetables' (although he is aware that they are supposed to be good for him), but nor does he like red meat.

> I hate mushrooms and cabbage, and potatoes and, er, one of the most valuable vegetables, er, broccoli. I hate onion but I like fruit. I'm a cereal person, but some people call me a vegetarian. I used to be into fishcake, but now I don't like that because of the fish. I don't like lasagne because it's got little red things in it. Do I ever eat proper meals? Probably not. I eat toast.

He eats in a succession of crazes, often sparked off by television advertisements. His older siblings, Carl and Tracy, both date their own 'fussy eating' from the change from primary school, where they had to eat everything up, to secondary school, where they were allowed to choose what they liked. 'And then when we went home, we used to say, don't like this, don't like that, want something different.' Now Carl loves any sort of pasta, but the only Italian food Tracy will eat is pizza. 'Chicken Kiev is my thing at the moment,' she says. 'I'll probably eat it for a couple of weeks, and then get fed up with it, so we'll find something else.'

Interestingly, this now very common behaviour among children – a few weeks exclusive enthusiasm for one item, and then an absolute rejection of it – closely resembles food experiments with tiny babies carried out by Dr Clara Davis in the 1950s. Her trials showed that, given a wide range of choice, tiny babies would select a balanced diet although they might spend a week on nothing but egg and the next devoted to carrot purée. It was this discovery, coupled with a determination to avoid the psychological traumas associated with eating identified by Freud and his followers, that formed the basis for the permissiveness in eating habits recommended by Dr Spock and most other childcare experts.

But what would have happened if Dr Davis had offered the babies only the crisps and lemonade, coco pops and burgers that now seem to dominate children's food preferences? Spock advises parents to 'stay firm on the fizzy pop' (without saying how) and Penelope Leach's best-selling baby care manuals tell parents to be wary of convenience foods. 'Although frozen foods can have the same nutritional quality as fresh food, canned and dehydrated foods are often nutritionally poor. A bowl of tinned tomato soup may fill your baby's stomach but it will not provide many calories or many useful nutrients'. But Leach too is sanguine that most children will eat a balanced diet if they are offered enough good things and left to themselves, especially if multivitamin drops are provided.

Parents remain anxious but confused. Didn't they say on Radio 4's trusty *Food Programme* that vitamin pills and drops were useless? Or will that be disproved in another survey, probably financed by the billion-dollar vitamin supplement industry, next week? Others put their feet up after reading Dr Spock's opinion that 'Children have a remarkable inborn mechanism that lets them know how much food and which types of food they need for normal growth and development. It is extremely rare to see serious malnutrition or vitamin deficiency or infectious disease result from a feeding problem.'

Although parents see the evening meal as an essential focus for family life, most teenagers thoroughly enjoy the independence of choosing food for themselves from the refrigerator or freezer. Kathryn Dodd's research into the eating habits of 64 London families with teenagers aged between 15 and 17 found that half of the adults said it was 'very important' to eat together, but only a quarter of the children did so.

'We got used to using the microwave when Mum was on evening shifts,' says Carl. 'If it didn't have a ding at the end of it, we wouldn't eat it!' Ian and Neil also like to choose what they eat for themselves – Saturday night's meal is their decision, and Rosie's choice of meal during the week is governed by their shifting likes and dislikes. But the range of foods that all the children select from is far more varied than anything that was offered in the old days of 'eat up your greens or there won't be any pudding.' 'My favourite starter is cantaloupe melon and Parma ham,' says Neil. 'I know it's quite expensive, but it tastes really good.'

Dodd's research team identified five different ways in which teenagers handled the domestic eating situation. 'Integrators' allowed their parents to keep a close grip, accepting the adult view that 'eating together as a family' was an essential forum for communicating and dealing with problems. The children's escape from parental control was postponed, perhaps indefinitely. 'Resisters' were teenagers who used the rejection of the family meal to rebel against their upbringing and the family itself, often by announcing that they were vegetarians, or on a diet. Conflict in these cases 'was associated with a sense of powerlessness in respect of family events'; most were girls from Asian backgrounds whose parents were uneasy about Western customs.

A third 'spoilt' group opted out of family meals partially or totally, but continued to be serviced by their mothers, often with separate meals. This created much more work for her but was seen as a 'gift' to the young people, a way of keeping them attached in the future. Such children were often the youngest in the family, and much more likely to be boys, and their mothers were generally at home rather than working. There was also a small group of 'detached' young people, who ate completely autonomously except on Sundays.

But by far the largest group was the 'delegated'. In these families, parents had voluntarily handed over responsibility for diet to the young people, or it had been unproblematically negotiated, and the work of cooking was often shared. In most cases, the fact that the mother was employed precipitated a more equitable distribution of work.

In reconstructed families, especially if fathers (who very rarely read childcare manuals) are preparing food for children they are not used to cooking for, new

Television has done as much to change family eating habits as convenience foods: programme times rather than meal times determine who will eat when

tensions can arise. Kathryn Dodd remembers a father who used to race home from work to cook for the teenage children of his first marriage after he had taken over custody of them.

> He was outraged if the children didn't eat up the food he'd cooked for them, or if they took their plates off the table and sat in front of the television. He felt they were abusing the effort he had made. It was as though the children were much younger, you know, when parents feel they can say, 'Eat your dinner up', as part of the socializing and disciplining of children.

Negotiations of this sort are becoming more necessary as it becomes more common for older children to remain at home, either because of the high cost of alternative accommodation or because they have no job. Failure to negotiate such situations successfully is one cause of such conditions as food refusal, anorexia and bulimia; it is also reflected in the number of young people who would rather live on the streets than with their families – or who have been thrown out by them in anger.

Where does this leave table manners? 'The more you try to impose rules and regulations on eating and table manners, the clearer it becomes to the toddler that the meal table is a marvellous place for a fight,' warns Leach.

Of course, it is up to parents to choose how and when to discipline their own children, but if you choose mealtimes you may pay a high price. I have known families who had got themselves into such a vicious circle over a toddler's meals that the whole family's life was ruined by it, often for months at a time.

Both the families interviewed see the meal table as a good place for teaching 'basic manners' and values. They are conscious of not being as strict as their parents were, but they believe that children should behave respectably. 'Our boys are veterans of restaurants,' says Rosie. 'You could take them out to dinner and they wouldn't disgrace us. Manners are very important – it's about being civilized. They give you an edge on life.' John remembers taking Carl away with him when he was a little boy of 12. 'We went for a meal in a restaurant,' says John, 'and it dawned on me, of course, at home he only ate with a fork, because we hadn't said this is how you eat, we'd just let him get on with it. After that we made a point of teaching him to eat properly.'

KEEPING SUNDAYS SPECIAL

I was talking to a couple of the lads, and they said to me, 'Oh, we don't have Sunday roast any more; we just have spaghetti bolognese or something.' I said, 'Ugh, how could you do that on a Sunday?' It's the climax of the week, when you can come in and say, 'Where's my Sunday dinner? I like my roast parsnips and the taste of gravy on a Sunday; it stems back to when my mum used to make it every week.'

JOHN

For most families, the Sunday meal cooked at home is still sacred in theory at least. The Surrey family regard it as an important ritual but they have moved it to the evening because of hobby and sporting commitments during the day. The children (young enough still to be model 'integrators', in Dodd's terms) are enthusiastic, and help to prepare it.

IAN: We have a proper, big dinner on Sunday evening ... And me and Neil help with the cooking by peeling the vegetables, and laying the table.
NEIL: We like all the trimmings, stuffing with roast chicken, Yorkshire pudding with beef, because we've liked that all our lives, and it's nice to have a Sunday meal, anyway.

IAN: We feel that if you don't eat together as often, then families just start falling apart.

NEIL: Yes, they'll start to drift if they don't communicate and eat together and things.

IAN: And if we don't help, we'd get lazy.

NEIL: And also the parents start to get a bit annoyed, because they're doing everything and we're not doing anything so we feel it's a bit necessary to help to stay out of trouble. But it is nice to have a good traditional meal on Sunday, because it sort of sums up the whole week. It's relaxing as well.

But Sunday lunch seems to be easier to keep going when children are small, or as a means of entertaining friends, than when teenagers are tugging at their familial leashes. 'They always did eat Sunday dinner with us, but they don't any more,' acknowledges Margi. 'They've changed; they're growing up.'

Sunday is changing too. Because of the enormous increase in car ownership, it is now a day for excursions rather than simply spending the morning cooking and the afternoon sleeping off lunch. Now that more and more shops are staying open, Britain's main leisure activity, mooning round the shops pretending to be hunter-gatherers, can take place on its main leisure day. This does not necessarily mean that families are spending less time together: it is just that the places where they are spending it are different.

They are still likely to look for a 'proper meal' somewhere. Fifteen years ago Sunday was a culinary desert. Today Alton Towers and garden centres, National Trust properties and shopping malls all take pains to offer good family food at week-ends. In pubs, children are no longer classed with dogs as undesirables and the old, bleak, closed-off 'family room' merges imperceptibly with the rest of the establishment. Restaurants are finding Sunday lunch big business, and their menus are rapidly adapting to the new situation, making it easier and cheaper than it ever has been for families to go out and eat 'as a family', with junior menus and half portions, even free meals for children.

Swinging singles, busy all week being different and original, turn surprisingly traditional on Sundays. Nigel Slater lives in a house full of bachelors who all cook Sunday lunch for friends in their individual flats.

It's the focus of the week, the big Sunday meal. The structure is the same – it's always lunch, not an evening thing. But it's friends coming over rather than family, and it won't necessarily be, in fact it inevitably isn't, the roast and two veg. And it's more relaxed, more informal. I actually find sharing food with friends more enjoyable than sharing food with the family. There is no pressure, the conversation is different, less inhibited. And it's the best way to get to know people. Much better than the forced sociability of family eating.

Christmas is Sunday writ large, the most important family ritual of the year. 'It's the Sunday dinner to beat all Sunday dinners,' says John. For him, having all the children and the family present is an essential part of the celebrations. Nigel Slater is more iconoclastic. 'When you bring together aunts and uncles and grannies and grandads who normally wouldn't spend any time together at Christmas, they don't necessarily want to be there. They just feel they have to be because of this ritual. It's rather controlled, rather contrived.'

COOKING FOR FRIENDS

Eating without conversation is only stoking.
MARCELINE COX, *Ladies Home Journal*, 1943

My friends are like family. When I'm alone I'll eat on the sofa, but I really enjoy the ritual of sharing a meal with friends at the table. It's a way of cementing relationships, an offering of friendship, whether it's a cup of tea or shepherd's pie.

BARRY DAINTY

Casual eating with friends has increased enormously in popularity. The elaborate dinners given by the cook-hostesses of the 1950s and 1960s ensured that she got plenty of recognition for the new domestic role she was forced to adopt once domestic servants disappeared. But as 'cooking for compliments' declined, and life for men and women alike moved into the fast lane, new solutions to socializing have been developed. Co-operative efforts are the key to success as far as Rosie and Paul are concerned. 'We have a large circle of friends who regularly go round to each other's houses, but you never think now of not taking something with you in the way of food. Once upon a time you would just take flowers for the hostess, or a bottle of wine. Now everyone comes and brings a curry, or a cheesecake, depending on the evening. It makes it less expensive and less effort and more fun, so you do it more often.'

By contrast, single men seem to pride themselves on their ability to cook lavish dinner parties for their friends unassisted. Barry Dainty admits that he gets 'real pleasure in planning, shopping and cooking for a dinner party – sometimes five courses!' He enjoys putting out the traditional dinner service he inherited from his mother and laying the table properly, but the meals he creates are more elaborate than anything his family used to eat. 'I suppose as I've grown up, I've got used to better things. But I like traditional food from the past too – good solid northern food like meat puddings.' Barry's speciality is buffet meals.

I tend to have a couple of buffet suppers each year, one on New Year's Eve, and the other after St Margaret's Day at church. I do tend to pull out all the stops on that – I have a wide selection of meats, lobster, salmon, salads, and puddings and they always seem to go down well. People always seem very surprised that I manage to do it all myself. But I get a lot of pleasure in seeing a lot of people happy. And if you're going to do a buffet, you might as well do a proper one, not just sandwiches and a few sausage rolls.

Clearly, cooking for friends allows a bachelor to demonstrate his competence in the kitchen, disproving the popular myth that he can't look after himself. Parents likewise tend to entertain more once their children have grown up and away from the family table. Starved of reflections of themselves in their children's eyes, they revive old friendships and make new ones. This is the second most common time for marriages to break up (the first is within five years of marriage, mainly for childless couples). Those who stick together allow their interests to graduate from the family to the wider community. 'Fifty is the joining age', runs the proverb. Finally, the wheel turns full circle: they become grandparents and are drawn back into Dodie Smith's 'dear octopus, from whose tentacles we never quite escape, nor in our innermost hearts, would ever wish to'. Eating rituals mark all these stages: twenty-first birthdays, wedding breakfasts, christening feasts and the regular annual heartbeat of Christmas.

ME TARZAN, YOU JANE?

Men were on the higher wages, weren't they, until they brought women in line with wages, so maybe it was because they were the bigger bread winners that they got the respect, more so than women did. But I think all that is changing, because women are earning now.

MARGI

I find cooking very therapeutic. I spend a large part of my day, like many people, at a desk, at a typewriter, on the phone, or rushing into town doing interviews, going to press conferences… And it's nice to stop, and do something with your hands other than type. I think my husband finds gardening therapeutic; cooking's my equivalent. I make more effort than most people, I think, because it's my hobby.

ROSIE

There was a time in the 1970s when women frantically attempted to be all women to one man. Shirley Conran's *Superwoman* outlined a gruelling agenda of competence in every sphere, disguised as a lighthearted guide to the short cuts that would make it all possible. It didn't last long. In 1980, Caroline Blackwood and Anna Haycraft published *Darling, You Shouldn't Have Gone to So Much Trouble*, a definitive cookery book for cheats that was intended to laugh the ogre of guilt out of the kitchen forever. It opened:

In the 1950s and 1960s it was the fashion to cook the 'back to nature' and 'old-fashioned' way. Women were encouraged, and were therefore prepared, to bake not only their own bread but their own brioches. They sweated their own vegetables; they marinated for several days; they chopped and peeled and grated by hand; they worried as they weighed extremely complex ingredients on inaccurate and wobbly scales. They infused, dredged, strained, double-boiled and parboiled, clarified and leavened; they cut bloody raw meat into segments; they blanched, basted, chined, piped and stiffened, and they took the beards off mussels. They were quite ready to embark on dishes so ambitious that the culinary procedures involved took up most of the day.

Now they are all in a state of mutiny. They recognize cookery to be an art, but they find it an art which becomes increasingly personally unfulfilling.

A year later, *Options* magazine was launched, aimed at 'an entirely new breed of consumer,' the kind of woman who had 'a calculator in her handbag, a stereo in her car, a note recorder in her office'. It was addressed to 'busy women with open minds who will take advantage of every technological advantage to make work more efficient and play more fun: the first generation of women for whom freezers, dish-washers and microwave ovens are not luxuries but essentials.'

As more and more women took up paid work, the idea of delegating or sharing cooking became generally acceptable. 'Men don't expect their wife or partner to come home and cook after they've been working themselves, though there's still a hardcore of men who want their supper cooked for them and there it is on the table at the same time every day, and woe betide their wives if it isn't,' says Slater. 'But the new thinking is that there should be a little bit of effort from both of them. Whoever is home first will cook – or whoever wants to cook.'

It is also now acceptable for women who do not like cooking, and whose part-ners do, to swap roles completely. But in practice women are still responsible for most of the cooking that takes place in Britain. Although men are no longer the only breadwinners, they remain the primary wage-earner in most households. Both Margi and Rosie do the lion's share of the cooking in their respective families, though they have quite different ways of describing their situations. Margi started cooking for her mother when she was 13 and got married when she was 16. She feels that with John, Carl and Tracy at work and Mathew at school, doing the housework and the cooking is obviously her job. Even when she worked evening shifts at the local factory she used to leave complete evening meals ready to be microwaved when the other members of the family came home. She says jokingly that 'a mum's a slave', but she clearly likes the feeling that she is indispensable. 'When John and I went to Butlins for the weekend, Carl and Tracy couldn't really cope. They left a waffle under the grill and nearly set the house on fire.' She still cooks a 'proper meal' every night, even though half the family choose something different from the freezer or order a take-away.

Rosie probably spends even more time than Margi on preparing meals, but she calls cooking 'playing'. 'It's my hobby, really,' she says. 'I love it. I'm not a house-wife. Paul and I are both professionals. I cook for the family because I want to, and the boys know that.' Paul makes no claims to the chef's baton, and there is a family joke about him feeding the boys on tinned potatoes when Rosie was working away from home. She keeps Marks & Spencer ready meals in the freezer, so the family can help themselves, but if she's away in the evening, she tends to leave them a pasta dish that she's made herself, which they can heat up.

> Waiting on my family hand and foot is the last thing I'd do. Having said that, I still do a larger proportion of it than anybody else simply because, as I mostly work from home, it is easier for me to go shopping, or to cook, while I'm doing other things. During the week the boys have homework, and it's far more important to me as a mother that they do their homework and get it right than that they empty the dishwasher. But when they've fin-ished their homework, they will lay the table and empty the dishwasher, and if they leave the place scattered with crisp packets or dirty glasses they will feel my wrath.

Short cuts and convenience foods have given women the time to enjoy the creative side of cooking. In the 1990s they can take possession of a newly enjoyable have-it-both-ways gourmet high ground which is both a lot less dull than being a housewife and considerably more fun than being a feminist. Best of all, men and women can come together again over the dining-table. Or the barbecue. Nigel Slater:

> Male cooking is about display. The barbecue is a classic example. They make a lot of fuss, plan it, do it in the garden where all the neighbours can see. They make lots of smoke, lots of sizzling ... It's their way of showing everybody that they're cooking, providing for their family. It's their annual display – the closest that twentieth-century man gets to spearing a mam-moth, dragging it home and roasting it in front of the village.

Men of all ages are now learning to cook. Rosie is teaching her 81-year-old father-in-law the finer points of the sauté and the simmer. 'When Paul's mother died, he didn't know how to switch on the cooker. It sounds a joke, but he couldn't even boil an egg! You won't get that in the next generation.' When Rosie gives an 'alternative' dinner party, the men do all the shopping and cooking and the women dress up to the nines. They are waited on hand and foot and not even allowed to get up from the table. The deliberate formality in reconstructing ladies of leisure hints at a nostalgia that is not for the idealized families of the 1950s but for the tradition-al pre-war order of things for the middle classes. The husbands are not so much changing places with their wives once a year as expressing a longing for the leg-endary cooks of the 1930s.

Male cooking still tends
to concentrate on display,
the barbecue is almost
invariably the occasion on
which Dad takes over

The newest upper-middle-class domestic trend, made possible by high rates of unemployment and a large floating unofficial pot of willing workers, is the return of the domestic servant, tactfully rechristened 'contract cleaner' or 'dinner-party professional'. Carl could be more realistic than we think when he talks about 'getting a slave' to cook for him.

THE STRANGE CASE OF STICKY TOFFEE PUDDING ◼️

In a time of recession, no work and nearing the millennium, things are a bit scary. A lot of people who thought their lives were secure and safe are finding that everything is very fragile. And one way to comfort yourself is to return to a modern version of your grandparents' food. That's why you get restaurants serving Thai followed by Sticky Toffee Pudding.

NIGEL SLATER

My mother is, without question, the best domestic cook I have ever come across. Food – solid, delicious, thought-about food – comes out of her kitchen, out of her hands, in a never-ending flow of gastronomic pleasure. She is not a fancy foody cook, but a real one. Abundance, that beautiful, biblical concept, is the word for her cuisine. Neither extravagance nor fuss, but excellence.

SARA MAITLAND, quoted in *Loaves and Wishes*, 1992

One of the most popular television cookery series ever was *The Victorian Kitchen*, which featured Ruth Mott as everyone's dream of a traditional cook to a wealthy household. Why are we suddenly so interested in the history of English food, so nostalgic for our recent past? There has been something of a backlash against convenience foods recently, although it seems to be among single men rather than families. 'Every fish finger you put in front of someone is seasoned with a little bit of guilt,' says Slater. 'It's that sense of letting yourself down and other people.' Sales of Slater's three books on 'real fast food' have endorsed his hunch that the weathercock of fashion was swinging away from ready-to-eat sole *goujons* and seafood tagliatelle. Could the generation of Thatcher's bachelors be warming up to proposing marriage to a cohort of nice, traditional girls from the shires? Or is it tastebuds as much as guilty consciences that rebel? 'There's just something about microwave food,' says Barry Dainty. 'It's a bit bland. And I'm never sure what's in it – just odds and ends, not the whole fish or the whole meat.'

Ruth Mott, the comforting, motherly image of the Victorian cook

Kathryn Dodd regards the 1990s as 'a most exciting time ... People are re-defining themselves and Englishness is changing. We're entering a phase where the idea of a traditional English diet is disappearing – but what do we put in its place? We've moved from the old traditions; we've got many many different groups of people from all over the globe living in Britain now, and they've brought their own ideas about food. The English are very good at picking new things up, but it raises questions about who we are as English people. That's why we want to see the subject historically.' In fact, she points out, the food that most people were eating in the 1930s and 1940s, described scathingly by George Orwell in *The Road to Wigan Pier* (1937), was distinctly unattractive.

In 1991, Arabella Boxer published her *Book of British Food*. Its subject was not the ghastly diets behind Orwell's aspidistras, but upper-class food: the 'brief flowering' of informal and elegant eating that came after the Edwardian pomposities of Mrs Beeton and before the austerity of the Second World War. According to Boxer, the most important influences on food at that time were the odd combination of dishes from America's colonial past via the fashionable table of Wallis Simpson and Marcel Boulestin's popularization of French cuisine, *Simple French Cookery for English Homes*. She was not the first to rediscover past traditions. In 1942, Constance Spry had looked back at the 'high epicurean taste' of the decade before the war. 'The criterion of good food was subtlety of flavour and contrast, combined with that perfection of simplicity which is the hardest thing to achieve.' Theodora Fitzgibbon's *The Art of British Cooking* (1965) and Jane Grigson's *English Food*

(1974) were both deservedly popular, but did not stem the tide of enthusiasm for Italian, Indian and finally Thai food.

But in the last five year, there has been a very high degree of interest in combining the best British traditions with the fascinating contributions made by the international influences around us. Spry, Fitzgibbon and Grigson have all been reprinted and dozens of other paeans of praise for all things British have appeared. 'This is the "Year of the Tigers",' announced the 1989 *Good Food Guide*, 'of the breakthrough of young British chefs, an economic maelstrom. The industry is doubling its size every four years. Fifty restaurants are said to be opening in Greater London every month.'

The best new restaurants are international in reference but rooted in their local economy. Pierre and Jill Labat of Water Yeat, at the foot of Lake Coniston, run a guesthouse restaurant that is more like a large family dining room than a public place to eat. Fish is from the nearby sea, lamb from the lakeland hills. Vegetables come from local allotment-owners, cheeses and smoked meats from local smokeries. At the other end of the country in Dartmouth, Joyce Molyneux' famous Carved Angel draws visitors from hundreds of miles away; it, too, prides itself on using what the region, rather than international food processing plants, can offer.

ENVOI

A group of closely related persons living under one roof; it is a convenience, often a necessity, sometimes a pleasure, sometimes the reverse; but who first exalted it as admirable, an almost religious ideal?

ROSE MACAULAY, *The World My Wilderness*, 1950

Far from being the basis of the good society, the family, with its narrow privacy and tawdry secrets, is the source of all our discontents.

EDMUND LEACH, Reith Lectures 1967

Facing page:Joyce Molyneaux collecting herbs in the beautiful garden of her Dartmouth restaurant

In an age when everybody can, for technological reasons, survive independently, individual members of families have taken the opportunity to express and enjoy that independence. But do separate menus really mean selfish lives? Response in times of crisis may be a more accurate measure of family health these days than the sight of father, mother and children saying grace around the Sunday lunch table. Janet Finch's book *Family Obligations and Social Change* (1989) rightly questions our tendency to assume that golden ages for family life existed in the past, and paints a reassuring picture of how families do in fact support and provide for their members. Eighty per cent of children under the age of 16 live under the same roof as both their parents. Only 6 per cent of people over 65 are in residential care and only 48 per cent of those over 90.

There is, of course, no cause for complacency when we consider the amount of domestic violence, juvenile crime and child abuse reported in the newspapers. But remember those long-forgotten anxieties over the post-war 'crime waves' and the gruesome anecdotes of the 1950s told by Robert Fabian in *London After Dark*. They suggest that what has changed is the frequency and explicitness with which such cases are now reported, as much as any increase in the number of crimes that are committed. In the past, no one took much notice of the horrors of private life, let alone measured them. 'No family can hang out the sign, nothing the matter here,' runs an old Chinese proverb. The open wound of divorce may be better than the secret poison of being chained to physical or mental oppression for life. The truth is that today our expectations of human behaviour are as perfectionist as our standards of food hygiene and nutrition. It is important not to confuse that entirely laudable fact with a panic over social breakdown.

Investigating how the majority of families now eat together and live together is not the depressing exercise that one would have expected it to be, given the gloomy prophesies that abound. What emerges is that pragmatic solutions to old sources of tensions are being discovered. The famously uncomfortable strait-jacket of dependencies that used to be the family is easing up, turning into a comfortable stretchy pullover with lots of room for growth. For a minority of us, it is a garment that can be changed at will for something that suits its wearers better. For most of us family life, like the food we eat, has never been more rewarding.

BIBLIOGRAPHY

Addison, Paul, *Now the War is Over, a Social History of Britain 1945-51*, BBC/Cape, 1985

Anderson, Verily, *Spam Tomorrow*, Rupert Hart Davis, 1956

Asian Voices, Life stories from the Indian subcontinent, Ethnic Communies Oral History Project, Borough of Hammersmith and Fulham, 1993

Barker, TC, McKenzie JC, and Yudkin, J, *Our Changing Fare*, 1966

Barr, Ann, and Levy, Paul, *The Official Foodie Handbook*, Harpers & Queen, 1984

Bateman, *Cooking People*, 1966 London

Beck, Simone, Bertholle, Louisette and Child Julia *Mastering the Art of French Cookery*, Knopf 1961, Cassell 1963

Belasco, WJ, *Appetite for Change - How the Counter-Culture took on the Food Industry 1966-1988*, NY Pantheon, 1989

Bendit, Phoebe and Laurence, *Living Together Again*, Garmol1, 1946

Blackwood, Caroline, and Haycraft, Anna, *Darling, You Shouldn't Have Gone to So Much Trouble*, Futura, 1980

Blishen, Edmund, *A Cack-handed War*, 1972

Booker, Christopher, *The Neophiliacs, A Study of the Revolution in English Life in the Fifties and Sixties*, Pimlico, 1970

Brannen, Julia and Wilson, Gail (eds) *Give and Take in Families: Studies in Resource Distribution*, Allen & Unwin, 1987

British Nutrition Foundation, *Why Additives? The Safety of Foods*,1977

Burnett, John, *Plenty and Want, A Social History of Diet in England from 1815 to the Present Day*, Routledge, 3rd ed, 1989

Calder, Angus, *The People's War*, Jonathan Cape, 1969

Cantor, David, *The Story of Cranks*, 1982

Carson Rachel, *Silent Spring*, Penguin, 1963

Choudhury, Yousuf, *The Roots and Tales of the Bangladeshi Settlers*, Sylheti History Group, 267 Malmesbury Rd, Small Heath, B10 0JE, Birmingham, 1993

Colpi, Terri, *The Italian Factor* Mainstream, 1991

Corbishley, Gill, *Appetite for Change*, English Heritage, 1993

Cowie, Evelyn, *Breakfasts*, Herbert Jenkins, 1958

Coxhead, Elizabeth, *Constance Spry,a Biography*, Luscombe, 1975

Curtis-Bennett, Sir Noel, *The Food of the People, Being a History of Industrial Eating*, Faber, 1949

David, Elizabeth, *French Country Cooking*, Michael Joseph, 1951

David, Elizabeth, *French Provincial Cookery* Michael Joseph, 1960

David, Elizabeth, *Italian Food* MacDonald, 1954

David, Elizabeth, *Mediterranean Food*, John Lehman, 1950

David, Elizabeth, *Summer Cooking*, Museum Press, 1955

David, Elizabeth, *English Bread and Yeast Cookery*, Allen Lane, 1977

Davies, Jennifer, *The Wartime Kitchen and Garden*, BBC, 1993

Davis Adèlle *Let's Cook Right*, Harcourt Brace, NY, 1947

Davis Adèlle, *Let's Eat Right to Keep Fit*, Harcourt Brace NY, 1954

Delafield, E M, *The Provincial Lady in Wartime*, MacMillan, 1940

Driver, Christopher *The British at Table*, Chatto & Windus 1985

Drummond, J, *The Nation's Larder and The Housewife's Part Therein*, G Bell, 1940

Ellis, Alice Thomas, *The Twenty-seventh Kingdom*, Duckworth, 1982

Finch, Janet, *Family, Obligation and Social Change*, Polity, 1989

Finkelstein, Joanne, *Dining Out, a Sociology of Modern Manners*, Polity, 1989

Gardiner, CG, *Canteens At Work*, OUP 1941

Gavron, Hannah, *The Captive Wife*, Routledge 1966

Golding Louis and Simon, André, *We Shall Eat and Drink Again*, Hutchinson, 1944

Grieve, Mary, *Millions Made My Story*, Gollancz, 1964

Griggs, Barbara, *The Food Factor*, Viking, 1986

Grigson, Jane, *English Food*, MacMillan 1974

Hardyment, Christina, *Perfect Parents* (originally *Dream Babies: child-rearing theories from*

Locke to Spock, 1983), new edition OUP, 1995

Hardyment, Christina, *Mangle To Microwave: the mechanization of the household*, Polity, 1989

Harrison, Ruth, *Animal Machines*, 1964

Hinton, James, 'Militant Housewives: The British Housewives League andthe Attlee Government', *History Workshop* pp129-156, Autumn, 1994

Hiro, Dilip, *Black British, White British*, 1991

Holdsworth, Angela, *Out of The Dolls House*, BBC, 1988

Hopkins, Henry, *The New Look, a Social History of the 1940s and 1950s*, Secker 1963

Hubback, Judith, *Wives Who Went to College*, Heinemann 1957

Klein, Josephine, *Samples From British Cultures*, Routledge, 1965

Klein, Viola, *Working Wives*, 1959

Lacey, Richard, *Unfit for Human Consumption - Food in Crisis - the consequences of putting convenience before safety* , Souvenir, 1989

Lacey, Richard, *Hard to Swallow, A Brief history of Food*, CUP, 1994

Laski, Marghanita, *Love on the Supertax*, 1944

Law, J, 'How much can the Sociologist Digest at One Sitting? The Macro and the Micro revisited for the Case of Fast Food', in *Studies in Symbolic Interaction, vol 5*, ed N Denzin, Jai Press Connecticut, 1985

Leach, Penelope, T*he New Baby and Child*, Michael Joseph, 1988

Lewis, Jane, *Women in Britain since 1945*, Blackwell 1992

Lewis, Peter, *The Fifties: Portrait of a Period*, Cupid, 1989

Lo, Kenneth, *Chinese food*, Penguin, 1972

Lucas, Diore, *Cordon Bleu Cook Book*, Dent 1953

Mabey, *Food For Free*, Collins, 1972

Mennell, Stephen et al, *The Sociology of Food*, Sage, 1992

Mennell, Stephen, *All Manner of Food*, Blackwell, 1985

Merriman, Nick (ed) *The Peopling of London*, London Museum, 1993

Minns, Raynes, *Bombers and Mash: The Domestic Front 1939-1945*, Virago, 1980

Mitchison, Naomi, *Among You taking Notes*, Gollancz, 1985

Mo, Timothy, *Sour Sweet* , André Deutsch, 1982

Montanari, Massimo, *The Culture of Food*, Blackwell, 1994

Murcott, Anne, 'Food and Nutrition in Postwar Britain', in P Caterall and J Obelkevietch, *Understanding Postwar British Society*, Routledge,

Murcott, Anne, *Sociology of Food and Eating*, Radcliffe, 1983

National Food Survey Committee, *Annual Report* (various dates)

Obelkevitch, Tim *Understanding Postwar British Society*, Routledge, 1994

Oddy, DJ and Miller, DS(eds), *The Making of the Modern British Diet*, Croom Helm, 1976

Orbach, Susie, 'A Language all of its Own', in Till, Antonia, ed, *Loaves and Wishes*, qv.

Panter Downes, Mollie, *One Fine Day*, 1947, reprinted with an introduction by Nicola Beauman, Virago, 1990

Patten, Marguerite, various cookery books (1949-54)

Patten, Marguerite, *Cookery in Colour*, 1960

The Pub and The People, Mass Observation, Gollancz, 1943

Pyke, Magnus, *Technological Eating*, John Murray, 1972

Revel, J, *Culture and Cuisine, A Journey through the History of Food*, trans Helen Lane, Doubleday, 1972

Robins, Joan, *Common-Sense Cooking and Eating*, Odhams Press, 1953

Sargent, S, *The Foodmakers*, Penguin, 1985

Schrank, J, *Snap, Crackle and Popular Taste*, Delta NY, 1977

Seymour, John and Sally, *Self-Sufficiency, The Science and Art of Producing and Preserving Your Own Food*, Faber, 1973

Shrapnel, Norman, *The Seventies: Britain's Inward March*, 1980

Sissons, Michael and French, Philip (eds) *The Age of Austerity*, Hodder, 1963

Social Trends, various editions, HMSO.

Spencer, Colin, *The Heretic's Feast*, Fourth Estate, 1993

Spock, Benjamin, and Rosenberg, Michael, *Dr Spock's Baby and Childcare for the Nineties*, Simon and Schuster, 1992

Spry, Constance, and Hulme, Rosemary, *The Constance Spry Cookery Book*, 1956

Till, Antonia (ed), *Loaves and Wishes, Writers*

writing on Food, Oxfam/Virago, 1992

Valery, Ann, *Talking About The War*, Michael Joseph 1991

Van Den Berghe, Pierre, 'Ethnic cuisine, culture in nature', *Ethnic and Racial Studies* 7(3), 387-97

Vincent, Gerard, and Prost, Antoine, *History of Private Life volume V: Riddles of Identity in Modern Times*, Harvard University Press, Massachusetts and London, 1991

Visram, Rozina, *Ayahs, Lascars and Princes*, Pluto Press, 1986

Visser, Margaret, *The Rituals of Dinner*, Viking, 1991

Whitehorn, Katharine, *Kitchen in a Corner*, 1962, renamed *Cooking in a Bedsit*, Penguin, 1963

Williams, Gertrude, *Women and Work*, Nicholson and Watson, 1945

Willmott, Peter, and Young, Michael, *Family and Kinship in East London*, Routledge, 1957

Willmott, Peter, and Young, Michael, *Family and Class in a London Suburb*, Routledge, 1960

Wilson, Elizabeth, *Only Halfway to Paradise*, Tavistock, 1980

Winship, Janice, *Inside Women's Magazines*, Pandora, 1987

Yarwood, Doreen, *The British Kitchen*, Batsford, 1981

Zeldin, Theodore, *An Intimate History of Humanity*, Sinclair Stevenson, 1994

Zihlman, Adrienne, in Dahlberg, (ed), *Woman the Gatherer*, Yale, 1981

INDEX

PICTURE CREDITS

BBC Books would like to thank the following for providing pictures and for permission to reproduce copyright material. While every effort has been made to trace and acknowledge all copyright holders, we would like to apologize should there have been any errors or omissions.

Page 8 Imperial War Museum; 9 from *Good Housekeeping* magazine August 1949; 11 Hulton Deutsch Collection; 13 & 17 Topham Picturepoint; 18 Popperfoto; 21 Syndication International; 24 Hulton Deutsch Collection; 25 *left* cartoon by Giles *Daily Express* 4.7.46, *top right* Hulton Deutsch Collection, *bottom right* Topham Picturepoint; 28 Retrograph Archive; 30 title page *Venus in the Kitchen* by Norman Douglas, William Heinemann Ltd *1952*; 32 Topham Picturepoint; 33 *left* British Film Institute, *right* & 35 Topham Picturepoint; 36 & 40 Hulton Deutsch Collection; 42 *left* from *Good Housekeeping* magazine February 1951, *right* Retrograph Archive; 45 Hulton Deutsch Collection; 46 cartoon by Graham, *Punch* magazine; 47 BBC; 49 *left* Hulton Deutsch Collection, *right* & 51 Retrograph Archive; 53 *main picture* Topham Picturepoint, *inset* BBC; 54 Hulton Deutsch Collection; 59 Retrograph Archive; 60 Hulton Deutsch Collection; 63 BBC; 70 & 73 Hulton Deutsch Collection; 78 J. Lyons & Co. Ltd; 81 & 84 Hulton Deutsch Collection; 85 Copyright © 1979 Len Deighton, 1990 BV Holland Copyright Corporation. Reprinted by kind permission of Jonathan Clowes Ltd on behalf of Pluriform Publishing Company BV; 89 *top* Hulton Deutsch Collection, *bottom* Barnaby's Picture Library; 93 *left* from *French Country Cooking* by Elizabeth David, Penguin Books 1959, *right* Topham Picturepoint; 95 from *Petit Propos Culinaires 41*, Prospect Books 1991; 97 Imperial War Museum; 98 Popperfoto; 99 Advertising Archives; 100-1 *top left* Hulton Deutsch Collection, *bottom left & right* from *The Daily Mail Book of Britain's Post-War Homes* 1944; 102 Retrograph Archive; 103 Birds Eye Wall's; 104 from *The Daily Mail Ideal Home Book 1951-52*; 105 *top* Barnaby's Picture Library, *bottom* cartoon by Merrily Harpur, *Punch* magazine, 106 Tim MacPherson; 107 Robert Harding Picture Library; 108 Anthony Blake Photo Library; 109 *top* cartoon by Albert, *Punch* magazine, *bottom* Barnaby's Picture Library; 110 Mike Abrahams/Network; 111 S. & R. Greenhill; 112 Holt Studios; 113 cartoon by Duncan, *Punch* magazine; 116 Hulton Deutsch Collection; 117 J. Sainsbury plc; 121 *both* from *Good Housekeeping* magazine 1949; 122 Retrograph Archive; 123 Watford Observer; 124 Steve Pyke/Network; 127 Hulton Deutsch Collection; 128 Topham Picturepoint; 129 Hulton Deutsch Collection; 135 *main picture* Popperfoto, *inset* Topham Picturepoint; 140 Mike Abrahams/Network; 143 BBC; 146 Paul Mellor; 147 Yang Sing Restaurant; 149 *top* Martin Mayer/Network, *bottom* Advertising Archives; 152 Chris Fairclough Colour Library; 154 Ulrike Preuss/Format; 157 *top* S. & R. Greenhill, *bottom* Press Association; 160 Topham Picturepoint; 164 cartoon by Merrily Harpur, *Punch* magazine; 168 from *Self-Sufficiency* by John & Sally Seymour, Faber & Faber 1973; 171 Popperfoto; 174 Denis Doran/Network; 177 *left* Weightwatchers (UK) Ltd, *right* Topham Picturepoint; 182 *left* cartoon by Dickinson, *Punch* magazine, *right* Anthony Blake Photo Library; 183 Barnaby's Picture Library; 184 Network; 187 & 193 *both* BBC; 194 *left* Union Pictures, *right* Oxford College of Further Education/Rebecca van der Putt; 195 S. & R. Greenhill; 197 Brenda Prince/Format; 198 & 200 Barnaby's Picture Library; 202 Brenda Prince/Format; 203 Jenny Woodcock/Bubbles; 204 Jenny Mathews/Network; 207 S. & R. Greenhill; 214 Chris Fairclough Colour Library; 215 BBC; 217 from *The Carved Angel Cookery Book*, Harper Collins 1990, *Photo*: Martin Brigdale.